MAN-EATER

HAROLD SCHECHTER has been a professor of American literature and culture at Queens College, the City University of New York, since 1975. The author of more than thirty books, he has been widely praised for his historical true crime narratives. His two reference works, The *A to Z Encyclopedia of Serial Killers* and *The Serial Killer Files*, are standard works in the field. He is also the editor of the landmark Library of America volume, *True Crime: An American Anthology*, described by the *Washington Post as* 'almost obscenely entertaining'. Harold Schechter's essays have appeared in the *New York Times*, the *Los Angeles Times*, the *Wall Street Journal* and the *International Herald Tribune*. He lives in Brooklyn and Mattituck, New York with his wife, the poet Kimiko Hahn.

ALSO BY HAROLD SCHECHTER

NONFICTION

Psycho USA: Famous American Killers You Never Heard Of

Savage Pastimes: A Cultural History of Violent Entertainment

Fatal: The Poisonous Life of a Female Serial Killer

Fiend: The Shocking True Story of America's Youngest Serial Killer

Bestial: The Savage Trail of a True American Monster

Depraved: The Shocking True Story of America's First Serial Killer

Deranged: The Shocking True Story of America's Most Fiendish Killer!

Deviant: The Shocking True Story of Ed Gein, the Original "Psycho"

The Whole Death Catalog: A Lively Guide to the Bitter End

The Serial Killer Files: The Who, What, Where, How, and Why of the World's Most Terrifying Murderers

NARRATIVE NONFICTION

Killer Colt: Murder, Disgrace, and the Making of an American Legend

The Devil's Gentleman: Privilege, Poison, and the Trial That Ushered in the Twentieth Century

The Mad Sculptor: The Maniac, the Model, and the Murder That Rocked 1930s America

FICTION

The Tell-Tale Corpse

The Mask of Red Death

The Hum Bug

Nevermore

Outcry

Dying Breath

HAROLD SCHECHTER

MAN-EATER

The Saga of **ALFRED G. PACKER,**

AMERICAN CANNIBAL

HEAD
of ZEUS

ISBN (HB): 978178185703
ISBN (E): 9781781857397

Printed and bound in Germany by GGP Media GmbH, Pössneck

Head of Zeus
Clerkenwell House
45-47 Clerkenwell Green
London EC1R 0HT

www.headofzeus.com

In memory of
Kurt Brown

Six miners went into the mountains
To hunt for precious gold;
It was the middle of the winter,
The weather was dreadful cold.
Six miners went into the mountains,
They had nor food nor shack—
Six miners went into the mountains,
But only one came back.

—"The Lost Miners" (nineteenth century)

PROLOGUE

CANNIBAL COUNTRY

In 1620, before embarking on their epochal voyage to New England, the members of the Scrooby Congregation—that intrepid band of believers we know as the *Mayflower* Pilgrims—took sober account of the hardships that lay before them. There was—as their chronicler, William Bradford, wrote—the ocean crossing itself, whose grueling demands were "such that the weak bodies of women and other persons worn out with age and travail could never be able to endure." Those who survived the perilous journey would find themselves faced with "the miseries of the land . . . liable to famine, and nakedness, and the want, in a manner, of all things. The change of air, diet, and drinking of water would infect their bodies with sore sickness and grievous diseases."

Daunting as these physical challenges seemed, however, an even graver threat remained. Those "who should escape or overcome these difficulties," wrote Bradford, "should yet be in continual danger of the savage people, who are cruel, barbarous and most treacherous, being most furious in their rage, and merciless where they overcome; not being content only to kill, and take away life, but delight to torment men in the most bloody manner that may be; flaying some alive with the shells of fishes, cutting off the members and joints of others by piecemeal and broiling on the coals, eat the collops of their flesh in their sight whilst they live."

Here, then, was a prospect unnerving enough to "move the very bowels of men to grate within them, and make the weak to quake and tremble": enduring sickness, starvation, exposure, and other "lamenta-ble miseries," only to fall victim to cannibals.[1]

Ever since Columbus reached the New World, Europeans had thought of America as the home of cannibals. It was through Columbus, in fact, that the word "cannibal" entered the English language. Having made landfall in the West Indies, the legendary explorer encountered a warlike tribe who were reputed to devour their captives and whose name—Carib—he mistakenly recorded as "Canib." Before long, the Spanish word *caníbales*—"cannibals" in its Anglicized form—had become synonymous with the man-eating "savages" of the New World. By Shakespeare's time, the association between cannibalism and the Americas was so complete that, when the Bard conjured up his imaginary "brave new world" in his final play *The Tempest*, he populated it with two indigenous beings, the fairylike Ariel and the bloodthirsty brute Caliban, whose name is an anagram of *caníbal*.[2]

Whether the Caribs actually engaged in anthropophagy (the technical term for man-eating) remains a matter of dispute among scholars. There is no doubt, however, that the Indian atrocities described by William Bradford were more than mere rumor. Male prisoners of the Iroquois were subjected to hideous tortures. After having their fingers "chopped or bitten off," their bodies flayed, and their genitals scorched with red-hot coals, they were generally "burned to death after disembowelment, some parts of their bodies having been eaten and their blood drunk in celebration by their captors."[3] Other North American tribes also engaged in cannibalism. Archaeological evidence—heaps of chopped, butchered, and roasted skeletal remains recovered from various sites—strongly suggests that the Anasazi, the supposedly peace-loving ancestors of today's Pueblo Indians, routinely dined on human meat—"man corn," as they called it.[4]

As it turned out, Bradford's darkest forebodings proved unfounded. As all American schoolchildren know, far from "fill[ing] their sides full of arrows"—as Bradford feared—the native inhabitants of the New World came to the Puritans' aid, teaching them "how to set their corn, where to take fish, and to procure other commodities." Though half of the new arrivals perished during the first brutal winter, Bradford and the others lived to celebrate their survival with a harvest festival, inviting their Indian neighbors to join them in a three-day feast of native fare: wild turkey and water fowl, venison and shellfish, pumpkins, beans, and corn.[5]

The situation was very different for the Puritans' English predecessors, the shipload of adventurers who, thirteen years before the *Mayflower* landed, had established the Jamestown settlement in Virginia. Despite sporadic stretches of peaceful coexistence between the newcomers and the surrounding tribes, relations grew increasingly hostile. By 1609, conditions were so dire that any white man who ventured outside the fortified confines of the settlement was likely to meet the fate of one unfortunate British captive: "At a leisurely pace, his extremities were cut off with mussel shells and tossed into the fire before him; he was flayed—the skin was torn from his face and head—then disemboweled while still alive; and finally burned to ashes."[6]

Hunkered within their ill-provisioned palisade during the brutal winter of 1609–1610, the Jamestown colonists quickly found themselves facing starvation. George Percy, youngest son of the eighth Earl of Northumberland and one of the original band of settlers, later recounted the torments he and his companions endured. After consuming their "horses and other beasts," they were driven "to make shift with vermin as dogs, cats, rats, and mice." When no more rodents could be found, they began "to eat boots, shoes or any other leather some could come by." At length came the ultimate horror. Maddened with hunger, some of the colonists resorted to "things which seem incredible, as to dig up dead corpses out of graves and to eat them. And some have licked up the blood which hath fallen from their weak fellows." One man—later burned at the stake for the atrocity—murdered his pregnant wife, "ripped the child out of her womb," then "chopped the Mother in pieces and salted her for his food." When the supply ship finally arrived, Jamestown's population had been reduced from five hundred men, women, and children to sixty-four near-skeletal survivors.[7]

In the summer of 2012, four hundred years after the Jamestown colonists suffered through their catastrophic "starving time," scientists made a grim discovery at the site of the settlement. Excavating a trash pit containing the bones of dogs, cats, horses, and other animals consumed during the crisis, a team of archaeologists came upon the skeletal fragments of a human being.

Through state-of-the-art forensic analysis, the investigators determined that the remains were those of "a female, roughly fourteen years old (based on the development of her molars) and of British ancestry ... either a maidservant or the child of a gentleman." Telltale cut marks on the skull and shinbones made it incontrovertibly clear that the girl had been butchered for food.

At a press conference held at the Smithsonian National Museum of Natural History in Washington, DC, Douglas Owsley, the physical anthropologist who analyzed the remains, explained that "the chops to the forehead are very tentative, very incomplete. Then the body was turned over, and there were four strikes to the back of the head, one of which was the strongest and split the skull in half. A penetrating wound was then made to the left temple, probably by a single-sided knife, which was used to pry open the head and remove the brain." It seemed likely, Owsley went on, that the brain was eaten first, "because it decomposes so quickly after death," followed by her "tongue, cheeks, and leg muscles."[8]

The announcement that the centuries-old stories of Jamestown cannibalism had finally been corroborated by science generated headlines on both sides of the Atlantic. In reporting the news, more than one commentator noted an "ironical" dimension to the findings. Like William Bradford and his fellow Pilgrims, George Percy and the other members of the Jamestown settlement had left England with their heads full of stories about Native American cannibalism—of New World "savages" who "eat their enemies when they kill them, or any stranger if they take them." In the end, however, it was the English themselves who resorted to cannibalism, driven to this extremity by a harsh and unforgiving wilderness that could strip a man of all civilized restraint.

Part One

DEAD MAN'S GULCH

1.

THE PATHFINDER

Asked to name the greatest explorers of the American West, most people—at least those with a modicum of historical awareness—would answer Meriwether Lewis and William Clark. By the mid-nineteenth century, however, Lewis and Clark had been largely forgotten by their countrymen, their achievements overshadowed by those of another trailblazer, John C. Frémont. Remembered today by few outside the ranks of professional historians, Frémont was hailed in his lifetime as "The Great Pathfinder" and "The Hero Who Started Civilization in the West." One contemporary proclaimed that, along with Columbus's first voyage to the New World and George Washington's military triumphs in the Revolutionary War, Frémont's deeds were "the greatest events in the world . . . connected with the rise and progress of the United States."[1]

His renown rested on a series of surveying expeditions he undertook with the legendary scout and Indian fighter Kit Carson. In the course of these journeys, Frémont "covered more ground west of the Mississippi than had any other explorer," mapped most of the Oregon Trail, and played a leading part in wresting California from Mexico.[2] The published reports of his adventures, packed with vivid descriptions and thrilling incidents, became instant bestsellers, inspiring thousands of settlers to migrate out west.

Such was Frémont's fame that, in 1856, he was nominated as the Republican Party's first presidential candidate. The ensuing campaign was "one of the nastiest in the nation's history." Indulging in the kind of unbridled calumny that makes modern-day mudslinging seem like the height of civility, Frémont's adversaries branded him "a secret papist" (a harsh accusation in an era of virulent anti-Catholic bigotry), a bastard, an adulterer, a native-born Frenchman, and the son of a prostitute. They also alleged that, during his last expedition, his men had resorted to cannibalism.[3] Unlike some of the other imputations leveled against him, this one happened to be true.

In 1848, at the behest of his father-in-law, US senator Thomas Hart Benton, Frémont—with three triumphant expeditions behind him—undertook a journey to chart a route for a transcontinental railroad. The proposed path, following the thirty-eighth parallel, would cut through the Sangre de Cristo and San Juan ranges of the Rockies, Colorado's "roughest mountains." Though urged by trappers familiar with the region to wait until spring thaw, Frémont and his party of thirty-three men forged ahead in one of the worst winters in living memory. Either through incompetence or (as some researchers believe) deliberate treachery, their guide, a sixty-one-year-old mountain man named "Old Bill" Williams, eccentric even by the standards of his breed, consistently chose the "worst possible routes." Trapped in the snow-choked mountains, the men froze, starved, and began dying off one by one. After exhausting their food supply, devouring the pack mules, and consuming their own boots, belts, and knife scabbards, some survived on the flesh of their dead companions. In the end, ten of the thirty-three men perished in the disaster.[4]

Frémont failed in his presidential bid, losing the 1856 election to his Democratic opponent, James Buchanan. While other factors contributed to his defeat—among them his staunch antislavery stance—historians agree that the rumors of cannibalism associated with his "fatal fourth" expedition helped put an end to his political career.

Twenty years later, in the same region of Colorado where the Pathfinder's men suffered their harrowing ordeal, another episode of cannibalism occurred, inciting widespread horror in the American public. In contrast to the now all-but-forgotten Frémont, however—who had already begun his long slide into obscurity—its perpetrator would achieve lasting notoriety, becoming a permanent part of our national folklore.

His name was Alfred Packer, though—as the West's most infamous cannibal—he was known by a variety of epithets: Packer the Ghoul. The Human Hyena. The Man-Eater.

2.

THE NEW ELDORADO

On January 24, 1848, James W. Marshall, a transplanted New Jersey carpenter hired to construct a sawmill on the American River near Coloma, California, spotted some glittering flakes in the water. "It made my heart thump," Marshall later recalled, "for I was certain it was gold."[1] Despite efforts to keep the find a secret, word of the discovery quickly spread, unleashing a worldwide epidemic of gold fever and instigating a mass invasion of California.

The earliest arrivals found nuggets for the taking. Within a decade, however, the rivers were panned out. Disillusioned miners began searching elsewhere. In 1858, a party of prospectors led by a Georgian named William Green Russell turned up a few small deposits of gold dust in the Pikes Peak country of the Southern Rocky Mountains. Newspapers trumpeted the discovery, touting the region as "The New Eldorado." Heeding the rallying cry of "Pikes Peak or Bust!" tens of thousands of treasure hunters swarmed to the Colorado Territory in the second-greatest gold rush in US history. Mining camps sprouted throughout the mountains. In less than a year, Denver grew from a small cluster of mud-chinked log cabins and ramshackle lean-tos into a bustling settlement with a population of close to five thousand.

While most of the newcomers ended up with nothing but "broken hopes and busted fortunes," some became rich overnight. "Millionaires were made in a matter of moments," writes one historian, "as the born lucky swung their picks and felt the rock give way to . . . pay dirt—a pocket of mixed sandstone, clay, and quartz, impregnated with flour gold." From a high-grade vein, a man could realize as much as $1,500 a day, at a time when the average American laborer earned less than one-third of that amount in a year.[2]

The outbreak of the Civil War temporarily halted the stampede. With the war's end, a new army of hopefuls flocked to the region. By then, the gulches and streams of the Rockies had yielded much of their precious yellow ore. Gold, however, wasn't the only mineral treasure to be wrested from the mountains. In 1860—so one story goes—a prospector named Sam Conger, while camping on a meadow near Boulder Creek, fished out a nugget of silver from the water. Since Conger was hunting for gold, he attached little value to the specimen, though he kept it as a curio. Nine years later, however, after learning of the wealth issuing from Nevada's fabled Comstock silver lode, he and some partners returned to the spot, where they quickly uncovered a rich vein of the precious white metal, setting off a second frenzied rush to the Colorado Rockies.[3]

From the older mining districts north of Denver, this new wave of fortune hunters poured over the mountains until it reached the mineral-rich wilderness of the San Juans. Situated in the southwest corner of Colorado, the San Juan country is an area of spectacular beauty, its towering peaks among the highest in North America, its slopes and alpine valleys heavily forested with native conifers and deciduous trees: pine, spruce, fir, cedar, aspen, box elder, and more. With its jagged peaks, deep canyons, sheer rock walls, and dizzying gorges, it is also a notoriously harsh environment, particularly during its prolonged, brutal winters. For John C. Frémont, whose fourth expedition met its terrible fate in the area, the San Juans were "the highest, most rugged, most impracticable, and inaccessible of the Rocky Mountains."[4]

The natural obstacles presented by the San Juan range, however, did nothing to stem the tide of migrants. When one early pioneer, Enos Hotchkiss, uncovered a high-grade claim east of Lake San Cristobal, thousands of silver seekers swarmed to the area in a matter of weeks.[5] The dream that possessed them was described by an earlier would-be miner "smitten with silver fever," the young Sam Clemens. "I would have been more or less than human if I had not gone mad like the rest," he recalled in later years when the world knew him as Mark Twain. "I succumbed and grew as frenzied as the craziest. . . . I expected to find masses of silver lying all about the ground. I expected to see it glittering in the sun on the mountain summits."[6]

For countless men lured to the "Silvery San Juans" by a similar fantasy, the quest for instant riches would end in abject failure. For a few, it would lead to something far worse.

3.

DRIFTER

In early October 1873, the *Denver Tribune* ran a piece that was reprinted in newspapers throughout the Southwest. Headlined "The San Juan Silver Mines," it reported the recent find of a lode "that surpasses the Comstock of Nevada in richness" and hailed the "San Juan District" as a land of "immense and apparently inexhaustible mineral resources" where "hundreds of rich discoveries" remained to be made.[1]

Residing in the vicinity of Salt Lake City, Utah, at the time this article appeared was a thirty-one-year-old drifter named Alfred G. Packer. He was born in Allegheny County, Pennsylvania, on November 12, 1842, one of eight children of a carpenter named James Packer and his wife, Esther (née Esther Griner).[2] Throughout his life he claimed—falsely—to be closely related to his native state's most prominent citizen, Asa Packer, railroad pioneer and founder of Lehigh University. James Packer himself would achieve a notable distinction at the very end of his life. When he died on February 23, 1902, at age ninety-six, he had broken a local longevity record, having "reached an age," as his obituary put it, "not attained by any other in this county."[3] By then, of course, he had long since achieved another, far less enviable distinction—as the father of one of the nation's most notorious murderers.

Shortly after Alfred's birth, James moved the family to LaGrange, Indiana, where he found work as a cabinetmaker and became an active member of the Methodist Episcopal Society.[4] About his infamous son's boyhood virtually nothing is known. At some point in Alfred's early adolescence, he was apprenticed to a shoemaker, acquiring a skill he would use throughout his life, leatherworking. He also suffered a string of violent seizures, the first symptoms of the disorder that would afflict him throughout his life—grand mal epilepsy, a condition for which no effective treatment existed at the time.

Packer was six months shy of his nineteenth birthday when the bombardment of Fort Sumter ignited the Civil War. Exactly one year later, in April 1862, he joined the Sixteenth Regiment of the US Infantry at Winona, Minnesota. His enlistment form describes him as just over five feet eight inches tall, with a fair complexion, blue eyes, and light hair (oddly, since it is clear from both photographs and eyewitness testimony that his hair was, as more than one observer described it, "coal black").[5]

The regiment immediately left for North Columbus, Ohio, where Packer spent the summer months in Camp Thomas, a Union training base for new recruits. Shortly after his arrival, he proudly adorned his right arm with a military tattoo that identified him as "Alferd Packer" of the "Second Battalion, 16th Infantry." Some historians blame the botched first name on the unknown tattooist, but the truth is that Packer, at this stage of his life, possessed such rudimentary writing skills that he couldn't correctly spell his own first name (a trait he shared with at least one of his siblings; extant letters of his older sister, Melissa, are consistently signed "Malissa").[6] Eventually, he would get it right. Documents from his later years, when he had achieved a far higher degree of literacy, are all correctly signed with his baptismal name, Alfred.

Following his stint at Camp Thomas, Packer accompanied his regiment to Camp Douglas, just south of Chicago—at that time a training facility for Union soldiers, later a prisoner-of-war camp so squalid, disease-ridden, and overcrowded that its Confederate inmates called it "Eighty Acres of Hell." Years afterward, in applying for a government disability pension, he would claim that he had contracted typhoid fever while performing "constant, prolonged, and unnecessary guard duty" at the camp and that the prolonged illness was the cause of his epilepsy—one of Packer's many flagrant falsehoods.[7]

Though he had enlisted for three years, Packer's time in the Sixteenth Regiment came to an abrupt end shortly after Christmas 1862, when he received a disability discharge at Fort Ontario, New York. The official certificate states that he was "incapable of performing the duties of a soldier because of epilepsy." In the blank space where the examining physician was to indicate the number of days that "said soldier has been unfit for duty," the doctor wrote, "all the time."[8]

Making his way westward, Packer enlisted again, this time in Company L of the Eighth Regiment of the Iowa Cavalry. In keeping with his penchant for self-serving fabrications, Packer would maintain that he spent time as a scout for George Armstrong Custer, a claim for which no evidence exists. Shortly after his enlistment, the regiment was sent to Tennessee, where it was attached to the defense of Nashville. A surviving company muster roll from this period offers the first documented evidence of a predatory streak in Packer's behavior. In the space reserved for "Remarks," the regimental scribe noted that, in November 1863, Private Packer's salary had been docked $2.50—roughly equivalent to fifty dollars today—"for plundering citizens of N[ash]v[ille]."[9]

Packer's regiment was still in Tennessee the following April when his illness brought a permanent end to his military career. "This soldier has been unfit for duty for sixty days in consequence of epilepsy," the regimental surgeon wrote on Packer's disability discharge paper. "The paroxysms occur once every 48 hours and sometimes as often as two and three times every 48 hours."[10]

In the following years, Packer drifted ever farther west, working variously as a harness maker and saddler, trapper, teamster, hunter, and wilderness guide. As the 1860s drew to a close, he, along with hordes of other young army veterans, found himself in Colorado, prospecting for gold. After losing parts of two left fingers in an accident while mining near Breckenridge, he worked for a time as a "jack whacker," leading long strings of pack mules laden with supplies—food, lumber, tools, and dynamite—up the perilous mountain trails.[11] He remained subject to violent epileptic seizures. "At frequent intervals," recalled a mining partner named George Riley, Packer would "fall to the ground and struggle to a terrible degree. . . . He would then be prostrate for several days, unable to perform any labor."[12]

Though Packer's precise movements in the decade following his discharge are impossible to trace with precision, it is certain that by

1871, he was seeking his fortune in Utah. Eventually, he made his way to Bingham Canyon, where he worked at copper mining until he was sickened with lead poisoning. Back on his feet, he moved to the tiny town of Sandy—hardly more than a general store and a few ramshackle buildings, about twelve miles south of Salt Lake City—and worked in one of the many small smelters just outside of town. It wasn't long, however, before he "got leaded again." The illness, Packer later testified, "throwed me into fits. They thought I was going to die." Under the care of the local sawbones, one Dr. McCann—who treated him with liberal doses of castor oil—Packer was back on his feet by the fall of 1873, when newspapers spread the word of the latest silver strikes in the San Juan Mountains of Colorado.[13]

+ + +

Among the army of fortune hunters working in the vicinity of Bingham Canyon at that time was a fellow named Bob McGrue, who had come over from Oregon with his partner, George Tracy. McGrue was the owner of two wagons drawn by a pair of four-horse teams and—his prospecting ventures having come to nothing—was making a meager living by hauling freight "where I could get freight to haul." Sometime toward the end of October, he began to hear talk "about this San Juan country, where it was represented that rich lodes had been found and that many were going there." When Tracy suggested that the two of them join a company that was organizing for the journey to southwestern Colorado, McGrue replied that he "would just as soon go there as anyplace else." "Times were dull, not much to do, and winter coming on," he later recalled. "Any place that showed a chance to make some money would do me."

One evening, shortly after McGrue arrived at this decision, a strapping young man with long black hair and a small goatee showed up at the spot in Bingham Canyon where McGrue and Tracy were camped and introduced himself as Alfred Packer. As McGrue recounted, "He said he would like to go with me to this San Juan country, that he was broke, had no way to pay his passage, that if I would let him go he would help and do all he could along the road, that he had lived and worked in

Colorado and knew considerable about the country and that he would be useful as a guide." McGrue was impressed not only with Packer's seemingly robust health—"he appeared as though he might be an active athlete"—but with his intelligence. "While he was generally quiet and reticent," said McGrue, "he loved to go among the Mormons and argue religion with them. I often listened to him and thought he was smart and a fine talker." In exchange for Packer's help with the horses and service as a guide, McGrue agreed to pay his fifty-dollar "grubstake."[14]

Before setting off, McGrue and Tracy, along with the other members of the Colorado-bound party, spent several days in Salt Lake City stocking up on supplies. The dangers of getting caught on the trail with inadequate provisions were well known to experienced prospectors, many of whom had heard the harrowing tale of Daniel Blue.

Fourteen years earlier, in February 1859, Blue and his two brothers, Alexander and Charles—"infatuated" with dreams of gold—had set out from Illinois for Pikes Peak. Traveling by railroad and boat, they made their way to Lawrence, Kansas, where they purchased a packhorse and, after loading it with woolen blankets and some sacks of flour, proceeded onward by foot. Before long, they were joined by other young men bound for "the new Eldorado."

Disaster struck when they found themselves lost in the wilderness, "completely confused as to [their] course." To make matters worse, their pony broke free of its tether and vanished, carrying most of their provisions with it. Slinging their few remaining supplies onto their backs, the three Blue brothers and a man named Soley pushed ahead.

Unable to find any game besides a few rabbits, they quickly exhausted their meager rations. After eight days without food, "except boiled roots and grass and the snow," Soley died of starvation, "requesting us, with his last words, to take his body and eat as much as we could, and thus preserve our lives." Daniel and his brothers, "lying helpless on the ground" beside the corpse of their companion, resisted for three days before succumbing to desperation. "Wild with hunger," they cut the flesh from Soley's arms and legs and devoured the meat "with eager relish."

Alexander Blue was the next to go. "Before his death," Daniel wrote in his memoir, "he, like Soley, urged us to eat his body for our own preservation. After he had been dead two days, the uncontrollable and maddening cravings of hunger impelled Charles and I to devour a part of our own brother's corpse!"

Taking "a part of our brother's body with us to eat thereafter," Daniel and Charles resumed their journey until the latter collapsed "from sickness and exhaustion" and died, leaving Daniel "alone in company with my dear brother's corpse—alone in a boundless waste of prairie, weak, helpless, and starving." Once again, Daniel was "impelled by the terrible pains of hunger" to feed on the flesh of his own sibling.[15]

He was finally rescued by an Arapaho brave, who came upon him gibbering in the woods. Carried back to the Indian's camp, the skeletal gold seeker—"so weak that his limbs flopped grotesquely each time he attempted to move"—was nursed with "warm antelope blood and some raw antelope liver" until he was strong enough to make the trip back to civilization. Transported by stagecoach to the little mining settlement of Auraria, "Daniel Blue slowly regained his physical health, but his mind never fully recovered from the ordeal."[16]

+ + +

Their provisions loaded onto wagons and pack animals, McGrue, Tracy, Packer, and the rest of the expedition—nineteen men in all—set out from Bingham Canyon on the first of November.[17] Before they had gotten very far, two other prospectors were added to the group: Preston Nutter, who threw in with the expedition at Provo, and Oliver D. Loutsenhizer, formerly sheriff of Bozeman, Montana, who joined at Salina.

From the first, Nutter felt that the party was "poorly provisioned" for the journey. The other men, however, seemed unconcerned. Packer, after all—who insisted that he "knowed all the country" well—assured them that they would have no trouble reaching their destination, roughly four hundred miles away, in only twenty days' time.[18]

4.

PARIAH

The going was easy at first, the party of twenty-one men with their wagons and pack animals following the Old Spanish Trail southeast toward the Colorado border. Eventually they came to the old Mormon fort on the banks of the Grand River, a walled mission established in 1855 by a band of Brigham Young's followers. Once across the river, however, it quickly became clear that, as Loutsenhizer later put it, "Packer did not know the way and . . . was lying when he said he could guide."[1]

By then, Loutsenhizer had already developed a powerful dislike of Packer. Soon after joining the group, "Lot" (as his friends called him) heard whispers that Packer had spent time behind bars in Salt Lake City, a rumor confirmed by Packer himself, who confessed that he had "been in the county jail for ninety days" after being "caught in a house of prostitution."[2] The revelation reinforced the growing impression among certain members of the party that—as Preston Nutter put it—Packer was "a man without a character." As the little wagon train trudged onward, he grew increasingly "sulky, obstinate, and quarrelsome," grumbling loudly about the rapidly diminishing provisions.[3] It didn't help matters that he vented his complaints in an unusually grating voice, described by some as "high-pitched and whiny," by others as "not high, not low, but hollow-sounding."[4]

Lot, Nutter, and others made no effort to conceal their frank dislike of Packer. He was accused of being a petty thief—"willing to take things that did not belong to him whether of any value or not"—and of hogging the dwindling supply of rations. Even as their "flour grew scarce," Loutsenhizer bitterly recounted, Packer "would build up a fire, bake up a great cake of bread bigger than a dinner plate, and sneak off with it under his coat to eat it because the other fellows jeered him for his greediness." According to both Nutter and Lot, Packer also displayed a disquieting interest in the amount of money that the other men were carrying, repeatedly "inquiring round to see how much [they] all had."[5]

At least one member of the party felt differently: Bob McGrue, who was paying Packer's way and sharing a wagon with him at night. McGrue could never understand the other men's antipathy toward his traveling companion, particularly in light of Packer's illness.

McGrue became aware of Packer's condition early on in the trip. One evening, while the party was camped just outside Provo, Packer hunkered down by the fire alongside eighteen-year-old George Noon, a San Francisco native nicknamed "California." McGrue, who was tending his horses, happened to glance toward the campfire and—as he afterward recounted—saw "Packer with a wild stare in his eyes looking into the fire . . . All of a sudden he fell over partly into the fire and in his fit or convulsion knocked the coffee pot over, the water from which on the hot coals and ashes caused a steam that scalded and freckled up Packer's face and eyes considerable. I shouted at once to George Noon to catch Packer when he was falling, but he being a young man appeared to become scared and paralyzed and could not or did not move, and I ran up and pulled Packer out of the fire and that steam. Packer remained in the fit quite a while and was a bad sight, his eyes having an open, glaring, dead cast."

Once revived, Packer resorted to one of his habitual lies, assuring McGrue "that that was the first fit he ever had in his life." From that point on, recalled McGrue, "he had them repeatedly. In the daytime I could tell when they were coming on, as he would glare into the fire with an insane stare from which nothing could attract him. At such times I would catch him, lay him down, and hold him till he came out of the fit."

Sometimes, the seizures would happen in the middle of the night. Packer, who slept beside McGrue in one of the wagons, would "get up for some call of nature. . . . Just as he got over the end gate of the wagon, he would fall in the fit inside of the wagon, sometimes nearly onto me. I always in those cases held him till the fit was over, then put him to bed."

The first time this happened, McGrue—suddenly roused from his slumber in confusion and alarm—"grabbed Packer and shouted for help" to the men sleeping round the campfire outside. McGrue was stunned when, "as with one voice, they all shouted, 'Damn you, you wanted him along, now take care of him.' Nor would they ever help me take care of him."

"Why all the outfit hated Packer so I never knew," said McGrue. "All or nearly all of the company asked me to drive him out of the company and not let him go along. I answered that, with the exception of George Tracy, I knew Packer as well as I did any of them, that he done his part and behaved himself as well as any of them, that he had just as good a right to go along and over the route as they had."

As for Packer himself, he responded to their treatment of him in kind. Knowing that "they hated him so," he "stayed apart from the balance of the men," nursing "a cordial hatred" toward most of them and a particularly "vindictive and unforgiving hatred" of the two who "were hardest on him"—a Scotsman named Cooper, who claimed to be an MD, and a German butcher, Frank "Reddy" Miller.[6]

+ + +

Arrived at the Green River, about eighty-five miles from the Colorado border, the party, unable to find a shallow enough spot to cross, was forced to dismantle the wagons and ferry them across on crudely made rafts. Once on the opposite side, it became clearer than ever that Packer, in McGrue's words, "did not know the country or route better than the rest of us." It fell to Nutter and Lot, mounted on horseback, to scout ahead for a suitable route. "For long stretches," McGrue recalled, "we could see no road or trail on account of snow." From time to time, the group would encounter an Indian or two and "pay them to guide us on. Sometimes they would go for a day or so, tell us there were some Indians up ahead who were their enemies, and they would go no farther."[7]

With their food running out and no game to be found beyond the occasional snowshoe rabbit, tensions mounted among the men.

One evening, as the group was gathered around the campfire, a Philadelphian named George Driver exchanged hard words with Jean Cabazon, a Frenchman known inevitably as "Frenchy." When Driver sneeringly called Frenchy a "puppy," the latter replied, in his heavily accented English, that if he was a puppy, Driver was a son of a bitch. Only the swift intervention of several of their companions kept the two men from coming to blows.[8]

By then, the men were famished enough to consider eating one of their horses. For five days, as they pushed on to the San Juan country, they subsisted on nothing but chopped barley. They were on the brink of starvation when, on January 25, 1874—almost three months after they had set forth from Utah—they suddenly found themselves surrounded by a band of "whooping and yelling" Indians, decked out "in war array."[9]

5.

OURAY

For centuries before the arrival of the white man, the land that would later become the Colorado Territory was occupied by scattered bands of a single nomadic tribe. Short, stocky, and so dark skinned that other Indians called them "the Black Faces," they were known to themselves simply as *Nuchu*—"the People"—and to early Spanish explorers as the *Yutas*, from which their ultimate name derived: the Utes.

Until the mid-seventeenth century, these sturdy hunter-gatherers traveled in small family groups of ten to forty people. Following a seasonal cycle, they ranged on foot from mountain slope to river valley, the men hunting deer, elk, antelope, and jackrabbits, the women gathering pine nuts, berries, grass seeds, and tubers. Their lodgings were hide-covered teepees and thatched wickiups. Once a year, in early spring, members of the various bands would gather to take part in the Bear Dance, a sacred ritual that lasted four or five days and culminated with a great feast. When the celebration was over, the groups would disperse, heading off to their separate hunting grounds.

This age-old way of life underwent a dramatic transformation in the mid-1600s, when the Utes came into contact with the Spanish colonists of Taos and Santa Fe and first set eyes on the miraculous four-legged creatures that the Europeans had introduced to the New World. Entranced by these "magic dogs"—as the Utes called horses—the Indians began to acquire them, initially by bartering buckskins, eventually through more aggressive means: raiding Spanish settlements or trafficking in slaves, generally children captured from enemy tribes. Within a few generations, the Utes had been transformed from passive wanderers—reduced in times of want to feeding on rattlesnakes and lizards—into feared, warlike horsemen who claimed a vast expanse of Western territory as their own.[1]

In 1848, when America won possession of the entire Southwest from Mexico, the Utes fell under the authority of the United States. One year later, the government entered into a "friendship treaty" with the tribe. According to its provisions, the Utes recognized the sovereignty of the United States and agreed not to roam beyond their "accustomed territory." Since that territory was deemed "unsuitable for Anglo-American settlement" at the time, the government did not feel it necessary to confine the Indians to a specifically defined reservation.[2]

All that changed a decade later. With the discovery of gold in Colorado and the onset of Pikes Peak mania, the Utes found themselves in increasing conflict with the hordes of white miners swarming over their ancestral land. In January 1868, a delegation set out for Washington, DC, to negotiate a new treaty between the United States government and the Indians. Mediating between the two parties was the legendary scout Kit Carson. Representing the Indians was the chief of the Tabeguache Utes, the largest of the seven tribal groups. His name was Ouray.

Much about Ouray's background is obscure, including the meaning of his name, which most sources claim translates as "the arrow," though Ouray himself reportedly explained that it derived from "ooay," the first bit of gibberish to issue from his mouth as a child.[3] His father was a Jicarilla Apache who had been stolen and brought up by the Utes, his mother a member of the Tabeguaches. Raised in Taos, Ouray grew up fluent in Spanish, as well as Apache and the various Ute dialects. How well he spoke English is another matter of dispute. Certain accounts describe him as a flowery orator, though most agree that he had limited command of the language.[4]

After a boyhood spent herding sheep in New Mexico, the young Ouray—short, barrel-chested, physically powerful, and fearless—left for Uncompahgre Valley on the Western Slope of Colorado, where his widowed father had gone to rejoin the Ute tribe that had raised him. He soon distinguished himself not only as a superb horseman and fierce warrior against the Cheyennes and Sioux but as a charismatic leader with an uncommon gift for diplomacy. By 1863, at the age of thirty—when he made his first trip to the nation's capital to observe, at first hand, the sheer numbers and might of the white man—he had been generally recognized as the head chief of the Ute nation.

Ouray and his fellow members of the 1868 delegation arrived in Washington in early February. A photograph Mathew Brady took at the time shows the Ute chief surrounded by a group of much taller, formally dressed government officials sporting various styles of facial hair—full beards, muttonchop whiskers, and walrus mustaches. Ouray poses front and center, fixing the camera with a formidable stare and radiating an almost palpable air of dignified authority. He is dressed in traditional tribal garb—a fringed and ornamented buckskin shirt that descends to his knees, buckskin breeches, and moccasins—and wears his hair in two long braids that are wrapped in otter fur and hang down either side of his outthrust chest.

After two months of negotiations—during which Ouray "met President Johnson, General Grant, John C. Frémont and scads of other celebrities"—the treaty was ready to be signed.[5] In return for relinquishing a vast tract of their traditional hunting grounds, the Utes were guaranteed "absolute and undisturbed" ownership of slightly more than fifteen million acres of southwestern Colorado—roughly one-quarter of the territory—to be known as the Confederated Ute Reservation. No whites would be allowed "to pass over, settle upon, or reside in" the reservation. As additional compensation, the government agreed to pay the tribe $30,000 per year for thirty years in clothing, blankets, and other "articles of utility" and another $30,000 in food—beef, mutton, wheat, flour, beans, and potatoes.

To distribute these annuities, handle any complaints from the tribe, and resolve all conflicts between Indians and whites, two agencies would be established. At each, the government was to build a schoolhouse, where Ute children between the ages of seven and eighteen could learn to read and write English. To promote further assimilation, each agency would also house a farmer, a blacksmith, and a miller who would offer aid and instruction to all adult male Indians willing to abandon their traditional hunting ways for homesteading.[6]

No sooner had the treaty been ratified than the San Juan silver rush brought thousands of new miners flooding onto the Ute reservation. Ouray complained to the US authorities, but his protests were in vain. In the interest of avoiding armed clashes with the ever-growing population of whites, he offered to allow prospectors to enter the reservation during summer months and work their mines, so long as they established no permanent homes. For white Coloradans, however, the San Juan range and its mineral bounty were theirs by right of Manifest Destiny. "An Indian has no more right to stand in the way of civilization and progress than a wolf or a bear," thundered the *Boulder News*, while the *Rocky Mountain News* vilified the Utes as a "dissolute, vagabondish, brutal, and ungrateful race that ought to be wiped from the face of the earth."[7]

Faced with a grim choice—leading his braves in a hopeless war against a vastly more powerful adversary or giving up the San Juan silver fields to secure a reduced but still extensive reservation for his people—Ouray, ever the clear-eyed realist, opted for the latter course. In an agreement reached in September 1873, the Utes ceded to the United States four million acres of San Juan mineral lands. In return, the government agreed to pay the Indians an additional $25,000 a year above the amount granted in the treaty of 1868. The Utes would be allowed to hunt on the surrendered land as long as they maintained peaceful relations with the whites. A final provision—one that would generate lasting controversy in the life of Chief Ouray—granted him an annual stipend of $1,000 for his part in hammering out the agreement and persuading his fellow Ute chiefs to accept it.[8]

Though believing he was acting in his people's best interest, Ouray was derided by some as an "'apple' Indian, red on the outside and white on the inside"—a traitor who had sold out his tribe for a few pieces of silver. After several failed attempts on his life, he took to traveling with a Mexican bodyguard, who "slept outside his door at night." To the white settlers, on the other hand, his efforts to promote peaceful coexistence would earn him praise as a farseeing, statesmanlike leader—"the greatest Indian of his time," as one national newspaper put it, the stead-fast "friend of the white man."[9]

+ + +

Ouray was among the band of war-painted braves that surrounded Packer's prospecting party on January 25, 1874. As trespassers on the Ute reservation, the whites had little reason to expect kindly treatment from the Indians. Frenchy Cabazon—who, in addition to his native tongue and English, spoke fluent Spanish—explained to Ouray that he and his companions had no intention of settling in the area. Satisfied that the gaunt and bedraggled men were transient fortune hunters, Ouray—in a characteristic display of hospitality—advised them against traveling any farther in the snow-packed mountains and invited them to remain with his tribe until the spring thaw.[10]

When the twenty-one exhausted men agreed, Ouray led them to a spot within two miles of his own village—"a spring where there was wood and plenty of grass" for their animals, as Bob McGrue described it. Putting up a variety of shelters—tents, shanties, and dugouts—they settled in for the winter, pooling their money to buy flour, coffee, sugar, and tobacco from the Indians, along with three goats to be butchered for their meat. There was steady contact between the whites and their Ute hosts, who paid regular visits to each other's camps. "We was generally pretty sociable with each other," Packer later recalled. As for Ouray, he would earn the lasting gratitude of the prospectors. "The chief," said Loutsenhizer, speaking for all the men, "treated us like brothers."[11]

Within a week, however, Lot and several others, Packer included, were already growing restless. With Frenchy serving as interpreter, they learned from Ouray that the nearest outposts were the Los Pinos Indian Agency, eighty miles to the east, and the cow camp, slightly closer, where the government maintained the livestock allotted to the Utes under the 1873 treaty. Ouray insisted, however, that—with the trails buried under three or more feet of snow—it was folly to attempt to reach either destination. His warnings went unheeded. On February 2, Lot and four others—Mike Burke, George Driver, and the Walker brothers, Isaac and Tom—set out by foot. Packer tried to follow, but when Lot aimed a six-shooter at him and told him that "if [Lot] saw him after [they] passed the point of the mountain there would be trouble," he returned to the camp.

Then, carrying enough food to last for a week, Lot and his companions headed into the wilderness, hoping "to make the cow camp in three or four days."[12]

+ + +

One frigid afternoon three weeks later, James P. Kelley and Sidney Jocknick, the cowboys in charge of the government cattle camp, were relaxing in their cabin when they were startled by a knock on the door. Opening it, they found two haggard men, "skin and bones from hunger and cold," who stumbled inside and sank down before the blazing fireplace. Revived with some warm milk and bread, the strangers—who gave their names as Oliver Loutsenhizer and Mike Burke—explained that three members of their party were still stranded out in the snow. Hitching up a sled and loading it with provisions, Kelley and Jocknick followed Lot and Burke's tracks back to where the two prospectors had last seen their companions. They found the three men, "more dead than alive," huddled around a small fire. After "livening them up a bit" with some coffee and a few pieces of meat "roasted on a stick Indian style," Kelley and Jocknick managed to get them back to the cabin, where, the following day, Lot narrated the harrowing tale of their ordeal.[13]

Lost in the snow after exhausting their food supply, the five men were reduced to subsisting on rosebuds and wild berries. They were temporarily saved from starvation when Lot spotted a coyote with something clamped in its mouth. Lot took aim with his six-shooter and fired at the animal. The shot missed, but the coyote dropped what it was carrying before bolting away. It turned out to be the foreleg of a sheep, which provided the men with enough meat to keep them going for a few more days.

The men staggered onward in temperatures that sometimes dropped to ten degrees below zero. In places the snow was three feet deep with a crust that couldn't support their weight, and they sank up to their knees with every step. They tried fashioning crude skis out of cottonwood, but these "Norwegian Snow-shoes" (as the miners called them) simply "wore down in the snow instead of staying on top." Before long, they were scrounging for berries again.[14]

When three of the party announced that they could go no farther, Lot decided to press ahead with Burke, vowing "to use all the strength left in his body to find the camp and get help." The two men floundered onward in the snow. They were near starvation when they came upon a cow stuck in a snowdrift. It took thirteen shots for Lot to kill the animal. Cutting its throat with a knife, he and Burke drank some of the warm blood, then sliced off a chunk of flesh and ate it raw. Revitalized, they staggered on. They had reached a point of exhaustion again when they spotted a curl of chimney smoke rising from the cabin.[15]

+ + +

The prospectors remained at the cow camp for several weeks, gradually regaining their strength. At the time, they had no idea that, just a few days after their own departure from Ouray's camp, Alfred Packer and five other men had struck out into the wilderness, following the trail blazed by Lot's party.

6.

THE SIX

In addition to Packer, the party that set out from the Ute camp in the second week of February consisted of both the oldest and the youngest of the prospectors, Israel Swan, a man in his sixties, and sixteen-year-old George "California" Noon; the German butcher, Frank "Reddy" Miller; Shannon Wilson Bell of Michigan; and a Philadelphian named James Humphrey. Ouray urged the men not to leave. "He told them," recounted Bob McGrue, who was present at the scene, "that they would find those men that had gone before dead in the snow, and that they would all die, and that he had not an Indian in the band that would go to show the route . . . as they were afraid of the deep snow."

When he saw that the six men would not listen to reason, Ouray squatted on his haunches and, using a stick to draw a map in the ground, "gave them all the directions he could as to the route."

The following day, February 9, McGrue, who had agreed to accompany the men as far as he could, loaded their blankets and other provisions onto two of his horses. The party left around noon and walked until sunset, then camped for the night, Packer laying out his bedroll "apart from the balance of [them]." At dawn the following day, they set out again.

By midafternoon, McGrue would go no farther. Already "the snow was so deep that I could not get the horses through it." Unpacking the men's supplies from his horses, McGrue "delivered them their outfit and turned back."

Except for Alfred Packer, McGrue later testified, "I never seen any of the party since."[1]

+ + +

Sometime in late March or early April—the date is uncertain—a small party of Utes, several women among them, came upon a white man camped by the Gunnison River. He was seated on a log, preparing his dinner. A piece of meat, skewered on a stick, was roasting in his fire.

After a minute or two, having evidently judged the meat done, he began to remove it from the fire. Suddenly, he became aware that the Indians were watching him. Leaving the meat on the coals, he hurriedly picked up something lying on the ground beside him and threw it into the river.

Later, the thing washed up on the riverbank and was found by one of the Indian women. It was a human arm, missing much of its flesh.[2]

7.

LOS PINOS

Situated near the foot of Cochetopa Pass, about twenty-five miles south of the cow camp, the Los Pinos Indian Agency consisted of a cluster of rough-hewn buildings arranged around a two-hundred-foot quadrangle. A schoolhouse large enough to accommodate up to forty children occupied the center of the square. The agent's house—a three-room cabin built of "logs sawed on two sides and chinked with wood chips and mud"—stood at the northern end. Other buildings included a combined carpenter and blacksmith shop, a sawmill, a warehouse, a stable, and a communal mess hall.[1]

In the early hours of April 16, 1874—"a spring-like" morning when the "snow was getting soft"—Alonzo Hartman, one of the agency's employees, left his bunkhouse to collect some firewood. A direct descendant of Daniel Boone on his mother's side, the twenty-four-year-old Hartman had migrated from Iowa with his family a dozen years before and settled in the Denver area. After working as a cowboy on the Western Slope, he had been hired at the agency cow camp, where, along with James Kelley and Sidney Jocknick, he managed the three thousand head of cattle, riding out each day to move the herd from one grazing area to the next.

In late 1873, Hartman had left his coworkers to handle matters at the cow camp while he wintered at the agency. He was standing by the woodpile on the morning of April 16 when, as he later wrote, he "noticed a man coming down the little creek, walking leisurely on the ice." In one hand the stranger carried a Winchester rifle; in the other, a coffee pot that—as it turned out—held a clump of live coals, used for starting campfires. A little pack was strapped about his shoulders. "I knew the man did not belong to the agency," wrote Hartman, "for there were only a few of us staying there that winter, and the others were all sitting about the fire reading or playing cards."

Hartman's first impression of the fellow was that "he didn't seem different from any other man who had been exposed to the cold winter weather." Though his beard was shaggy even by frontier standards and his long black hair unkempt and matted, he "showed little sign of having been . . . lost in a wild, uninhabited country with the thermometer showing between 30 and 50 degrees below zero every morning." Whatever hardships the stranger had endured, he seemed "none the worse" for them.

"Hello," said Hartman. "Are you lost?"

"Is this the agency?" asked the stranger. When he spoke, Hartman saw that his two upper front teeth were missing.

"It is," said Hartman. He put a few questions to the fellow—Where was he heading? How far had he come?—but couldn't get a straight answer. "His mind was all right, but he just didn't want to be questioned," Hartman recalled. Assuming the stranger was hungry, Hartman then "hustled him" to the mess hall.[2]

Four other agency employees were just digging into breakfast when Hartman entered with Packer: clerks Stephen Dole and Herman Lueders; Constable Herman Lauter; and Major James P. Downer, a one-time Pennsylvania congressman now serving as justice of the peace. Their subsequent accounts of Packer's arrival would differ in significant ways. One claimed that he was wild-eyed and haggard, another that he looked "hearty and well fed." According to a third, he was ravenously hungry and, when offered a platter of beefsteak, wolfed the meat down. Another insisted that he turned nauseated at the sight of food and requested whiskey instead.[3]

All agreed, however, that—as Lauter later testified—Packer claimed to have set out from Chief Ouray's camp two months earlier with "five other men . . . and that he had became snow-blind and footsore, and they left him somewhere in camp with a few days' provisions while they was to go down to find the settlement and come back for him. They had not come back, so he laid there sometimes and he struck out for himself and come to the agency."[4]

+ + +

Among the men who had listened to the wise counsel of Chief Ouray and remained camped near the Ute village until the snow began to melt were the Scotsman Dr. Cooper, Preston Nutter, and a prospector known to history as "Italian Tom." On April 2, the trio bid farewell to their Indian hosts and set out on horseback for the Los Pinos Indian Agency. They reached it two weeks later, arriving, by an odd coincidence, just hours after Packer made his appearance.

At the sight of the men, Packer grew visibly agitated. When Nutter asked "where the rest of the party were," Packer "said he didn't know" and claimed, once again, that his five traveling companions had left him behind after he went out to hunt game and "got his feet wet and frozen."[5]

After a short stay at the agency, Packer announced that he "was tired of Colorado and wished to return to his family and friends in Pennsylvania." Claiming to be broke, he sold his Winchester rifle to Major Downer for ten dollars. Accompanied by Nutter and the other two members of the original party, he then set out by wagon for the town of Saguache, forty-five miles away.[6]

In the course of the eleven-day journey, Nutter noticed something strange. Packer was in possession of a big skinning knife that had belonged to the German butcher, Frank "Reddy" Miller. When Nutter asked where he had gotten it, Packer explained that Miller "stuck it in a tree, went off and left it."

Nutter said nothing in reply. Privately, however, he had already begun to harbor serious doubts about Packer's story—to "misbelieve" him.[7]

8.

SAGUACHE

Pronounced "sah-WATCH," the county of Saguache derives its name from the Ute word *saguaguachipa*, generally translated as "water at the blue earth." Early trappers and traders, who found the Indian word a mouthful, abridged it to "Saguache"—a name, as Otto Mears later recalled with some asperity, that "means absolutely nothing."[1]

Mears's life story could easily have borne the title of one of Horatio Alger's rags-to-riches fables: *Bound to Rise, Do and Dare, Forging Ahead, Luck and Pluck, Making His Mark, Strive and Succeed*, or any of a dozen others. Born to Jewish parents in a province of present-day Latvia, he was orphaned at three and spent the next eight years being shuttled from one unwelcoming relative to the next, first in Russia, then in England, and finally in the United States. In 1851, still only eleven, he found himself stranded in San Francisco, living on his own in a Barbary Coast boarding house. Supporting himself at a variety of odd jobs—newsboy, store clerk, tinsmith, milkman, hotel worker—he eventually made his way to the mining camps of Nevada, where he discovered that the people profiting most handsomely from the gold rush were not the prospectors but the entrepreneurs who furnished them with supplies and transportation: "the store and saloon keeper, and the teamster and the freighter."[2]

Following a three-year stint in the Union army—during part of which he served under Colonel Kit Carson in the campaign against the Navajos—Mears drifted out to Santa Fe, where he found work as a clerk in a trading post. His ferocious drive and business acumen quickly drew the attention of rival traders, who put him in charge of their newly established store. One year later, tired of working for others, Mears relocated again, this time to the town of Conejos in the Colorado Territory, just across the border from New Mexico, where, in partnership with an old friend, Isaac Gotthelf, he opened a general store.

To supply its troops at Fort Garland, an outpost situated in the vicinity of Conejos, the US Army was paying a premium for flour. With his keen eye for the main chance, Mears promptly built a gristmill. Partnering up with another Colorado pioneer, a rancher named John Lawrence, he bought more than twelve hundred acres of government land at the site of present-day Saguache and began cultivating wheat. When the army suddenly dropped its price, he turned to another market: the booming mining camps in the area later known as Leadville, 135 miles away from his gristmill. Since there were no existing roads through the rugged mountain passes, Mears, after obtaining the appropriate charter, constructed a toll road, the first step in a storied career as a road and railroad builder that would earn him renown as "The Pathfinder of the San Juans."

Moving his store to his new homestead, he—along with John Lawrence and a few other early settlers—not only secured passage of a bill creating the town of Saguache but managed to have it made the county seat. Before long he had gotten himself elected county treasurer; founded the town's first newspaper, the *Saguache Chronicle*; won a government contract to deliver the mail; and helped negotiate the 1873 treaty with the Utes—all the while continuing to operate his store, which quickly grew into the area's largest emporium, stocking everything from groceries, whiskey, and cattle feed to mining tools and Levi's "best California riveted overalls," priced at $2.50 a pair.[3]

+ + +

"During early days, Saguache led a riotous existence," notes one official history of Colorado. "Every other building was a saloon."[4] It was to one of these establishments, run by a fellow named Dolan, that Packer repaired immediately upon his arrival in town.

Described as an "Irish wag of rare and sometimes profane and vulgar wit,"[5] Dolan—known to everyone as Larry, though his Christian name was James—took an immediate shine to the scraggly-bearded, gap-toothed prospector, in large part, no doubt, because Packer, who had claimed to be penniless just days before, seemed to have money to burn. During his nearly two-week stay in Saguache, he spent $100 at the saloon, by Dolan's estimate—a considerable sum in 1872, equivalent to roughly $2,000 today. Most of the money went for liquor, though (according to Dolan) he also lost $37 in a single game of "freeze-out" poker.[6]

Packer's free-spending ways aroused the suspicion of other members of the original prospecting party, who had been arriving in Saguache from Ouray's camp and who recalled that Packer had been broke when the expedition left Utah. As more of them showed up and found lodging at the town's only boarding house, Packer asked Dolan if he could move into the saloon, explaining that "the boys didn't like him very well and that he would like to sleep with [Dolan]." Though warned by Dolan that "it would be a very disagreeable place to sleep," Packer camped out at the saloon for the rest of his time in Saguache, eating canned food—mostly oysters and peaches—sleeping beneath a blanket on the hard-packed mud floor, and occasionally taking over the bartending chores when Dolan had to run an errand.

When business was slow, the two men filled the empty hours with talk. Packer described his weeks alone in the wilderness, where he subsisted largely on rosebuds. To Dolan, however, his new friend "did not look as if he had starved at all. He simply looked rough, as one would after a mountain trip." At one point, they "got to talking about money matters." As the saloonkeeper later recalled, Packer "told me if I was short of money, he could spare me three hundred dollars."[7]

Six days after moving into the saloon, Packer—made increasingly uneasy by the growing doubts about his story voiced by Nutter and others—decided to get out of town. Heading over to Mears's general store, he purchased a pair of brogan shoes, a cheap shirt, two pairs of canvas overalls—"a common pair, not California made"—and some tobacco, for a total of eight dollars.[8] Then, after some haggling with the merchant, he agreed to pay seventy dollars for a horse and bridle.

Extracting some bills from his wallet, he handed them to Mears, who had heard rumors that Packer once spent time in jail for passing counterfeit money. When one of the ten-dollar bills struck Mears's practiced eye as fake, Packer fished out a second billfold stuffed with money and gave him another greenback.[9]

By the time Packer was ready to leave town, feelings against him were running dangerously high among his former traveling companions. All the members of the original Utah party had made it safely by then to either Saguache or the Los Pinos Indian Agency. All, that is, except the five men who had set out from Ouray's camp in the company of Alfred Packer.

9.

ADAMS

On May 1, 1874, while Packer was making preparations for his departure, General Charles Adams, head of the Los Pinos Indian Agency, stopped off at Saguache on his way back from Denver, where he had gone on some official business. With him was his wife, Margaret, sister-in-law of the territorial governor, Edward McCook.

Just three years earlier, Adams was still known by his original name, Karl Adam Schwanbeck. Born and raised in the city of Anklam in the province of Pomerania, Germany, he was educated in the local secondary school (or *Gymnasium*), where he excelled in classical languages. Shortly after graduating in 1862, he emigrated to the United States and immediately enlisted in the Sixth Massachusetts Regiment. He fought bravely in the Civil War and was wounded twice in battle. Following his discharge, he headed west, where he served in the Third US Cavalry against the Kiowa and Comanche Indians in New Mexico and Texas. Appointed brigadier general of the Colorado Territory militia by his brother-in-law in 1870, he jettisoned his Germanic family name and assumed his new Americanized one, a change ratified by the Colorado legislature in 1871. The following year, he became Indian agent at the Los Pinos Agency.[1]

Arrived at Saguache early on the morning of May 1, Adams and his wife were having breakfast at the house of Otto Mears when Packer appeared and joined them at the table. "He began talking mostly with my wife," Adams later recalled, "about his experiences in the mountains."

Packer's story was essentially the same one he had been telling since he emerged from the wilderness: "that he and five men had left the encampment of the Utes some time in February and they had wandered in the mountains for several days and he had frozen his feet. That his comrades had stayed in camp with him a few days, that he was unable to walk and could not keep up, so they had to leave him on the mountainside. One of the party gave him his rifle to procure food and after a few days he was able to walk again—he lived on a rabbit that he killed and afterwards on rosebuds till he managed to reach the agency."[2]

Packer was still regaling Mrs. Adams with the details of his ordeal when Adams excused himself and went over to the general store, where Mears apprised him of the dark rumors swirling through town: "that Packer, who had no money when he parted from [Ouray's camp], seemed to be well supplied with that commodity, that he had shown things belonging to his companions, such as knives and purses, that in gambling and carousing he had already spent a great deal of money at Saguache."[3]

Reasoning that, if Packer had survived on rosebuds, his five companions might have done the same, Adams proposed "fitting out a party" to hunt for the missing men. "I asked Packer to be the guide," Adams afterward testified. "He said that he had no objections, only he had no money. He had spent what money he had and must go to work. I told him I would give him work and in capacity of employee send him out on this expedition." Packer agreed.

The next morning, Adams and his wife left for the Los Pinos Agency in a buggy, with Otto Mears and Packer accompanying them on horseback. Halfway there, they encountered one of the men who had traveled from Utah with Packer: Bob McGrue's partner, George Tracy, on his way into Saguache for provisions. Packer dismounted to exchange a few words with Tracy. When Tracy asked him "what became of the boys," Packer offered the usual tale, with one significant difference. This time, as Tracy testified, "he said that old Swan had died."[4]

+ + +

Several members of the original Utah party were present at the agency when Adams and the others arrived. As the general told it, the men lost no time "in accusing Packer of having murdered their friends" and demanded that he be handed over to them. Adams, however, would have no part in a lynching. Taking Packer into his office, he pressed him to reveal "where he got the money he had spent" in Saguache. At first, Packer insisted that "he had no money except the ten dollars" he had gotten from selling his rifle to Major Downer. When Adams asked about the purchases he had made from Otto Mears—including the horse and bridle—Packer, claiming that it had slipped his mind, suddenly recalled having borrowed it from a blacksmith named Kincaid in Saguache, "an old family friend" who had "let him have this money to go home on."[5]

Adams immediately dispatched one of his employees to Saguache. Sometime later that day, while awaiting the man's return, Adams noticed Packer wandering toward Los Pinos Creek, about a quarter mile from the agency buildings. Not long afterward, one of Adams's staff members "saw Packer throw something into the stream." Packer would later be searched for the two billfolds that Otto Mears had seen in his possession, but they would never be found.[6]

+ + +

The messenger sent to Saguache returned the following day. After hearing his news, Adams called Packer back to his office, seated him in a chair, "and again asked what had become of his comrades." Packer announced that "he had nothing more to say."

"Not in regard to the money either?" asked Adams.

"No," said Packer.

"Well then," said Adams, "I will tell you that you have lied to me. I know that Kincaid gave you no money. I will ask you again: where did you get the money? You might as well tell me the truth. I believe these men are dead and you know something about it. If the matter is as I suspect, you are more to be pitied than blamed. But I wish to get the whole truth of this thing because I do not care to send out a party into the mountains to search for dead men."

For a long moment, Packer "sat silent." When he finally spoke, his voice was thick with emotion. "It wouldn't be the first time," he said, "that people had been obliged to eat each other when they were hungry."

"No," said Adams. "I have heard of such occurrences. But is this the case in this instance?"

Tears sprang to Packer's eyes. "I will tell you the whole story," he cried. "But I am afraid of the boys!"

Adams assured him that he "need not be afraid of the boys." He continued, "If you tell the truth, there is no danger."

Then, "crying and blubbering like a child most of the time," Packer "commenced to tell the story."[7]

10.

FIRST CONFESSION

Having gravely misjudged the time it would take them to reach the government cow camp, Packer and his five companions found themselves out of provisions "almost before we knew it." For the next few days, they "struggled along the best we could," barely subsisting on "roots dug out of the frozen ground." Ten days after leaving Ouray's encampment, sixty-year-old Israel Swan died from starvation. The others immediately set upon his body, cutting away chunks of his flesh, which were roasted on a campfire and greedily devoured.

Provisioning themselves with strips of his flesh, the men then set out again. After four or five more days of trudging blindly through the snowbound wilderness, James Humphrey collapsed and died. He was butchered and eaten "in the same way, as the men were out of food again and hungry." Packer also confessed to having taken $133 from a billfold he had found on Humphrey.

Besides Packer, there were now three remaining members of the party: Shannon Wilson Bell, George "California" Noon, and Frank "Reddy" Miller. A few days after the death of Humphrey, Packer wandered off from the others to gather wood for a campfire. He returned to find that, in his absence, Bell and Noon had murdered Frank Miller, "who had been sick of rheumatism and delayed the party on the march." His body was "dissected and the best parts eaten." Like the corpses of the two men who had preceded him, Miller's was "left lying [at the spot] where the meat was taken off."

Their strength temporarily restored, the three survivors pushed ahead. "Several days after that," Packer continued, "Bell shot 'California' with Swan's gun." Packer and Bell then "both together had eaten his flesh."

There were now only two men left of the original six. After making "a solemn compact . . . not to kill each other for food," they forged ahead until they "came to a grove of timber near the banks of a lake." Their pledge was speedily broken. They were warming themselves around a campfire when, according to Packer, "Bell arose and taking his rifle aimed a blow with the butt end at me. The blow missed and the stock, striking a tree, broke off." Grabbing his own rifle, Packer shot and killed Bell in self-defense. "There was nothing I could do," he insisted. "In only a few seconds he was dead and couldn't utter a sound."

Packer remained at the campsite for several days, living on Bell's flesh. Then, taking "some of the flesh along with him," he continued on his way, reaching the agency two weeks later, just "a day or so" after he ran "out of meat."[1]

+ + +

Following the recital of this confession, Adams summoned his staff into his office, along with Otto Mears and several of Packer's original traveling companions—a dozen men in all. He then had Packer repeat the story in the presence of these witnesses. It was nearing midnight by the time the "tale of horror" was done. Fetching a sheet of official stationery engraved with the agency's name and logo—an Indian warrior in a buffalo headdress, mounted on a charging pony and clutching a lance—Adams wrote out an "extract" of the confession, which was signed and sworn to by Packer and certified by Justice of the Peace James Downer:

> Old Man Swan died first and was eaten by the other five persons about ten days out of camp. Four or five days afterwards Humphreys died and was also eaten; he had about one hundred and thirty three dollars ($133). I found the pocket book and took the money. Some time afterwards, while I was carrying wood, the butcher was killed—as the other two told me

accidentally—and he was also eaten. Bell shot "California" with Swan's gun and I killed Bell. Shot him. I covered up the remains and took a large piece along. Then traveled fourteen days into the agency. Bell wanted to kill me with his rifle—struck a tree and broke his gun.[2]

A few days later, Adams sent a letter to his superior in Washington, DC, Edward Parmelee Smith, commissioner of Indian affairs. In it, he relayed Packer's story and affirmed his faith in its basic accuracy. "I believe this to be in the main correct," wrote Adams, "as Mr. Packer looked quite fat when he arrived here and has since shown traces of mental aberration, which is said to be the consequences of eating human flesh."[3]

+ + +

Packer may have persuaded Adams that he was telling the truth, but Preston Nutter and his fellow prospectors remained unconvinced. One of them—James Montgomery, who had grown close to Shannon Bell during the journey from Utah—bitterly accused Packer of lying, insisting that "it was impossible for Bell to injure anyone" or "participate in the cannibalism as described." Nutter himself scoffed at Packer's earlier claim that he had found Frank Miller's butcher knife stuck in a tree and "pronounced his affidavit a tissue of lies."[4]

There seemed one sure way to corroborate the story. At the suggestion of Adams, Packer agreed to guide a search party back to his camp. If Bell's body was found there along with his broken rifle, then Packer was telling the truth. Adams pledged to set him free and even offered to bankroll his trip home to Pennsylvania.[5]

A day or two later, the party set out. Besides Packer, it consisted of three members of the original Utah group—Nutter, Dr. Cooper, and James McIntosh—an Indian known as "Captain Billy" and two other Utes, and the agency constable, Herman Lauter, there both to keep a watchful eye on Packer and to make sure that he came to no harm at the hands of the three other miners.[6]

It was Lauter himself—so he afterward claimed—who nearly came to harm. About four days out from the agency, he noticed that Packer had the butcher's skinning knife tucked under his shirt. When Lauter "demanded it of him," Packer "rushed at me with that knife." Grabbing his wrists, Lauter managed to wrest the weapon away and subdue Packer.[7]

As the party drew close to Lake San Cristobal, Packer—who had proved a willing guide up to that point—suddenly claimed that he had "no knowledge of the country" and "was entirely lost." When he refused to go any farther, Nutter, as he later put it, "had some controversy with Mr. Packer." He continued, "I told [him] I was satisfied that he had killed these men and ought to be hung for it."

"If you are satisfied that I killed the men," Packer replied, "*you* find them."

Adamant in his refusal to continue, Packer, guarded by Lauter, was sent back to the Los Pinos Agency, where he was placed in the custody of Sheriff Amos Wall of Saguache while the investigation into the affair proceeded.

Pressing on by themselves, Nutter and the remaining members of the search party finally came upon Packer's camp. It was immediately clear that it had been inhabited "for quite a length of time" and that its occupant "was used to camping." A neat bark shelter, big enough to accommodate one man, had been erected against one tree. In front of the lean-to "was a very neat fire place," made by someone "very partic- ular in gathering flat rock." A "small path" running "fifteen or twenty steps away from the camp" led to a spot that had been obviously "used by the individual who camped there to answer the call of nature."

Nutter would claim that "in looking around," he found a pillbox, which "convinced me that Packer had camped there." There were also unmistakable signs that, during his weeks in the camp, Packer had suf- fered grand mal seizures. As one witness reported, "the bed was the pure earth, no pine boughs, leaves, or grass. It appeared as though the man who used it had lain in it a great deal and in one position, and it appeared as though he might of been in delirium and had hallucina- tions. . . . The bed of earth showed the print of a man's head, his shoul- ders, and hips, and his heels had worn holes of oblong shape, as though in his delirium he would keep pulling up and stretching out his legs so that each foot would push out a little dirt each time, and finally made quite a large hole with quite a pile of dirt behind each heel."[8]

There was, however, no sign of either Shannon Bell's body or the rifle he had supposedly broken while trying to club Packer to death.

Still convinced that Packer had murdered all five of his companions, Nutter and others thought that he might have "thrown the bodies into the lake. So we drained the lake by cutting a beaver dam across the stream." They "searched up and down the lake . . . for several weeks from the time we got there." But they "found nothing."[9]

11.

THE SWEETEST MEAT

Packer was immured in the Saguache jail—nothing more than a crude log cabin—when his story first made the news. A recap of Packer's Los Pinos confession, the account—printed in the July 11, 1874, issue of the *Rocky Mountain News* and headlined "Man-Eaters in Colorado"—struck a bizarrely flippant tone.

Following Israel Swan's "death from exhaustion," explained the anonymous writer, "the remaining five cooked and ate their defunct companion." James Humphrey—"whose digestive organs don't seem to have relished human flesh"—was the next to go, "and soon his bones were picked as clean as those of the unfortunate he had assisted in picking." Once Humphrey's body was thoroughly defleshed,

> the rest began looking at each other with hungry glances, wondering which would be so kind as to die next. As no one of them proved to be accommodating enough in this particular, Noon made a virtue of necessity and, some ten days afterwards, shot Miller. His two remaining companions condoned the offense by accepting the invitation to dine on Miller, but, after all that was eatable about Miller had been eaten, it occurred to Bell that "he that sheddeth man's blood, by man his blood shall be shed," and accordingly he shot Noon and shared him at the Noon-day meal with Packer. By the time Noon was digested, Bell became convinced of the truth of the apothegm that self-preservation

is the first law of nature, and, not having any powder, he made for Packer with the butt of his gun. Packer was smart enough to get out of the way, and Bell struck a tree instead. Packer, indignant at this attempt on his life, killed and ate Bell, and two weeks afterward crawled into the Indian agency in a state of starvation.

Packer, the article concluded, was expected "to survive the fearful ordeal, although, strange to relate, he professes to prefer the human food he then became accustomed to, to the ordinary fare of civilized and Christian people."[1]

This final, outlandish observation became the source of one of the many sensational rumors that would surround the Packer case for years to come: that, during his original confession, Packer "acknowledged that he had grown quite fond of human flesh, and coolly said that he found the breasts of man the sweetest meat he had ever tasted."[2]

12.

THE DISCOVERY

To this day, no one knows exactly who found the bodies.

According to the August 28, 1874, issue of the *Rocky Mountain News*, it was a prospector named C. H. Graham who, two weeks earlier, had stumbled "across the corpses of five men lying at the foot of a lofty pine tree in a secluded valley" on the south branch of the Gunnison River. "The bodies," the article continued, "were all more or less mutilated. The head of one had been severed from the body; the head of another was badly crushed, while the flesh had been cut in huge masses from the breasts, thighs and the fleshy parts of the legs of all. . . . The bodies of two were in a state of perfect preservation so as to be easily recognized, but the remaining three were mutilated so that their own mothers would not have known them."[1]

Another contemporary swore to a different version. According to this account, Graham and two other prospectors, George Nichols and P. P. Wells, "were sitting around their campfire smoking and exchanging stories, when a dog belonging to one of them brought in a bone of suspicious appearance. This they examined with enough care to convince them that it was from the arm of a human being. They had heard of the disappearance of Packer's companions and they immediately began a search of the vicinity which was soon ended by the revolting discovery of the remains of the missing men . . . in a clump of pine trees under a bluff and near the water."[2]

Most historians, however, credit the grim discovery to someone entirely different: John A. Randolph, an artist on assignment for *Harper's Weekly*. Advertising itself as "the best family newspaper in the world," the *Weekly* commenced publication on January 3, 1857. Featuring "essays on various subjects, verse, some humor, a page or two of news, serial novels and short stories," it quickly caught on with the public, reaching a weekly circulation of one hundred thousand within a few years of its launch. Crucial to its appeal were its illustrations. Sometimes filling entire pages—or even two-page spreads—these engravings were produced by some of the best American artists in the field, including Winslow Homer and the great political satirist Thomas Nast.[3]

On or around August 20, 1874, Randolph, an artist who regularly provided illustrations of western mining life for the *Weekly*, was hiking through a densely shaded spruce grove about two miles north of Lake San Cristobal when he came upon a grisly tableau: a bunch of corpses clustered at the foot of a steep bluff near the Lake Fork of the Gunnison River. Randolph lost no time in alerting a prospector named Hezekiah Musgrave, who was camped nearby. Going to investigate, Musgrave, as he later testified, "seen five men lying there as though they had been killed by some sharp instrument, looked like it might be a hatchet, struck in the head."[4] Uncertain of what to do, Musgrave and Randolph hurried off to spread the word.

A party of miners, including a young man named John R. Pond, was camped not far away on Henson Creek. Years later, Pond vividly remembered the afternoon when Randolph and Musgrave appeared in the camp: "They told us that they had found some dead bodies up near the river close to the San Cristobal Lake. I and a number of others went up to see them."

As they approached the spot (soon to be named and forever after known as Dead Man's Gulch), "the stench . . . and the apparent desolation sickened me and I could not go in to examine the bodies closely," Pond recalled, "But I noticed that four of them were laying close together, and where the blanket of one was turned up—probably by the wind—the thigh looked as though a piece had been cut out. All those four men were covered with blankets. The fifth one lay out quite a ways from the others and the head was gone." Pond, who could barely look at the rotting remains, was amazed to see John Randolph coolly making pencil sketches of the gruesome scene.

Two months later, an engraving based on Randolph's drawings would appear in the October 17 issue of *Harper's Weekly*. Accompanying an article headlined "A Colorado Tragedy," the image depicted the five murdered prospectors lying among their blankets, some reduced to little more than spinal columns, rib cages, and leg bones, some with ghastly bearded heads atop their skeletal remains. When John Pond saw the issue, he found the picture "a high stretch of imagination." Gruesome as it was, it couldn't begin to capture the sheer horror of the reality.[5]

+ + +

Bob McGrue, the man who had been kindest to Packer during the journey from Utah, was camped at Antelope Park with Preston Nutter when C. H. Graham showed up and informed them that the remains of their missing companions had been discovered. McGrue remained with the wagons and gear, while Nutter went off with Graham to view the scene.

When Nutter returned three days later—as McGrue recalled—"he told me they were the bodies of the party, that four of them lay close together covered with their blankets, that those four had been hit in the head with a hatchet, that the other layed off some distance apart, that he had been shot but that his head was missing, that some of them showed that some meat had been cut out of them."

Contrary to the report in the *Rocky Mountain News*—which claimed that two of the bodies "were in a perfect state of preservation," Nutter told McGrue that "all were a decayed bad smelling mess and [it was] hard to tell much about them." With the exception of the one decapitated body, however, they retained enough of their features to make identification possible. As for the headless one, Nutter could tell from what remained of the clothing that it was the corpse of Frank Miller.[6]

+ + +

Following an inquest presided over by Hinsdale County coroner W. F. Ryan, the fetid remains of the five murdered prospectors were carried to the bluff overlooking the crime scene and laid, side by side, in a shallow grave. Like Dead Man's Gulch directly below, the burial place soon acquired a name that it retains to this day: Cannibal Plateau.[7]

13.

ESCAPE

In stark contrast to our own high-speed information age, when we learn about the latest crimes and catastrophes the instant they happen, news traveled slowly in the old days. It wasn't until the second week of September that papers across the country carried front-page stories of the slaughter in the San Juans. Unlike the news media today, more-over—which takes care to refer to suspects as "alleged" criminals—the nineteenth-century press did not hesitate to describe Packer as a "murderer and cannibal," a perpetrator of "one of the most dreadful and diabolical crimes on record," and a "fiend" who had killed the sleeping victims for their money and "lived off the flesh of his dead comrades."[1]

Even the *New York Times* felt no scruples about flatly declaring that Packer—who had not yet been tried, let alone convicted—"murdered those men by chopping their heads off with a hatchet, robbed them of money and other property, and then told the story of cannibalism to hide the crime." Fortunately, the article concluded, "Packer has been arrested and is now in jail."

About that final point, however, the *Times* article was badly out of date. By the time it appeared—September 9, 1874—Packer was long gone from the Saguache jail.[2]

+ + +

Blame for Packer's escape has been laid on various individuals. Sheriff Amos Wall has been accused of not keeping a watchful enough eye on his prisoner; it has even been suggested that he accepted a bribe to set Packer free. Fingers have also been pointed at an eighteen-year-old dishwasher named Grimes, reportedly placed in charge of the Saguache jail when Sheriff Wall was called away to Del Norte on official business. According to rumor, Packer slipped Grimes some money in exchange for a penknife, then used the blade to pick the flimsy jail lock.[3]

The surprising truth, not revealed until a quarter century after the fact, appears to be that Packer was set free by the two men regarded as the main founders of Saguache: Otto Mears and John Lawrence.

Orphaned—like Mears—in early boyhood, the Saint Louis–born Lawrence was consigned to a Dickensian orphanage, from which he absconded at fourteen. After laboring as a farmhand in Iowa and Minnesota, he got swept up in the Pikes Peak gold rush of 1859. Failing as a miner, he worked as a freighter, driving ox wagons laden with supplies between Omaha and Denver. After serving in the New Mexico Volunteers during the Civil War under the command of Kit Carson, he turned his hand to farming and stock raising in the vicinity of Saguache Creek at the northern tip of the San Luis Valley. Along with Mears, he was instrumental in establishing both the county and town of Saguache and became a member of the territorial legislature, the first of many official posts he held, even while building a ranch that eventually grew to more than 1,100 acres.[4]

He first became acquainted with Alfred Packer during the latter's nearly two-week stay in Saguache. "I seen him first in the saloon of Larry Dolan," Lawrence recalled.

> Mr. Dolan introduced me to him. I seen him and talked some with him for the next four or five days. At times I seen him playing cards and drinking some, and I smoked and drank some with him. Our talk was casual, no special importance. . . . I knew of the talk of his companions being lost in the mountains. I knew of his going back with a company to hunt his lost companions. Knew that they did not find them. Knew that he

was turned over to the sheriff to be kept till something might turn up.[5]

The bodies of the missing men had not yet turned up when Lawrence and Mears made their decision. Lawrence explained:

"Otto Mears come to me and talked the matter over in regard to Packer. This was our conclusion. . . . We were a young, poor county. It cost four or five dollars a day to keep Packer. We had no evidence that the men were dead or that Packer had done any wrong. We agreed to turn Packer loose. . . . In a day or so after, the sheriff having gone down to Del Norte, after night Packer was given provisions, etc. and turned loose."[6]

+ + +

On August 22, 1874, two days after the discovery of the bodies, Hinsdale County justice of the peace Orlando A. Mesler issued a warrant for the arrest of "one Al Packer," charged with the murders of Israel Swan, George Noon, Shannon Wilson Bell, James Humphrey, and Frank Miller "as appears by coroners inquest." The warrant, directed to the sheriff of the county, instructed him to bring in the fugitive "dead or alive."[7]

Relatives of the five slain men quickly put up a reward for Packer's capture. It was also rumored that Packer had a $500 bounty on his head for a triple murder he had committed four years earlier in El Paso County. With reward money totaling, by some accounts, as much as $5,000, "the whole town became man-hunters." For weeks, search parties scoured the mountains, canyons, and passes—but to no avail.

From time to time in the succeeding years, there would be a reported sighting of the fugitive. In 1879, for example, a stagecoach driver named Brayden, formerly a policeman in Pueblo, Colorado, spotted a man who bore an unmistakable resemblance to Packer in Wickenburg, Arizona. He alerted station agent James D. Martin, who had known Packer in Saguache, and the two immediately saddled horses and set out in search of the "much sought man." "We wanted him and wanted the reward," Martin recalled. By the time they arrived in Wickenburg, however, "the fellow had left. We rode a short distance along the road he was supposed to have taken, but did not find our man."[8]

+ + +

For the public at large, Packer gradually faded from memory. Occasionally, however, a story about him would appear in the papers. On July 31, 1875, for example, under the headline "A Dome of Thought," the *Lake City Silver World* reported that a man named G. A. Depping, while "prospecting on the mountain just east of town," had discovered a human skull about a mile from Dead Man's Gulch. Bearing "the marks of blows from a hatchet or some other sharp instrument," the skull was assumed to be that of Packer's victim Frank Miller, whose severed head had never been found.

"How the head came to be so far removed from the body, whether carried away by Packer or some less fiendish beast of prey," the article concluded, "will ever remain a mystery."[9]

Part Two

THE MAN-EATER

14.

SURVIVORS AND HEROES

In one of the less uplifting episodes in the Old Testament—2 Kings 6: 24–30—the king of Israel is confronted by a woman who entreats him to resolve a thorny dispute. During a recent famine, she and a neighbor had arrived at a novel solution to their predicament. As religious scholar Philip Jenkins paraphrases: "They had agreed to eat the son of one woman, then the son of the other, and they had already completed the first stage of the gruesome deal. Now, though, the second woman was reneging on the deal. Would the king not grant her justice by ordering the promised second act of cannibalism?"

For Jenkins, this passage illustrates the extent to which the Bible "overflows with 'texts of terror' . . . stories of casual murder, mass slaughter, rape, adultery and treachery." There are other lessons to be drawn from it, too, one of which is that not every woman in the Bible is endowed with a highly developed maternal instinct. Another has to do with prevailing attitudes toward survival cannibalism. That the aggrieved woman in the text so readily confesses to having eaten her own son (an act of "gastronomic incest," in the memorable phrase of one scholar) reflects the fact that, throughout history, people who could only save themselves from the agonies of slow starvation by consuming human flesh have rarely incurred social condemnation.

Among shipwrecked sailors, "the practice of eating each other when they became hungry" was so well established that it was widely accepted as an occupational hazard.[1] In November 1820, for example, the *Essex*,

a ship from Nantucket, sank in the South Pacific after being rammed
by a mammoth sperm whale (an incident that served as the inspiration for Melville's *Moby-Dick*). Though the twenty crewmen might have
easily sailed to the relatively accessible islands of the Marquesas, they
were terrified of falling into the clutches of the reportedly cannibalistic natives and chose instead to make for the coast of South America,
nearly three thousand miles away. After two nightmarish months adrift
on the ocean, the starving survivors turned cannibal themselves.

For the most part, they consumed the corpses of shipmates who
had perished of exposure or starvation. In one instance, however, a
seventeen-year-old seaman named Owen Coffin—cousin of the ship's
captain, George Pollard—was sacrificed for food after drawing a losing lot. When Pollard was finally rescued, he was found at the bottom
of his whaleboat, sucking marrow from his butchered cousin's bones.
Despite his having engaged in gastronomic incest, Pollard's townspeople absolved him of blame, the drawing of lots for the purpose of survival cannibalism having long been accepted as the "custom of the sea."[2]

Historians of maritime disaster have documented many similar cases. There was the *Nottingham Galley*, which ran aground on a
desolate isle off the coast of Maine, leaving survivors stranded without food. When the cook died, "the captain himself skinned, dressed,
and quartered the corpse," which was then consumed by the crew "with
the utmost greediness." Some years later, after the sinking of the timber
brig *George*, survivors—including the woman's husband—subsisted for
eleven days on the flesh and blood of a dead female passenger, Joyce
Rae. In 1826, the timber ship *Francis Mary* was disabled in a gale. After
more than two weeks adrift on their derelict vessel, the starving survivors began to feed on the corpses of the dead:

> John Wilson died on February 22 and was quartered and hung
> up for food; the next day, I. Moore died, and his liver and heart
> were eaten. Matters went from bad to worse, and when the
> cook, James Friar, died, Ann Saunders, his betrothed and a pas-
> senger . . . "cut her late intended husband's throat and drank his
> blood, insisting that she had the greatest right to it." . . . Ann
> Saunders was not the only woman to survive; the captain's wife,

Mrs. Patterson, did, too, and, having eaten the brains of an unfortunate apprentice who had survived no fewer than three previous shipwrecks, opined "it was the most delicious thing she had ever tasted."[3]

In these and similar instances, the survivors displayed little sense of shame upon rescue. Far from denying their actions, they freely admitted them, making no effort to conceal their cannibalism. "Rescuers found partially butchered bodies in lifeboats even when the remains might have easily been thrown overboard," one historian observes. "In one extraordinary case, survivors trapped on a derelict signaled to a passing ship by waving the hands and feet of a man they had butchered and eaten."[4] For the most part, those who had endured such ordeals could count on the sympathy of a forgiving public. Even on those rare occasions when survivors were brought before the law, they tended to be treated with leniency. After twenty agonizing days in an open dinghy, Captain Thomas Dudley of the British yacht *Mignonette*—which had foundered in a gale off South Africa—cut the throat of the dying seventeen-year-old cabin boy, Richard Parker. Over the next several days, until they were saved by a passing ship, Dudley and two other survivors "feasted off the body" (in Dudley's own words). Though the captain and his mate were charged with murder, "most public sentiment hailed the men as heroes for having done what was necessary. The dead man's father forgave them, and they were granted bail, which was unusual in a capital case. After they were convicted, Queen Victoria commuted their [death] sentences to just six months in prison. Shortly after their release, the British government restored their maritime credentials."[5]

Still, the public hasn't always extended its sympathies to those who have kept themselves alive on human carrion. Initially, at least, the survivors of the Donner Party found themselves the object of revulsion and scorn. Trapped by snow in the Sierra Nevada Mountains, the eighty-nine pioneers lost half their number to starvation and cold during the brutal winter of 1846–1847. When rescuers finally arrived at the encampments, they found evidence of widespread cannibalism. Newspapers described the discovery in the most sensationalized terms. "A more shocking scene cannot be imagined than that witnessed by the party of men who went to the relief of the unfortunate emigrants in the California Mountains," reported the *California Star* in April 1847:

> Bodies of men, women, and children with half the flesh torn from them, lay on every side. A woman sat beside the body of her husband, who had just died, cutting out his tongue; the heart she had already taken out, broiled and eat! The daughter was seen eating the flesh of the father—the mother that of her children—children that of father and mother.[6]

Thanks to such lurid accounts, the Donner pioneers were originally viewed as bloodthirsty ghouls who had no one to blame but themselves for their catastrophic plight. This perception was reinforced by the reported behavior of several survivors. Following his rescue, for example, Jacob Donner's teenaged hired hand, Jean Baptiste Trudeau, claimed, "with a perverted pride," that he had eaten a baby raw and roasted his employer's head, which tasted "like sheep with the rot."[7]

Most notorious of all was Lewis Keseberg. The last of the emigrants to be rescued, Keseberg was discovered lying beside a kettle full of human body parts. Members of the relief party reported that, far from feeling in any way abashed about his recourse to cannibalism, Keseberg "seemed almost enthusiastic" about it, remarking that human flesh was "tastier than California beef." Back in civilization, he continued to "flaunt his prowess as a cannibal [and] was heard boasting publicly in a bar-room that human liver was the best meat he ever ate."[8] Accused of having murdered George Donner's wife Tamsen for her flesh, he spent the rest of his increasingly embittered life as a marked man, shunned by his neighbors and taunted by children, who would sometimes throw rocks at him on the street.

+ + +

Though Lewis Keseberg ended his life as a social pariah, the cannibalistic behavior of other western adventurers did nothing to damage their reputations. On the contrary, it made them into objects of awed fascination, the stuff of frontier legend.

One of these characters was Charles Gardner, a transplant to the Colorado Rockies whose hulking physique and Philadelphia birthplace earned him the nickname "Big Phil." According to the most reliable sources, Gardner had been an instigator of the anti-Catholic riots that convulsed the City of Brotherly Love in 1844. Sought by the law for his part in the torching of several churches, he escaped to the West and took up the life of a mountain man. Among his fellow trappers and hunters, he quickly gained a reputation for outlandish behavior. Scalped and left for dead after an Indian skirmish, he wore a gruesome tonsure for the rest of his life and considered it the height of humor to doff his hat and bow deeply to every woman he met.[9]

It was his grotesque appetite, however, that brought him his greatest notoriety. He was a glutton for raw meat, which he devoured in such prodigious quantities that a single meal would keep him full for several days. His carnivorous craving, moreover, was not limited to beef. Stories abound of his cannibalistic habits. According to one account, after being stranded in a blizzard with an Indian guide, he emerged from the wilderness with a human leg thrown over his shoulder, the only uneaten remains of his companion. Other contemporary sources claim that, in the throes of hunger, he killed and ate his own Arapaho wife, Kloock. He is also said to have devoured a Frenchman. He spoke freely of his anthropophagous exploits and told anyone who inquired that human flesh, "when thoroughly cooked, tasted good, not unlike pork."[10]

Possibly because Gardner's victims were looked upon as a lower order of humanity—"redskins" and a "frog-eater"—he was viewed by his peers not as a criminal but as a colorfully eccentric, larger-than-life figure. Even some modern-day commentators share this view of "Big Phil the Cannibal," one starry-eyed historian of the Far West describing him as a "marvelous character."[11]

Another man-eating mountaineer, far more famous than Gardner, was John Johnson, a.k.a. Liver-Eating Johnson (or simply the Liver-Eater). Born John Garrison in 1824 in Little York, New Jersey, he went to sea as a young man, first on a whaling ship, later in the US Navy. After fighting in the Civil War, he drifted out to the northern Rocky Mountains, where he took on a new name and worked as a miner, trapper, teamster, hunter, whiskey trader, and occasional US Army scout.

He was renowned as an Indian fighter, having battled the Blackfeet and the Sioux. In later years, he served as a lawman, drove a stagecoach, and performed in a Wild West show before moving to Los Angeles, where he died in an old soldiers' home while planning his memoirs.

The exact derivation of his nickname remains in some dispute. The most authoritative sources claim that he became known as the Liver-Eater after removing that organ from a fallen Indian foe and consuming it, while others insist that he merely cut out the liver and—with that "rude sense of sport which had largely animated him throughout his life"—playfully "offered it to a friend as a choice morsel."[12]

Even in his lifetime, Johnson achieved the status of a wilderness demigod, a warrior-hero on the order of Beowulf and Achilles. According to widely promulgated legend, after Johnson's wife was slaughtered by a band of marauding Crows, he vowed vengeance against the entire tribe, embarking on a decades-long vendetta. To strike fear into the hearts of his foes, he not only scalped their fallen bodies but carved out their livers and devoured them raw.

"For almost forty years, Johnson stalked this tribe," relates one breathless chronicler, "and the Crows, in turn, stalked him":

> To have killed Johnson would have elevated any Crow warrior to chiefdom. The Crows hunted him in pairs and in small groups—no more than four or five in order to uphold their Indian code of fairness. Their quarry was too wise and wary for them. . . . On one occasion, he reportedly took on a band of six Crows, all top warriors, killing all in hand-to-hand combat, then cannibalizing their bodies and stringing up their remains from tree branches so that their tribesmen (and their ancient gods) could see them humiliated and disgraced in death.[13]

Though such tall tales have been thoroughly debunked by recent scholarship, they reveal an important truth. In the semicivilized world of the nineteenth-century western frontier, a cannibalistic killer could not only escape censure but be celebrated for his deeds—so long as his victims weren't white.

15.

FORT FETTERMAN

In the 1860s, impelled by both their lust for gold and their unquestioning sense of Manifest Destiny, hordes of white settlers flooded into the Montana Territory, provoking an inevitable conflict with the native inhabitants. To protect its citizens while they went about encroaching on Indian lands, the US Congress authorized the construction of three army posts along the Bozeman Trail, the primary overland route leading through Wyoming to the Montana goldfields: Forts Reno, Phil Kearny, and C. F. Smith.

No sooner had these forts been erected than they fell under constant attack by the Lakota Sioux, led by the legendary war chief Red Cloud. In November 1866, Captain William Judd Fetterman, a Civil War hero who had fought brilliantly under General Sherman, arrived at Fort Phil Kearny. Openly—and, as it turned out, fatally—contemptuous of his Indian adversaries, he boasted that "with eighty men, [he] could ride through the Sioux nation."[1]

On the morning of December 21, 1861, following an Indian attack on a party sent out to cut wood for the fort, Fetterman marched to its aid with eighty men under his command. Lured into a trap, they suddenly found themselves ambushed by more than one thousand Sioux and Cheyenne warriors. What happened next is vividly described by historian Donald McCaig:

Terrible yells drowned out the officers' commands. The cavalry apparently broke in terror and fled to refuge among rocks atop the spur a hundred yards above the infantry's position. The infantrymen kept their discipline longer, firing in volleys, then singly, until they began to run out of ammunition. The knife slash that cut Captain Fetterman's throat was deep enough to expose his neck vertebrae.

The cavalrymen loosed their horses, and for a few blessed moments fighting slackened while the Indians rounded up these prizes. When their scouts signaled that reinforcements were coming from the fort, the Indians attacked with knives and war clubs and lances and hatchets. Altogether, 81 soldiers fell to Red Cloud's onslaught. . . . Some 40,000 arrows were fired—a thousand for every minute the fight lasted.[2]

One year after the massacre, construction began on another fort in northern Wyoming—the last that the government would build in the Rockies. In keeping with military practice, it was named in honor of one of the army's fallen heroes: Fort Fetterman.

The soldiers stationed there had another name for it: the Hell Hole. Perched on a barren plateau and surrounded by a prairie wasteland, it was subjected to seasonal extremes of searing heat and subzero cold. In the winter, blizzards raged; in the spring, ferocious sandstorms buried the garrison in dust. Conditions were so primitive that Fort Fetterman quickly became known as a "hardship post." In a letter to the adjutant general, one cavalry officer, reporting on the dismal morale of his men, wrote that "they look upon being held so long at this post as an unmerited punishment. . . . Whenever men get to the railroad, there are some desertions caused by dread of returning to this post." In the span of a few months in 1873, four soldiers, desperate for medical discharges, shot off parts of their trigger fingers.[3]

For the fifteen years of its duration, Fort Fetterman served as an important supply base for the army and the launching point for various military campaigns against the Sioux and Cheyenne. With the final subjugation of the Plains Indians, however, the fort outlived its usefulness. In the spring of 1882, commanding officer W. H. Powell received orders to abandon the post. No sooner had it been vacated, however, than a flock of "squatters, entrepreneurs and other profit-seekers" moved in, swiftly transforming Fort Fetterman into a wide-open cow town, infamous for its saloons, dance halls, and bordellos.

Of the various dens of iniquity that flourished in this "sin city on the plains," the most notorious was an establishment known as the Hog Ranch, a pair of log buildings where cowpokes, trailhands, and traders could squander their pay on gambling, cheap whiskey, and a selection of women, ages twenty-five to forty-five, "whose affections were negotiable." Barroom brawls were commonplace and frequently escalated into bloodshed. On one notorious occasion, a "fine, upstanding" fellow named Dick Elgin, paymaster at the nearby Goose Egg Ranch, got into an altercation with a cowboy known as "Arkansas Red" Capps and ended up dead on the barroom floor, shot through the mouth. Capps attempted to flee but was caught when his horse bucked and threw him. He was consigned to the old military guardhouse that served as the town jail but, just two hours later, fell prey to frontier justice when a mob broke in and strung him up from a roof beam. A local rancher named John Hunton conveyed the prevailing sentiment about the lynching in his diary: "Dick Elgin killed at Fetterman yesterday. Murderer hung. Nice day."[4]

+ + +

Of the several lawmen tasked with maintaining a semblance of order in that "hell-roaring" town, the man who would ultimately win the greatest renown for his coolness and courage was Deputy Sheriff Malcolm Campbell. Born on a little farm in Ontario, Canada, the eldest of fourteen children, Campbell was twenty-five when his family moved to Iowa. Heading west on his own, he worked for years as a freight hauler—a "bullwhacker," in frontier parlance—before becoming a peace officer, a profession he would follow for the remainder of his working life.

One evening in January 1883, Campbell was about to sit down to his supper when a terrified waiter from the town's only hotel burst into his house to report that a drunken prospector had just drawn a gun and threatened to "plug him" when the waiter was slow in bringing the man a glass of water. Throwing on his coat, Campbell hurried over to the hotel, where he found the prospector standing at the bar, his revolver "shoved down the belt of his pants right near the front, so it was handy to get." Pulling his own six-shooter and telling the man to put his hands up, Campbell disarmed him, then escorted him to the old government jail and locked him up.

When the waiter decided not to press charges, Campbell had no choice but to let the man go. As he stepped from the cell and retrieved his weapon, the man—who gave his name as John Swartze—shot Campbell a look that the sheriff would never forget. He looked, Campbell later wrote, "as if he could butcher anyone who crossed him in anything."[5]

16.

SWARTZE

By 1883, Jean "Frenchy" Cabazon—a member of the twenty-one-man prospecting party that had set out from Utah for the San Juan silver country nine years earlier—had long since given up dreams of striking it rich and was eking out a living as a peddler in Wyoming. Loading up on household goods and sundries in Cheyenne, he would drive his covered wagon to Fort Fetterman, a distance of some one hundred and forty miles, stopping at all the ranches along the way.

In March of that year, during one of these trips, Cabazon put up for the night at a roadhouse run by a fellow named John Brown. As he arranged his bedroll on the floor and made ready for sleep, he heard someone in the adjacent barroom speaking in a distinctive, high-pitched voice.

Going to investigate, Cabazon saw that the fellow—who introduced himself as John Swartze—was missing parts of two fingers from his left hand and wore crudely fashioned false teeth in the space once occupied by his upper front incisors. Cabazon had no doubt who the man was, though the latter showed no sign of recognizing the little peddler. They chatted for a while, and "Swartze"—who explained that he'd been prospecting in nearby Spring Canyon with a father-son pair named Devoe—asked Cabazon to bring him some baking powder on his next trip from Cheyenne. Cabazon then bid the prospector good night and retired to his room.

The next day, Cabazon drove his wagon straight to the home of Deputy Sheriff Malcolm Campbell in Fort Fetterman and—as Campbell wrote in his memoirs—"laid out the facts before me, reporting Swartze to be the long-lost man-eater," Alfred Packer.[1]

Campbell, who remembered Swartze well from their run-in just two months earlier, knew the man was a rough customer. Still, he couldn't help wondering if Cabazon—who hadn't set eyes on Packer in nearly a decade—might not be mistaken. Among other things, rumor had it that Packer was long since dead, killed by Indians in Arizona.[2] Uncertain as to how to proceed, Campbell wrote that night to his superior in Laramie, Sheriff Louis Miller, apprising him of the situation and "asking for orders."

A week later, an answer arrived by telegram:

> Arrest Packer, alias John Swartze, at once, and take no chances whatever. Identification marks, the forefinger of the left hand off at the second joint and little finger of the same hand off at the second joint, the two upper front teeth gone and replaced by artificial ones. Wire me at once.[3]

By then, the man calling himself John Swartze had left Fort Fetterman and was lodging at the cabin of a prospector known as Crazy Horse on Wagon Hound Creek, thirty miles west of town. On Monday, March 12, the morning after receiving Sheriff Miller's telegram, Campbell, accompanied by his brother Dan, headed for the cabin in his buckboard.

It was late in the day by the time they arrived. As they drove up to the cabin, they saw Swartze emerge from the doorway and come striding toward them. Wheeling the wagon behind a haystack, the two men leapt to the ground. Campbell drew his six-shooter and ordered the man to stop where he was.

"What are you fellows fooling about?" growled Swartze.

Campbell told him he was under arrest and reached into his pocket for his handcuffs. As he did, Swartze dropped his own hands to his belt, as though going for a gun.

"Throw up them hands," shouted Dan, who was covering the prisoner with his Winchester rifle, "or I'll put a bullet right through you."

Campbell patted down his prisoner to make sure he was unarmed, then snapped on the cuffs.

"That's the first time in twenty years I didn't have my gun on," muttered Swartze. "If I had, you fellows never could've taken me. I would've gotten one or both of you for sure."

"What in the hell do you think we'd be doing all that time?" snarled Dan.

Once Swartze was handcuffed, Campbell pulled out Sheriff Miller's telegram from his shirt pocket and read it aloud. He then ordered his prisoner to hold out his shackled hands. The upper joints of the left index and ring fingers were gone. Like a horse trader examining a potential purchase, Campbell reached out and raised the man's upper lip. The missing two upper front teeth had been replaced with false ones.

There was no doubt about it. After nine years on the loose, Alfred Packer was in custody.[4]

+ + +

While Dan watered and fed the horses, Campbell led Packer into the cabin, ordered him to sit on a bench near the door, and asked where he kept his gun. Packer pointed his chin at a shelf, where Campbell found the weapon, a single-action .44-caliber revolver.

After refreshing themselves with some coffee and the uneaten food from the supper Packer had prepared just before the lawmen showed up, the brothers led him to the buckboard and headed back to Fetterman, with Campbell driving the team and Dan keeping watch over the prisoner. Arriving after dark, they locked him up in the old military guardhouse. Recalling what Cabazon had told him about Packer's escape from the Saguache jail nine years before, Campbell, as he later wrote, "put a guard in the corridor, for [he] knew Packer wouldn't stay in a place like that very long if [he] left him alone."[5]

Packer remained in the lockup until Wednesday, March 14, when the next stagecoach left town. By then, a press dispatch had gone out from Fort Fetterman, announcing the arrest of "Al Pacha, who nine years ago committed a horrible murder." Escorted by Campbell, he was taken by coach and train to Laramie. Much to his disgust, a large crowd of curiosity seekers was assembled at the Laramie station, eager to get a glimpse of "the man-eating murderer."

After an overnight stay in a local hotel, he and Campbell continued on by train to Cheyenne, where another mob of gawkers was waiting at the depot. As the train slowed to a stop, a bunch of them shoved their way on board and stood gaping at him.

"What are the damn fools looking at me like that for?" Packer growled to Campbell.

Elbowing their way onto the platform, Campbell and his prisoner were met by Cheyenne sheriff S. K. Sharpless and led to the jail, trailed by a procession of townspeople. Later that afternoon, several members of the press were permitted inside the jail for an interview. As Packer shuffled out of his cell, he "appeared to be a miserable, woe-stricken, unmanned wretch," wrote one of the reporters. Dressed in "a woolen shirt, a dark coat, and coarse pantaloons," all "much soiled," he had the "general makeup . . . of a laboring man who took no care of his person." To another reporter, everything about him—his "ungainly" physique, "lumbering movements," "small and sinister" eyes, "overlarge nose with thick nostrils," "black, unkempt" hair, "savage moustache," and "coarse, scraggy goatee"—gave him a "decidedly uninviting" appearance.[6]

Shifting nervously on his feet and speaking in a "thin, high key," Packer responded to questions with the longest speech he had made since his capture. "My name is Al Packer," he began. "I am from Harrisburg, Pennsylvania, my family living five miles from the city. I left there in '63. My relatives have nothing to do with the case. I don't want them to know anything."

He claimed to have no idea why he was under arrest. "I don't know what the charge is against me, only from what the telegram said," he insisted. He recalled very little of what had happened nine years earlier. "I was only a boy then; I'm thirty-three now," he lied, shaving eight years off his age. "I was the only man left out of a party of six that went out from the agency. We were out sixty or seventy days. We lived on buds and gum off the trees part of the time. When I got back, I was arrested. General Adams took my description when I came in and the route I took, that's all. I never made no statement. I've said more now than I ever did before."

Packer then blurted out a perfect example of what a later age would call a Freudian slip. "I plead guilty to the crime I am accused of," he declared.

"What?" the newsmen exclaimed in unison.

"I mean," he hurriedly amended, "I plead innocent. I did not murder the men. I may make a statement sometime. I'll not do it now. I calculate to tell all. If I'm going to be hung, I'm to be hung, but I'll make a statement at the right time."[7]

+ + +

Before Packer left Cheyenne, he was given a shave and a haircut and taken to the Jenkins & Howe gallery, where, handcuffed and shackled, he was photographed with his false teeth removed and his mutilated left hand resting upon his knee "so as to be plainly seen in the picture." Copies were quickly produced and offered for sale to the public, "Packer's pictures being in demand."[8]

A few hours later, Campbell and Hinsdale County sheriff Clair Smith—who had arrived from Gunnison a day earlier—escorted Packer to the train for Denver. As they stepped out of the jail onto Fifteenth Street, they were surrounded by "a swarm of men and boys" who followed them to the railroad yard, where an even larger crowd awaited. Led onto a car and seated across from the two lawmen, Packer kept his head low to avoid the stares of the townspeople who kept forcing their way onto the car for a final look at him.

All at once, someone addressed him in a heavily accented voice. "How are you, Packer?"

Packer looked up and stared at the man in silence.

"Don't you recognize me?" asked the fellow, a tall, distinguished-looking man in his forties.

"No, sir, I don't."

It wasn't until the man sat down beside him and looked directly into his face that Packer smiled in recognition and put out his manacled right hand to greet General Charles Adams.[9]

17.

REUNION

At the time of Packer's capture, General Adams, now serving as head post office inspector for Colorado, had been back in the United States for only a short time following a three-year stint as the US minister to Bolivia. He had received that plum appointment from President Rutherford B. Hayes for his role in resolving the crisis provoked by the notorious Meeker Massacre of 1879.

A journalist, poet, and social reformer aflame with utopian ideals, Nathan C. Meeker had migrated from New York to Colorado in 1869 and, with a band of fellow colonists, founded the town of Greeley, named for his boss, the famed newspaper editor who was the primary sponsor of the project. Eleven years later, having fallen deeply into debt, Meeker accepted the post of United States Indian agent at the White River Ute Reservation.

Determined to "teach the savages how to become civilized human beings," the blindly self-righteous Meeker made strenuous efforts to transform his charges—members of a proud, horse-based hunting culture—into Christianized farmers. His efforts provoked increasing resentment among the Indians, who saw agriculture as "squaw work" and valued their ponies above all other possessions.

The situation came to a boil when Meeker, in his typically misguided way, ordered a fifty-acre Indian horse pasture plowed up for farm ground. On September 29, 1879, twenty Ute warriors attacked the White River Indian Agency, slaughtering Meeker along with his ten male employees and taking the women and children hostage, including Meeker's wife, Arvilla, and their grown daughter, Josie.[1]

To secure the release of the captives, Secretary of the Interior Carl Schurz called on Charles Adams, who had won the trust and respect of the White River Utes during his tenure as Indian agent. In early October, Adams set out on "one of the most extraordinary treks in Western history," a nine-hundred-mile journey "mostly by horseback over an interminable labyrinth of mountain roads and Indian trails, lashed by hail and chilled by snow flurries." On October 21, accompanied by a party of thirteen Utes and five whites, Adams arrived at the Indian camp, where, to his great relief, he found the hostages safe and unmolested. After a long night of tense negotiation, the Indians agreed to release the prisoners. Within days, Arvilla and Josie Meeker—in a "highly nervous" but otherwise sound condition after their twenty-three-day ordeal—were back in civilization, while General Adams was acclaimed as a hero in the national press.[2]

+ + +

Immediately after hearing that someone alleged to be Packer had been taken into custody in Wyoming, Adams had traveled to Cheyenne to confirm the man's identity. Now, seated beside the prisoner on the Denver-bound train, the general was struck by the physical toll the years had taken on Packer.

"Packer, you've changed a good deal," said Adams.

"Yes, sir."

"Where have you been since you left Saguache?"

Packer answered with a brief rundown of his wanderings, which had taken him to Arizona, Nevada, Montana, and Wyoming.

Asked if he had anything to say about the crime he stood accused of, Packer shook his head. "Just the same as I told you that time before."

As the train rattled onward, however, he suddenly had a change of heart. He was ready "to take back his first statement" and "tell the whole truth." If Adams agreed to "protect him from the mob which he expected to take him from the officers upon [their] arrival in Denver,"

Packer would give "his true confession" when he was safely behind bars.[3]

There was, in fact, a horde of people awaiting Packer's arrival at Denver's Union Station—at least one thousand men, women, and children, eager for a glimpse of the "notorious murderer and outlaw." Hearing the bell of the approaching locomotive, they "made a grand rush" toward the track, crowding so eagerly about the cars that the passengers had trouble climbing down onto the platform when the train came to a stop.

When, moments later, General Adams appeared at the rear door of the third car, the crowd surged in that direction. Depot police struggled to keep them back as Packer emerged behind Adams. "Every eye [was] riveted" on what one witness called "the man-eating murderer's villainous and ugly face" as Packer stood on the platform of the car, "throwing terrified glances at the mob." Contrary to his fears, however, they were not bent on a lynching. Still, their demeanor was hostile enough to elicit a sympathetic response from one reporter:

> When he came out of the car, the poor Godforsaken creature looked around in a dazed way, finding not one friendly face in all that crowd. Not one person said a friendly word to him. Alone in the world with none willing or able to help him. Even though he deserved to be shunned by mankind, it seemed sad. Once he had been a little child with a home and someone who loved him. Now, he was an outcast.[4]

Reassured by Sheriff Smith that "no violence would be attempted against him," Packer, his arms and legs shackled, began to make his way laboriously down onto the platform, with Deputy Sheriff Linton and Deputy US Marshal Simon Cantrill helping to lift him down the final step. Flanked by the lawmen, he was led to the waiting room. As he passed among them, the crowd "fell back out of his path instinctively, as if the prisoner were a poisonous reptile."[5] Hurried onto a waiting hack, Packer was driven to the Arapahoe County jail, where—securely ensconced in his cell—he "drew a long sigh of relief." Not long afterward, General Adams arrived.

Then, with Sheriff Smith and Deputy Marshal Cantrill acting as witnesses and Adams transcribing the words "just as they fell from the mouth of the prisoner," Alfred Packer, under oath, made his second confession.[6]

18.

SECOND CONFESSION

"When we left Ouray's camp," Packer began, "we had about seven days' food for one man. We traveled two or three days, and it came a storm. We came to a mountain, crossed a gulch and came on to another mountain. We found the snow so deep that we had to follow the mountain on the top, and on about the fourth day we had only a pint of flour left. We followed the mountain until we came to the main range. I do not remember how many days we were traveling then. I think about ten days, living on rose buds and pine gum, and some of the men were crying and praying.

"Then we came over the main range. We camped twice on a stream which runs into a big lake; the second night just above the lake. The next morning we crossed the lake, cut holes into the ice to catch fish. There were no fish, so we tried to catch snails. The ice was thin. Some broke through. We crossed the lake and went into a grove of timber. All the men were crying and one of them was crazy.

"Swan asked me to go up and see if I could not see something from the mountains. I took a gun, went up the hill, found a big rose bush with buds sticking through the snow, but could see nothing but snow all around. I had been a kind of guide to them, but I did not know the mountains from that side.

"When I came back to camp after being gone nearly all day, I found the red-headed man, Bell, who acted crazy in the morning, sitting near the fire, roasting a piece of meat which he had cut out of the leg of the

German butcher, Miller. The latter's body was lying the furthest off from the fire, down the stream. The skull was crushed in with a hatchet. The other three men were lying near the fire. They were cut in the forehead with the hatchet. Some had two or three cuts.

"I came within a rod of the fire. When the man saw me, he got up with his hatchet towards me, when I shot him sideways through the belly. He fell on his face; the hatchet fell forward. I grabbed it and hit him in the top of the head with it.

"I camped that night at the fire. Sat up all night. The next morning I followed my tracks up the mountain, but I could not make it. The snow was too deep, and I came back. I went sideways into a piece of pine timber, set up two stakes and covered it with pine boughs and made a shelter about three feet high. This was my camp until I came out.

"I went back to the fire, covered the men up and fetched a piece of human meat that was near the fire. I made a new fire near my camp and cooked the piece of meat and ate it.

"I tried to get away every day but could not, so I lived on the flesh of these men the greater part of the sixty days I was out. Then the snow began to have a crust and I started out up the creek to a place where a big slide seemed to come down the mountain of yellowish clay. There I started up and got my feet wet, and having only a piece of blanket around them, I froze my feet under the toes. I camped before I reached the top, making a fire and staying all night. The next day I made the top of the hill and a little over. I built a fire on top of a log and on two logs close together I camped. I cooked some of the flesh and carried it with me for food. I carried only one blanket.

"There was $70 among the men. I fetched it out with me and one gun. The redheaded man, Bell, had a $50 bill in his pocket. All the other together had only $20. I had $20 myself. If there was any more money in the outfit I did not know of it and it remained there.

"At the last camp, just before I reached the agency, I ate my last pieces of meat. This meat I cooked at the camp before I started out and put it in a bag and carried the bag with me. Could not eat but a little at a time.

"When I went out with the party from the agency to search for the bodies, we came to the mountains overlooking the stream, but I did not want to take them farther. I did not want to go back to the camp.

"When I was at the sheriff's cabin in Saguache, I was passed a key made out of a penknife blade with which I could unlock the irons. I went to the Arkansas and worked all summer for John Gill, eighteen miles below Pueblo. Then I rented Gilbert's ranch, still farther down the river, put in a crop of corn, sold it to John Gill and went to Arizona."[1]

+ + +

For the most part, Packer told this story calmly, though—as had been the case when he'd made his previous statement nine years before—he grew extremely agitated when he described the extremes of suffering he and the others had endured. Asked to explain the discrepancies between the two confessions, he insisted that, at the time of the earlier one, he "was not himself, was, in fact, crazed and not responsible for what he said."[2]

Then, with Deputy Marshal Cantrill serving as notary public, he affixed his signature to Adams's handwritten transcription, spelling his name, as he consistently did during the first decades of his life, "Alferd Packer."

19.

THE HUMAN HYENA

For anyone who believes that we live in a particularly crime-ridden age, a look through old newspapers is an eye-opening experience.

In the month of March 1883, James Hyland of Des Moines, Iowa, recently separated from his wife, snuck into her bedroom and slashed, choked, and kicked her to death while she lay in bed, leaving the mattress a "perfect mass of blood." In Hall County, Georgia, a man named Herring, while drunk, "emptied a shovel of hot coals on his infant child burning it to death." Charles Smith, a well-to-do farmer living four miles north of Earlville, Iowa, hacked to death his two young sons as they worked in the barn, "killed his wife with the same weapon as she stood by the stove preparing breakfast," then attempted to murder his two daughters before cutting his own throat with a butcher's knife. Edward Rickert, a reporter for the *St. Louis Globe Democrat*, shot and killed Selina Wilson, "a married woman with whom he had very close relations." Emeline Meaker, dubbed "The Virago of Vermont" by the press, was hanged for the murder of her eight-year-old niece, Alice, a crime "so heartless and brutal that not a spark of sympathy was felt" for the executed woman.

A drunken dispute at a racetrack in Russellville, Illinois, ended in "a most atrocious murder" when a young man named Jim Davis shot to death an acquaintance, James Smith, over a five-dollar wager. Another drunken dispute, this one over a game of billiards, ended fatally when one Darius Davis of Guernsey County, Pennsylvania, crushed the skull of jeweler Jules M'Henry with his pool cue. And these were not the only homicides reported during this brief span of time.[1]

Overshadowing all these stories, however, was the news coming out of Colorado: the capture and confession of Alfred Packer, the "fiend who deliberately fell upon and butchered his five companions and for several weeks lived on flesh cut from their bones."[2]

In Colorado itself, of course, the Packer case was the biggest story in years, producing what one chronicler calls (somewhat hyperbolically) "a newspaper onslaught unequaled in the history of American journalism."[3] Papers throughout the Rockies trumpeted his arrest in luridly alliterative headlines: "Putrid Packer!" "Captured Cannibal!" "Man-Eating Murderer!" Though not yet indicted for any crime, he was openly accused of "the most atrocious and cold blooded murder ever committed in the West," "butchery without a parallel in Colorado history," and "the most revolting crime of the century."[4] To the editor of the *Gunnison Review*, Packer was a creature from the realm of gothic nightmare: "Once in a while, a tale of horror is told more dreadful than any that has ever been related. Once in a while a fiend makes his appearance upon the earth, seemingly for the express purpose of making mankind shudder at his crimes. . . . Such a man is Al Packer. . . . He is a man of whom when mention is made the world will grow pale, horror stricken, and amazed."

For sheer sensationalism, however, nothing surpassed the gleefully ghoulish headline of the *Denver Republican*'s March 17 edition:

Human Jerked Beef

—

The Man Who Lived on Meat Cut
From His Murdered
Victims

—

The Fiend Who Became Very Corpulent
Upon a Diet of Human Steaks

—

A Cannibal Who Gnaws on the
Choice Cuts of His Fellow
Man[5]

As for Packer's confession—a copy of which was immediately released to the press—the newspapers didn't mince words. "The cannibal is lying as villainously in his last confession as he did in his first," proclaimed the *Cheyenne Leader*. "That he is guilty of willful and premeditated murder there is no doubt. That he committed the crime in order to obtain possession of the money which his comrades carried is equally certain." The *Rocky Mountain News* was of the same opinion, stating unequivocally that "it is more certain than ever that Packer murdered the men for the purposes of robbery and to eat their flesh."[6]

While quick to condemn Packer for his supposed prevarications, the press had no qualms about publishing wholly unsubstantiated hearsay as confirmed fact. A long list of unsolved homicides—cold cases, in today's parlance—were attributed to the "unmanned wretch." He was said to have killed a miner named Blaisdell in 1872, a father and son in 1874, a trapping partner in 1875, and a young man named Harry Phillips in 1882, stealing money and property amounting to more than four thousand dollars. One rumor claimed that he carried morphine pills to treat his epilepsy and had made use of the drug to render his five prospecting companions powerless before hacking them to death. In an era rife with notorious gunmen and outlaws, from Billy the Kid to Frank and Jesse James, Packer, so the *Denver Republican* declared, was certainly "one of the most noted murderers the Nineteenth Century has produced."[7]

Avid for information about the Man-Eater, reporters sought out General Adams, who politely declined to be interviewed. He "did not think it proper to make any statements in advance," he explained, as he would undoubtedly "be one of the chief witnesses at the trial." Adams did, however, venture the opinion "that Packer would hang himself by the discrepancies of his statements."[8]

The general was not the only one to foresee that outcome. After complimenting Sheriff Smith on the "splendid judgment" he had displayed in "securing the fiend," the editor of the *Lake City Silver World* predicted, "the next chapter will probably be the trial and conviction of the ghoul; and the last his deserved death on the gallows." Other newspapers concurred. "The gibbet will surely be his portion," declared the *Saguache Chronicle*, while the *Montrose Messenger* wrote that Packer would unquestionably "expiate his crime upon the gallows." The *Rocky Mountain News* invoked Hammurabi's code—"an eye for an eye and a tooth for a tooth"—and confidently proclaimed that "the good people of Hinsdale County will execute it." The *Denver Republican* likewise cited ancient law. Packer's execution was ordained by God, said the paper, for as is written in scripture: "Whosoever sheddeth man's blood by man shall his blood be shed."[9]

20.

TWO TOWNS

In late summer 1874—not long after the remains of Packer's five missing companions were found moldering in their final campsite—a rich mineral lode was discovered just a few miles away from the crime scene. The lucky man who made the find was Enos Throop Hotchkiss. A veteran wagon-road builder and miner, Hotchkiss had been commissioned by Otto Mears to survey and construct a toll road from Saguache to the Lake Fork Valley, a 130-mile route through "some of Colorado's most tangled wilderness."[1] Pausing to do some prospecting at the north end of Lake San Cristobal, Hotchkiss struck a major deposit of silver and gold, staked a claim, and constructed the first log cabin in the area.

Anticipating a rapid influx of settlers, a company of speculators, largely financed by Mears, purchased and laid out a 260-acre townsite. Their investment paid off. In the spring of 1875, the town—christened Lake City—consisted of a saloon, two stores, and thirteen log huts with dirt floors and mud roofs. By the following fall, it had undergone an explosive growth, with a population of roughly 1,500 inhabitants. Touring the region in October 1876, a correspondent for the *New York Times* marveled at the dizzying transformation. "The first cabin was thrown together about two years ago. Now there are two banks, several large wholesale stores, a newspaper called the *Silver World*, real estate offices, club rooms, and a theater at which the 'San Juan Minstrels' hold forth nightly to crowded houses."[2] The following month, the editor of the *Silver World*—boasting that his town offered "nearly every luxury that gratifies the palate in New York or Chicago"—offered an even more detailed description:

> The town now contains ten assayers; three bakeries; two banks; three barber shops; two billiard halls; five blacksmith shops; three boot and shoe stores; two brick yards; two breweries; two cigar factories; one clothing house; five corrals and feed stables; two drug stores; one furniture house; fourteen stores dealing in general merchandise; four hardware stores; four hotels; two jewelry establishments; four Chinese laundries; fifteen lawyers; four meat markets; three new dealers; three painters; one planing mill; six restaurants (two open all night); seven saloons; four saw mills; one shingle mill; and nine surveyors.[3]

The year 1877 saw the construction of one of the town's architectural ornaments, a handsome county courthouse. Housing the offices of various officials—county clerk and recorder, county treasurer, assessor, clerk of district court, and county judge—the two-story wood-frame building also served as a venue for public lectures, beginning with a standing-room-only appearance by suffragette Susan B. Anthony, whose two-hour talk on women's rights on the night of September 20, 1877, "held the multitude with wondrous power."[4]

+ + +

After Packer gave his statement, plans were made to transfer him to Lake City, where his trial would be held in the county courthouse. For all the impressive construction that had taken place in Lake City, however, there was one building that, even as late as 1883, many locals viewed as woefully inadequate: the town jail. Just the year before, in April 1882, an enraged mob had encountered little difficulty in breaking into the lockup and dragging out a pair of lowlifes, George Betts and James Browning, proprietors of a seedy dance hall who had shot and killed Sheriff E. N. Campbell while burglarizing a house. Begging for their lives, the pair was marched out of town and hanged from a bridge spanning the Lake Fork of the Gunnison River. Far from decrying the deed, an editorial in the *Lake City Silver World* applauded it:

> During the past five years, several murders have been com-
> mitted in this county, and in but few instances have the per-
> petrators been brought to justice through the procedure of the
> courts. With crafty lawyers to defend them, who resorted to
> all the tricks of the profession . . . justice has been cheated of
> her rights and thereby criminals have become emboldened and
> vice and crime encouraged. . . .
>
> We fully and unequivocally endorse the recent action, not that
> we gloat in it but because it was a dire necessity. We rejoice in the
> evidence so sternly demonstrated that the people are not dead in
> spirit, calloused in nature, nor overawed by the baser elements pres-
> ent in the community, but that deep down in their natures be the
> seeds, the very foundation, of justice.
>
> The lynching of George Betts and James Browning was not the
> act of a wild and uncontrollable mob fired by excitement, revenge or
> liquor. It was the act of men, firm and determined, who saw that the
> higher law must be invoked, who recognized the fact that through
> the meshes and delays of the law as administered, the chances were
> greatly in favor of the escape of these criminals from conviction and
> punishment, or with the infliction of but a mild penalty for their
> crimes. . . .
>
> The recent lynching was the first in the history of the town. . . .
> The necessity which called it forth may never occur again. We hope
> it will not; but should it, we have faith that the people will answer to
> the call as determinedly as upon this occasion.[5]

With the local press crying for vengeance against the Man-Eater, there was legitimate reason to fear that the Lake City jail might not afford any more protection to Packer than it had to Betts and Browning. Packer's guardians decided that he would be safer in the neighboring town of Gunnison. One year earlier, after mortally wounding his boss during an altercation, an Italian railroad worker named Pete Theophil was brought to Gunnison, where a group of masked men wrested him from his guards, put a noose around his neck, and dragged him through the streets as he choked to death. Then, for good measure, they strung up his corpse from a livery stable sign. To prevent such outrages in the future, the town, at a cost of $8,000, erected a new brick jail, large enough to house one hundred prisoners and equipped with steel-barred cells.[6]

Late Saturday night, March 17, escorted by Sheriff Smith and his deputy, John O. Davis, Packer left Denver by train. Early the following morning, he arrived in Gunnison.

+ + +

Reminiscing about the early days of Gunnison, one old-timer—George A. Root, son of the founder of the *Gunnison Review*—recalled it as a "lively, booming" frontier town of three thousand residents. Its business district boasted banks, bakeries, blacksmiths, pharmacies, cigar stores, meat markets, tailors, telegraph offices, clothing emporiums, a photographer's studio, a brewery, two Chinese laundries, three real estate agencies, four barber shops, and more than a dozen saloons. Cowboys and miners could find female companionship at two "palaces of entertainment," the Red Light Dance Hall and Fat Jack's Place, where, on any given night, roughhewn men in buckskin breeches, blue flannel shirts, high-heeled boots with jangling spurs, and "a brace of six-guns strapped to their hips" went "tripping the light fantastic" with "'ladies' bedecked and bespangled in brief and extravagantly décolleté dresses."[7]

Visitors to the town could board at the forty-room Mullin House, a hostelry so popular that its lodgers typically consumed 125 pounds of beefsteak at breakfast each day. There was also a "high-class" eatery on Main Street called the Poodle Dog Restaurant that was "pretty well patronized," according to Root, "despite its name."[8]

For a town its size, Gunnison was well stocked with lawyers—nineteen in all. Immediately upon his arrival, Packer—using money accrued from "some interests in mines"—retained the services of four of the best: Aaron Heims and Thomas C. Brown of the law firm Heims, Brown & Kincaid; Frank C. Goudy, renowned as "The Silver-Tongued Orator of the Rockies" for his skills at public speaking; and a future judge named (ironically enough, given the circumstances of the case) Alexander Gullett.[9]

Later that Sunday, March 18, Packer—represented by attorney Brown—appeared before district judge Melville B. Gerry. Arraigned for the murder of his five companions, the prisoner was ordered to appear during the April term at the district court in Lake City, set to convene on the second of the month. He was then returned to the Gunnison jail to await the start of his trial.[10]

+ + +

During his incarceration in Gunnison, Packer was visited frequently by an old acquaintance, Nathaniel Hunter, who had been at the Los Pinos Agency when Packer first staggered out of the wilderness nine years earlier. Interviewed many years later about his relationship with the Man-Eater, Hunter related an anecdote that suggested Packer was not only counting on an acquittal but calculating ways to profit from his criminal celebrity.

"Once when he was locked up in Gunnison," recalled Hunter, "Packer proposed that the two of us go into the saloon business together."

"We will go to Washington, where I will be a drawing card because of my notoriety," Packer explained. "You have money and can start the business. I will let my hair and beard grow, dress up in Western style, put up a big sign announcing that the place is run by 'Packer, the Man-Eater,' and we will rake in more money than we know what to do with. They will come by the thousands, and all who come will be willing to pay a quarter for the drinks."[11]

+ + +

Packer wasn't the only one looking for ways to cash in on his notoriety. In the last week of March, shortly before the start of his trial, he was transferred to the Lake City jail, where he received a visit from Henry C. Olney, editor of the *Silver World*. Prepared to encounter a monster, Olney was surprised by the Man-Eater's unthreatening demeanor:

> We found him a somewhat different appearing man than we
> had expected to see or than he had been pictured. We confess
> we did not see that "fiendish look" or discover "nature's mark of
> a murderer, fiend, or ghoul" which the enterprising reporters of
> the Denver press tell us he carries in his face. On the contrary,
> he has a pleasant face and a mild gray eye—the latter not "deep
> set" and "gleaming with hate," as they have been pictured. He is
> in fact rather a mild looking person.

Confirming the account he had given to General Adams in Denver—the second confession—Packer clung "to the statement that he did not kill any of the company except Bell, and that was in self-defense." As for the catalogue of unsolved murders the press had laid at his door, he flatly denied the charges: "The newspaper men seem bound to make Packer out as the worst man in the world," he declared, referring to himself, as he sometimes did, in the third person. "I don't see why they should lie so, or what good it does them. Seems like every crime committed in the mountains by unknown men has been charged to Packer."

Though insisting on his innocence, he claimed to be "reconciled to his fate, even it be death of the gallows." Indeed, he suggested that such an outcome might be a relief, since the memory of killing Bell, even in self-defense, "had been with him night and day, so that he had had no rest or peace." He "regretted that he ever left the country without clearing up the whole matter." Time and again during the intervening years, he had resolved "to come back and give himself up, which he would have done within two months if he had not been arrested."

Looking forward to the approaching trial, Olney believed that the verdict might go either way. On the one hand, he said, "the testimony against Packer is almost wholly circumstantial." On the other, Packer's "own conflicting statements will no doubt weigh against him." In any case, Olney believed the proceedings would "be one of the most interesting in the annals of criminal trials."

Then, with an eye to exploiting the public's prurient fascination with the Man-Eater, he ended his article with a sales pitch. "We have received 2 doz. cabinet photographs of Packer to be sold," Olney wrote. "Price 50 cents each."[12]

21.

GALLOTTI

In 1875, Denver was the scene of a murder that—in the overheated words of Colorado historian Frank Hall—was "one of the most revolting and dreadful in the history of mankind," a crime rarely "exceeded in ferocity, cruelty, and incarnate fiendishness."[1]

In late October of that year, neighborhood residents became aware of "rank and extremely offensive odors" emanating from the modest house at 634 Lawrence Street on the outskirts of the city. Before long, the fetor had grown so overpowering that Mr. W. M. Failing, who lived directly across the street, summoned a policeman.

Breaking into the house, Failing and the officer were immediately confronted with the "sickening evidence of diabolical atrocity." Clotted blood was everywhere, spattering the walls and floors of all three little rooms as well as the connecting hallway. The place was clearly a shambles in the original meaning of that term: a slaughterhouse.

Fighting back their mounting nausea, the two men quickly located the source of the stench. A small trap door in the floor of the kitchen opened into "a sort of pit used as a cellar." Lighting candles, they descended the rickety stairway into the "foul, black, weird, and uncanny place."

There, piled in a heap, were four bodies "in the last stages of decomposition: cut, hacked, stabbed, and mangled, covered with filthy blankets and filthier mattresses." The throats of all had been slit from ear to ear. Lying nearby were "three large harps, two violins, a scissors-grinding machine, a hatchet, hammer, and several dirk knives all smeared and splashed with gore."

Within days of the appalling discovery, detectives under the supervision of Arapahoe County sheriff D. J. Cook had identified the victims as an Italian scissors grinder known locally as "Old Joe" and three young boys presumed to be his children or nephews, who earned their keep as strolling musicians. Investigators also managed to ascertain the names of the prime suspects: another band of Italians, acquaintances of the victims, who had recently fled the city and whose ringleader was a tinsmith named Filomeno Gallotti.

Taking off in pursuit of the fugitives, who had scattered in different directions, Cook and his two deputies, R. Y. Force and W. Frank Smith, ultimately captured the entire bunch. After a "long and arduous chase," Gallotti himself, who was headed for Mexico, was finally caught in Taos. Narrowly escaping a lynch mob, the killers were brought back to Denver, where one member of the gang, a young man named Leonard Allessandri, broke down and provided a detailed confession. His recital—according to historian Hall, a man not given to understatement—was among "the most devilish that has ever been told," a story ghastly enough to "fill the soul with unutterable dismay."

The elderly victim "Old Joe," ostensibly the relative of the three murdered boys, was actually one Joe Pecorra, "a padrone in Italy" and recent émigré to America. A kind of real-life version of Dickens's Fagin, he "had stolen the boys who played harps and violins, compelling them to earn money by any means, no matter how, and deliver everything to him. They were cruelly treated and forced to work day and night to satisfy his greed."[2]

Filomeno Gallotti, too, was a recent arrival from Italy, where he had been the leader of a "band of brigands which robbed and murdered travelers on lonely roads or held them for ransom." Fleeing the law, he had come to America and "drifted to New Orleans and at last to Denver," where he became acquainted with his countryman Pecorra. Before long, he had hatched a diabolical plot to "secure 'Old Joe's' money."

In his characteristically lurid style, Hall describes the ensuing massacre at Lawrence Street:

The old man and his boys with one or two others were playing cards in the front room. Gallotti stood like a death watch behind Joe, apparently interested in the game, but actually awaiting an opportunity to strike. Suddenly, and without the slightest warning, he drew from his coat a long, keen-edged butcher knife, and seizing the old man by the hair, drew back his head and with one stroke nearly severed it from his body. The blood spurted upon the table and into the faces of the players. Not content with this, as the quivering form fell to the floor, Gallotti jumped upon it and with fiendish glee plunged his knife into it as if it were a most delightful pastime to hack and mutilate. One of the others simultaneously seized the larger of the boys and endeavored to kill him in a like manner, but he fought desperately for his life. At last Gallotti, having satiated his appetite upon his first victim, arose and seeing the blundering work of his assistants, grabbed the boy and instantly slew him.

Minutes later, the other two boys, who had been out in the city with their instruments, returned home. "The smaller one came in first, carrying a violin under his arm. Gallotti seized him, and drawing a knife plunged it to the hilt just under the boy's right ear, cutting his throat." The second little boy, who was carrying a harp, tried to escape, but "Gallotti, the hell-born, caught him around the neck with one hand and with the boy's head under his arm slashed his throat from ear to ear."

To cap the horror, Gallotti "scooped up a handful of blood running from the big boy's throat and drank it" and made his confederates do "likewise as a pledge of fidelity." The four victims of the "infernal butchery" were then dumped into the pit beneath the kitchen floor.[3]

If ever a crime demanded the harshest punishment permitted by law, it was this "unparalleled massacre," perpetrated by a "self-confessed demon" who "poured out blood like water, reveled in it, and drank it fresh from the gaping wounds of the slaughtered."[4] To the howling indignation of the public, however, Gallotti and his "black-cursed" accomplices managed to escape the gallows.

They owed their salvation to a glitch in Colorado law. In 1868, the Colorado State Legislature established death by hanging as the penalty for murder. Two years later, the law was amended. According to the revised statute, the death penalty could only be imposed when "the jury trying the case shall in their verdict of guilty also indicate that the killing was deliberate or premeditated."[5]

Assigned by the court to defend Filomeno Gallotti was a young Georgia-born attorney, Charles S. Thomas, a graduate of the University of Michigan who had moved to Denver in 1871, seeking relief in the fresh mountain air from early-stage tuberculosis. In a cunning move, Thomas had his client plead guilty, thereby avoiding a jury trial. He then argued that, with no jury verdict, the defendant could not, under the wording of the 1870 statute, be condemned to death. Despite the cold-blooded premeditation of the atrocity, the presiding judge, A. W. Brazee, had no alternative but to sentence Gallotti to life in prison.[6]

The ruling provoked a public uproar, and, as Hall notes, "Judge Brazee was sharply criticized and fiercely condemned."[7] Still, it wasn't until 1881—five years after Colorado became the nation's thirty-eighth state—that the 1870 murder statute was repealed and a new one adopted that allowed for the death penalty even in cases where the defendant pleaded guilty.[8]

In drafting this amended statute, however, Colorado lawmakers committed another legalistic blunder—one that would have far-reaching consequences in the case of Alfred Packer.

22.

INDICTMENT

Though he lives on in legend as a comic stereotype, an ornery frontier hanging judge who talked like Rooster Cogburn, Melville B. Gerry was, in truth, a highly learned and eloquent individual whose speech sometimes verged on the florid. Born in Hamilton County, Florida, he fought gallantly for the Confederacy for the duration of the Civil War, winning two promotions in the field and mustering out with the rank of first lieutenant. After receiving his degree from Mercer College in Macon, Georgia, he practiced law in that city until 1873, when he migrated to Colorado for his health, residing first in Denver before moving to Lake City in 1877. Despite being "a lifelong Democrat . . . in a Republican stronghold," the thirty-nine-year-old Gerry was elected district judge by a large majority in 1882, a testament to "his personal popularity and well known reputation as a lawyer."[1]

+ + +

Under the theory that it would be easiest to convict Packer for the slaying of an elderly victim, prosecutors decided to try him for only one of the murders, that of sexagenarian Israel Swan, keeping the others in reserve in the unlikely event of an acquittal. On Thursday morning, April 5, with Judge Gerry presiding, a grand jury presented the indictment. Couched in the usual tortured legalese, it charged that

Alfred Packer, late of the County of Hinsdale, aforesaid, on, to-wit: the first day of March, in the year of our Lord, one thousand eight hundred and seventy-four, at the County of Hinsdale, in the State of Colorado, in and upon one Israel Swan, a human being in the peace of the said People then and there being, did then and there unlawfully, willfully, feloniously, and of his malice aforethought, make an assault; and, that the said Alfred Packer, with a certain hatchet, which he, the said Alfred Packer, in his hands, then and there had and held, in and upon the head and forehead of him, the said Israel Swan, did then and there, unlawfully, willfully, feloniously, and of his malice aforethought, strike, beat, and wound, then and there giving to the said Israel Swan, then and there with the hatchet aforesaid, upon the head and forehead aforesaid several mortal wounds and bruises of which said mortal wounds and bruises, he, the said Israel Swan, on the day and year last aforesaid, died.[2]

Representing Packer at the proceedings was his lead attorney, Aaron Heims, who immediately moved to quash the indictment, claiming that it was invalid on several grounds. To begin with, it specified that the crime had been committed in the "state of Colorado." In 1874, however—two years before it was admitted into the Union—Colorado was a territory, not a state. Similarly, the indictment specified that the crime took place in Hinsdale County, which did not exist at the time. Finally, argued Heims, "the court had no jurisdiction in the case," since the crime, "if committed at all, must have been committed on the then Ute reservation."[3]

The following morning, a new, amended indictment was presented. Once again, Heims strove to quash it, this time on a legal technicality ultimately stemming from the Gallotti case. According to Heims, his client could not be tried under the murder statute that had been adopted in 1881 "since the Swan homicide had been committed in 1874." Nor could Packer be tried under the murder statute of 1870, since—owing to a glaring oversight on the part of the Colorado legislature—that law had been repealed in 1881 without a provision known as a "savings clause." Such a clause would have preserved the right of the state to seek a murder conviction under the 1870 statute, even though that statute had subsequently been repealed.[4]

Though Heims's argument had significant merit—as later events would prove—Judge Gerry denied it. The following day, Saturday, April 7, another motion was filed by the defense, asking for a "reasonable adjournment" of the trial. An affidavit submitted by Heims and his associates argued that—thanks to the relentlessly shrill newspaper portrayal of Packer as a "ghoul," a "fiend," and a "human hyena" responsible for crimes of "unparalleled atrocity and enormity"—"public excitement in this county is so great against the defendant and . . . the inhabitants are so prejudiced against him that he cannot safely go to trial at the present term of this court."[5]

That many residents of Hinsdale County were baying for Packer's blood was unquestionably the case. In a letter penned years later, General Adams confirmed, "before . . . the trial, the miners from the surrounding country were determined to hang Packer without waiting for the law's delay, and it was only after a great deal of persuasion by the sheriff, some other county officials, other citizens and myself that the project was abandoned."[6]

Nevertheless, despite the defense team's legitimate fears that their client could not receive a fair and impartial trial under the current circumstances, the motion for an adjournment was denied. There was nothing more Packer's lawyers could do except prepare for Monday morning and the start of what the local press was already calling "the great Packer trial."[7]

23.

THE TRIAL: DAY ONE

The Hinsdale County Courthouse in Lake City hadn't drawn such a crowd since Susan B. Anthony's visit six years before. When the doors of the white clapboard building opened on the morning of April 9, 1883, the second-floor courtroom filled up within minutes—no surprise since the spectator section of the spartan little chamber was only large enough to accommodate a half dozen rows of bow-backed wooden chairs. One observer—who clearly had never attended a sensational murder trial before—was surprised to see how "many ladies [were] present" in the room. To ensure that the male members of the audience maintained a suitable decorum, signs were prominently posted on the walls: "No Spitting on the Floor."[1]

Those who were there for the titillating testimony about multiple murders and cannibalism endured hours of tedium before the first witness was called. It wasn't until four in the afternoon, after the questioning of nearly sixty candidates, that the all-male jury was selected and sworn in, each man affirming on a Bible that he would "well and truly try the matter at issue between the People of the State of Colorado and Alfred Packer, the defendant, and a true verdict render according to the evidence." Along with the judge, clerk, sheriff, bailiff, four lawyers, defendant, and a large potbellied stove, the jurors were crowded into a railed-off fifteen-by-thirty-foot area at the front of the room.[2]

Preston Nutter was the first to testify. In the years since he had come to Colorado as a member of the ill-fated prospecting party, Nutter had started an ore-freighting business and become a wealthy man. Much respected in the community, he had been elected to the state legislature in 1881 and had headed several house committees before quitting politics two years later to devote himself to cattle ranching, an enterprise that would occupy his prodigious energies for the next fifty years. At over six feet tall—"straight as a lodge pole pine and physically hard as the saddle he rode"—he cut an imposing figure and, like many westerners, was not a man to waste words. Frank in his undiminished loathing of Packer, he would prove a damaging witness against him.[3]

Under questioning by District Attorney John C. Bell, Nutter explained that he had first encountered Packer in November 1873. "I met him with a party of gentlemen going across the country. The party made up at Bingham Canyon, started for the San Juan country. Started ahead of us. I overtook them there." Asked about Israel Swan, Nutter confirmed that "there was a man by that name with the party I got acquainted with on the road."

And when, Bell inquired, did Nutter last "see Israel Swan alive?"

"Some time between the 7th and the 15th of February, 1875," said Nutter.

"You may state if you have since seen him," said Bell.

"I saw Israel Swan's body in August the same year," said Nutter, "about two miles or two miles and a quarter above here."

Was he "dead or living?" asked Bell.

"Dead," came the reply.

Asked to describe the condition of Swan's corpse, Nutter explained that it "was almost or nearly decayed." The body was partially covered with a blanket, one corner of which "lay across his head, and through that blanket into his skull was a cut, and on the blanket . . . there was left patches of matted hair, and blood soaked the blanket and showed the cut in the skull." He recalled, "[The cut] was at least nearly as long as my hand is wide" and "went clear down through the skull."

Though Nutter "could not perceive that flesh had been cut from Swan's body," he had observed something significant about the condition of the old man's clothes. They had been "cut and ripped up and piled on the body, or near the body," he said. "Looked as though the seams had been opened and the clothing cut right square where there wasn't a seam."

After giving the jury a moment to absorb the import of this testimony—which clearly suggested that the victim's clothing had been ransacked by the killer—Bell returned to the last time Nutter had seen Swan alive. "Who was with him?" Bell asked. "How many?"

Five others, said Nutter: "Wilson Bell, George Noon, Frank Miller, James Humphrey, and Mr. Packer." They were equipped "with their blankets, clothing, their provisions, and a couple of carbines and a hatchet." Miller "had a skinning knife about that long," said Nutter, extending his hands and holding them about eight inches apart. "He was a butcher and used that knife for skinning."

Nutter estimated that they had left Ouray's camp with "provisions enough to last a period of seven or eight days at least." Their destination was "where Gunnison City now stands. It was at that time a government cattle camp—cattle for the Ute Indians."

And when was the next time that Nutter saw Bell, Miller, Humphrey, and Noon?

"At the time when I saw Swan's body," answered Nutter. "They were there." All of them "showed hatchet wounds except one that I don't know if there was a cut in the head but the back of the head was entirely mashed in, as though struck hard."

Asked about the arrangement of the bodies, Nutter began to describe the scene but was interrupted by Bell, who handed him a stack of law books and suggested that he use them to demonstrate the position of the five sets of remains. Leaning forward in his chair, Nutter pointed to a crack in the wooden floor. "Make this mark the stream," he said. Then, setting down each book in turn, he indicated where the five bodies had lain. "They were a few feet apart," he said. "They were in a space half as large as this room. Not larger than that—not that large." Noon's body "laid nearest" to the vestiges of a campfire; the others "laid straight with the stream."

Backtracking chronologically, Nutter then described his arrival at the Los Pinos Agency on April 16 and his reunion with Packer, who initially claimed that Swan and the others had left him to fend for himself after he "got his feet wet and frozen" while out searching futilely for game. Packer's insistence that his party had been reduced to living "principally on beans" had struck Nutter as peculiar, since he himself had experienced "no trouble in killing all the mountain sheep we wanted anywhere over this country."

He had grown more suspicious after noticing Packer in possession of Frank Miller's skinning knife. Packer's explanation—that Miller had "stuck it in a tree, went off and left it"—seemed wildly implausible to Nutter. There was also the matter of the horse and saddle Packer had purchased from Otto Mears in Saguache. How did Packer—so devoid of funds when the twenty-one-member prospecting party left Utah that Bob McGrue had to cover his traveling expenses—manage to pay for the animal?

Eventually, Packer offered his initial confession and agreed to lead a search party to the site of his final camp. Whatever doubts Nutter may have been harboring about Packer's guilt were eradicated when, as quickly happened, Packer claimed to be "entirely lost." Angrily confronting Packer, Nutter denounced him as a murderer and declared that "he ought to be hung."

By the time Nutter finished recounting the story of his search for the missing men, he had been on the stand for nearly two hours. Before court was adjourned, Bell asked the witness a final question: "State what was said by Mr. Packer at different times during your trip from Utah relative to Mr. Swan's having money."

When Nutter replied that he couldn't "swear to anything having been said about Swan's having money," the DA rephrased the question: "You may state whether or not Mr. Swan had a general reputation among your party of having money or being a moneyed man."

Before Nutter could answer, attorney Heims was on his feet, objecting to the line of questioning as "incompetent and immaterial." Though the objection was sustained, Bell had managed to introduce the prosecution's theory of motive: that Packer had murdered Israel Swan for his money.[4]

24.

THE TRIAL: DAY TWO

General Charles Adams was the first to take the stand when court convened promptly at nine o'clock the next morning. In his heavily accented English, Adams described his first meeting with the defendant, over breakfast at Otto Mears's house in 1874, when Packer, seated beside Mrs. Adams, told the same story he had originally recounted after emerging from the wilderness: "that he and five men had left the encampage of the Utes some time in February and they had wandered in the mountains for several days, and he had frozen his feet—or the toes of his feet. That his comrades had stayed in camp with him a few days. That he had been unable to walk and could not keep up, so they had to leave him on the mountainside. One of the party gave him his rifle to procure food and after a few days, he being able to walk again— he lived on a rabbit that he killed and afterwards on rosebuds till he managed to reach the agency as he did."

Since Packer, according to this account, had managed to survive on little more than some meager vegetation scrabbled from the snow, Adams believed that "the others might be alive as well." He therefore proposed sending out "a party to hunt them up," with Packer as guide.

The next day, Adams, his wife, and Packer set out for the Los Pinos Indian Agency, where "several of the original party from Utah" had since arrived. Meeting with "two or three of these men," Adams learned of "several suspicious circumstances connected with this affair," particularly Packer's extravagant spending habits during his stay in Saguache.

"So I was induced to ask him where he got the money," Adams testified. When Packer's explanation proved to be a lie, Adams, after some cajoling, managed to extract a statement from him.

According to this initial confession, three of Packer's traveling companions—Swan, Humphrey, and Miller—succumbed successively to starvation and were eaten, each in turn, by the survivors. Noon was then shot for food by Bell, who subsequently attempted to club Packer to death with his rifle, breaking it against a tree when his intended target ducked. After shooting Bell in self-defense, Packer "lived on his flesh for several days," then took "some of the flesh along with him and finally reached the agency. He had been out of meat for only a day or so before he reached the agency." As for the money he had spent so freely in Saguache, he confessed to having scavenged it from Humphrey's body.

Adams explained that he then had Packer repeat the statement, this time in front of a dozen witnesses, including the men recently arrived from Ouray's camp. Though Nutter and several of the other miners dismissed the story as a lie, they agreed with Adams that if Packer could lead them to Bell's body and show them the shattered rifle, his story would be corroborated. "A few days after," said Adams, "I sent out this party in charge of [agency constable Herman Lauter]. . . . They returned in about twelve or fourteen days—maybe ten, I don't exactly remember—without having accomplished their object, so I advised the Justice of the Peace to send Mr. Packer to Saguache for safekeeping until the snows melted and the bodies were found."

Nine years would pass, Adams testified, before he saw Packer again. Following the latter's arrest near Fort Fetterman, the general had traveled to Wyoming, where the two had been reunited on the train carrying Packer from Cheyenne to Denver. After some initial hesitation, Packer suddenly seemed eager to unburden himself. "He said that he had always wished to talk to me ever since he had escaped from the sheriff in Saguache," Adams explained. "That his soul seemed to drive towards where I was in order to take back his first statement and tell the whole truth."

That evening in Denver, in the presence of Adams, Sheriff Smith, and Deputy Marshal Cantrill, Packer had made his second confession. Adams's handwritten transcription of the statement was entered into evidence as "Plaintiff Exhibit Number 1" and then, at the direction of Judge Gerry, read aloud to the jury. Following this recitation, Bell asked Adams if Packer had "given any reasons why he did not tell the truth at first."

"I asked him that question," said Adams. "I asked him why he did not tell the same story the first time that he told the second. He said he was very much excited, didn't know what he was saying at the time." Except for those moments when he recounted the killing of Bell, however, Packer—so Adams now testified—did not seem excited "at all during either statement. On the contrary, he seemed "perfectly cool," said Adams.

During a brief cross-examination, Aaron Heims attempted to get Adams to admit that Packer "was not in a proper frame of mind at the time he made the first statement." Adams, however, insisted that Packer had shown no signs "of an impaired mind" while making his first confession. Adams continued, "He told it in such a collected way, I thought it was so."[1]

This bit of testimony, which concluded Adams's appearance on the witness stand, contradicted an observation he had made back in 1874, when he reported to the commissioner of Indian affairs that Packer had "shown traces of mental aberration" at the time of his first statement.[2] Like Preston Nutter, Adams had proved an effective witness for the prosecution, conveying a strong impression of Packer not as a traumatized victim of horrific circumstances but as a cold and calculating liar.

+ + +

Adams was followed by his old friend Otto Mears. At the time, the little Russian émigré was deep into his career as Colorado's "transportation king," overseeing the construction of what would eventually be a 450-mile network of wagon roads through the fearsomely rugged San Juans. As one of the founders of Lake City and its largest property holder, he was a highly regarded figure in the county, and his words, as the prosecution well knew, carried a great deal of weight with the jury.

Speaking in his thick Slavic accent, Mears explained that "a week or two" after arriving in Saguache in the spring of 1874, Packer had "asked

[him] to sell him a horse and saddle and bridle." The price was "somewhere near a hundred dollars." Packer extracted a wallet from his pocket and passed the money to Mears, who, examining the cash, thought one of the ten-dollar bills "was a counterfeit." When Mears "told him I did not think it was good," Packer produced a second wallet. Inside, according to Mears, was a Wells Fargo money order.[3]

Under cross-examination by defense attorney Heims, Mears acknowledged that he had seen neither the amount of nor the signature on the money order. Still, the notion that Packer had lived it up in Saguache on money stripped from his butchered companions reinforced the widespread sense of his "mendacity and greed"—the bitter suspicion that "he had used his experience in the mountains to entice the men into the hills in order to murder them and steal their money."[4]

+ + +

Other witnesses called that morning lent support to the prosecution's theory that Packer had been motivated by "greed, not need." George Tracy, another member of the original Utah party, asserted that "all through" the trip to Colorado, Packer engaged in conversations about the money Israel Swan and Frank Miller had in their possession.[5] Saloonkeeper James "Larry" Dolan offered a vivid picture of the defendant's profligate ways during his time in Saguache, particularly his loss of thirty-seven dollars in a single game of "freeze-out" poker one long afternoon. In response to a question by Bell, Dolan recalled seeing Packer's wallet stuffed with "considerable money . . . twenty dollar notes and fifties." He also described the time "they got to talk[ing] about money matters" and Packer had offered to lend him $300.

Bell concluded his direct examination of Dolan by eliciting a particularly damning piece of testimony. "Have you seen [the defendant] since he came back this time?" he asked.

Dolan nodded. "I talked with him down at the jail one time. I come to see him."

"Did he tell you anything about the money matter?"

"Yes," said Dolan. "He said he wanted me, as one of the witnesses, to prove he did not have much money, only about a hundred dollars.

He said he wanted to prove he told me he had twenty dollars of his own money and seventy dollars of these men and that he sold his gun for ten dollars, which made one hundred."

"He wanted to show by you that he only had a hundred dollars?" asked Bell.

"Yes, sir."

"But you are positive that you saw more than a hundred dollars?" said Bell.

"Yes, sir," Dolan said emphatically. "I am."

During cross-examination, defense attorney Heims—seeking to cast doubt on Dolan's credibility—subjected him to an intense grilling about Packer's heavy loss at the long-ago game of poker. How, Heims wanted to know, did Dolan "recollect this thirty-seven dollar game so distinctly?"

"That was rather a large game for a man of small circumstance," came the reply.

Could Dolan recall another "individual who lost any considerable amount beside the instance you have given of this defendant?"

Dolan frowned thoughtfully for a moment, then mentioned a customer by the name of Brown who had once lost a good deal of money at a game of "freeze-out"—perhaps as much as forty dollars.

"Do you recollect exactly?" asked Heims.

"It may have been forty or more," said Dolan.

"But you recollect exactly the amount Packer lost?"

"Yes, sir."

"How comes it you recollect exactly the amount this man Packer lost but don't recollect just how much this man Brown lost? What causes you to recollect this and not the other?"

"I went over to Mr. Mears," Dolan explained. "We were talking about the matter of Packer's having no money. I made the remark that he lost that amount of money playing 'freeze-out.'"

Switching tacks, Heims asked Dolan about his conversation with Packer a few days earlier. "What reply did you make to him when he wanted you to testify as to the amount of money he had?"

Dolan shrugged. "I don't know that I made him any reply."

"You didn't say anything about the money matter?" Heims asked.

"I don't think I did."

"So your recollection isn't as clear in regard to that as to the game of 'freeze-out' nine years ago?" Heims asked, making no attempt to hide his disbelief.

His incredulous tone, however, had no effect on Dolan. The saloon-keeper's memory of the precise amount Packer had lost that afternoon in 1874 was, he insisted, "as clear to me now as at that day."[6]

+ + +

Grisly testimony was offered by Hezekiah "Hessie" Musgrave, the prospector who had been one of the first to examine the remains of Packer's murdered companions. Alerted to the presence of the corpses by the *Harper's Weekly* artist John Randolph, Musgrave proceeded to the campsite, where he saw "five men lying there as though they had been killed by some sharp instrument, looked like it might be a hatchet, struck in the head. Each were in their positions where they were killed. There was three of them seemed to be near together, the other two were off some distance from them."

"What indications did you see of flesh having been cut off from any of them?" asked Bell.

"The flesh had been cut off from one of them," said Musgrave, tracing a finger along his own torso as he spoke, "commencing at the breast and running down, also around, cut down that far and then cut across, and cut off also and down at an angle."

"Did you see any signs of violence upon each of the five men," Bell asked, "or did they seem to have died a natural death?"

"On three of them I took particular notice," said Musgrave. "There was a mark of the corner of a hatchet or some sharp instrument they had been cut in the head with." Another had his head completely "mashed in."

"Could you see any indications of there having been a struggle?"

"I could not," Musgrave replied, "unless it was the one who had his head mashed in. I thought that one might have had a struggle because he was—the way he met his death looked like that was the cause of it, he had his head mashed in on account of a scuffle, but the others did not."[7]

+ + +

To impress the jury with Packer's violent tendencies, Bell called Herman Lauter to the stand. After making his initial confession, Packer—so Lauter testified—was "turned over to my custody as Constable of that precinct." Lauter continued, "He volunteered to go out and show us where these things was, where his camps was. He said he could show us where each one of his camps was before reaching the agency until the final one."

About four days out from the agency, according to Lauter's recollection, he "found a knife on [Packer's] person and demanded it from him."

"Where did he have the knife concealed?" Bell asked.

"Under his clothes, next to his body."

"What kind of knife was it?"

"It is what a butcher calls a skinning knife," said Lauter.

"What did he do?" asked Bell.

"He rushed at me with that knife," said Lauter. "I clasped his hands and he laid the knife down."

To Lauter, the incident confirmed the prevailing sentiment about Packer among the search party. "The boys were in fear of him," he declared.

Lauter then added a sensational detail previously undisclosed. After bringing Packer back to the agency following the fruitless search, Lauter was told to escort him to Saguache and turn him over to Sheriff Amos Wall. Along the way they stopped to eat lunch. By the time they reached Saguache, Lauter "was very sick. A doctor was called, and I was declared poisoned."[8]

+ + +

Herman Lueders, formerly a clerk at the Los Pinos Indian Agency, was put on the stand to confirm the widely reported story that Packer had disposed of the two suspicious wallets by tossing them into the Los Pinos creek. Lueders recalled the morning that he and another employee, Stephen Dole, saw Packer wander "down towards the creek for a few minutes and then return." Though admitting that he had not actually seen Packer throw anything in the water, Lueders left no doubt that both he and Dole believed there was something suspect about the incident. "We had our own ideas about it," Lueders said. "We thought it strange."

Another employee of the agency, former justice of the peace James P. Downer, told of purchasing Packer's rifle for ten dollars. Downer, a Pennsylvania native and one-time member of the state legislature, explained that he "felt a sympathy for" Packer because he "was well acquainted with William F. Packer," a prominent Pennsylvanian who had served a term as governor between 1858 and 1861. Packer professed to be the former governor's nephew, an assertion that Downer saw no reason to question, though—like the similar claim the Man-Eater had made about Asa Packer—it was untrue.[9]

25.

THE TRIAL: DAY THREE

Wednesday's session began with the testimony of O. D. Loutsenhizer. Like Preston Nutter, Loutsenhizer had settled on the Western Slope and had played a pioneering role in its development. Along with a miner named Joseph Selig, he had founded the town of Montrose and, a year before the start of the trial, had been named a county commissioner by the governor.

Seeking to elicit additional testimony about Packer's supposedly mercenary motives, District Attorney Bell asked the witness if he "had any talk with Packer, or whether he had any in your presence, relative to money?"

"On the road somewhere near the Green River, we got out of provisions and there was some kicking," Loutsenhizer recalled. "Someone said it was a nice way of traveling, the idea of a man having nothing to eat and having plenty of money in his pockets. I think some of the parties were a little bit anxious to quarrel."

"What about Packer?" asked Bell.

"I thought he was particular about asking the boys questions."

"What kind of questions?" Bell prodded.

"About what so and so would have. Not only Packer alone, there were others in the party. They were in a bunch by themselves, all talking that way."

That others besides Packer had displayed an untoward interest in their traveling companions' money was not the kind of testimony that Bell was looking for. Hurriedly he asked, "Who was the party who attracted your attention most?"

"Mr. Packer," said Loutsenhizer.

"Why did he attract your attention?"

"Because he was inquiring so close about the money."

"How close?"

"He asked, 'How much money do you suppose this man has, and how much money do you suppose so-and-so has.' It only caused an impression on me from that time on. I had an impression in my mind that it looked a little strange, this talk."

Having coaxed forth the response he was looking for, Bell brought Loutzenhizer's testimony to a swift close. Following a brief cross-examination by attorney Heims, the prosecution then rested its case.[1]

+ + +

The dramatic high point of the trial—the moment the public had been waiting for—arrived at precisely 9:20 a.m., when the defense called Alfred Packer to the stand. Those who were hoping for a memorable appearance by the Man-Eater were not disappointed. Brooking no interruption, he would hold forth for two solid hours, delivering a rambling oration that, in the words of one chronicler, was "more like a harangue than coherent, calm, and collected testimony." His remarks were so meandering that observers likened them to the courtroom ravings of Charles Guiteau, the wildly erratic assassin of President James Garfield, whose trial had taken place less than two years earlier.[2]

Standing at the front of the room, Packer began with a series of demands. "I want to make a statement from the beginning, from the time I left Utah, Bingham Canyon, until we got here and I don't want to be questioned until after I get through with my statement," he announced. "And furthermore, I want four witnesses who were here yesterday. I want Mr. Mears for one, Major Downer for another, James Dolan the saloonkeeper, and that constable Lauter, that lame man. I would like it, if General Adams is around, I would like to have him. I would like to have these men come up here."

Speaking for the prosecution, attorney J. Warner Mills told the judge that the state had "no objection, but it is very irregular and the parties are not all here."

"I was here and I had to listen to twenty-seven witnesses, and I have no witnesses myself," said Packer. "I see a couple of them here now."

"Under the circumstances," said Judge Gerry, "I have no objection to their coming forward. Mr. Dolan and Mr. Nutter, you may come inside the bar."

"Nutter, I don't care for him at all," growled Packer. "I want Major Downer and that constable."

Having settled these preliminaries, Packer—clearly intent on having his say, no matter at what eye-glazing length—launched into his speech, addressing it at first to the assembled spectators until instructed by Judge Gerry to "direct it to the jury."

"I was working and got leaded," he began. "You miners all know what leaded is—being poisoned from the ore. I had a contract, was running a tunnel. There was about nine or ten men leaded when I was. I finished that contract and took another, but had to throw it up. I was not able to finish it, I run my tunnel twenty-five feet. They paid me and I left. It was getting then toward fall. I was sick."

Leaving for Bingham, he found lodging at a boarding house near some smelters. Before long, he "took the poison again—leaded, the same thing." He continued, "That was the third time I was leaded that summer. That threw me into fits. They thought I was going to die.

"I had a friend up there at Bingham, Dr. McCann. He had been treating me before. He gave me a dose of castor oil. Moved my boarding house from near the smelter to another boarding house in a little town called Sandy—just a store and a few buildings. After a time, I got strong. I heard of this outfit camped above. Heard they were coming over to Colorado. I had been to Colorado and I wanted to go back."

Packer then described his first meeting with Bob McGrue: "I went up and seen him. I told him my circumstances. I had been boarding, had been sick, been doctoring, that I was short of money. Told me he would like to have me go through to Colorado, and I asked how much he would charge me. I forget whether twenty or twenty-five dollars. I think twenty-five. He was to board me, and I was to help with his four horses. That was our agreement, and in a short time we started."

Contrary to the testimony of both Loutsenhizer and Preston Nutter, he claimed not to "remember whether I ever mentioned about moneys or money myself" during the trip. He admitted, however, that he had complained loudly when the party ran low on provisions near the Green River. "We got along all lovely until we run out of food," he recalled. "I expect I growled with the rest. I had paid my way and had lived on chopped barley. I am not much of a crank anyway, but I growled then, I know. Game was scarce. We didn't kill anything. Had seen no bear—no bear nor game." So dire was their situation that they raised the possibility of eating one of the horses. "I made a remark to Bob McGrue that we kill the lame horse. Bob said he couldn't eat a lame horse, but he could eat a nice little dark mare traded from the Mormons."

They were saved from their plight by the sudden appearance of a band of "whooping and yelling" Indians, led by Chief Ouray. Packer and his party quickly "corralled everything" and prepared for a fight, but Ouray, after satisfying himself that the prospectors had no designs on the Ute land, "invited us to his camp to give the Indians a chance to trade with us."

After deciding, at Ouray's suggestion, to "winter there," the twenty-one prospectors settled into a variety of makeshift shelters—McGrue and Tracy in a conical Sibley tent, Nutter and Cooper in a dugout, others in wagon sheds. As for Packer, he and Israel Swan "built a shanty out of brush and leaves. The other of the six boys that came with me built the same way." Though it was "pretty hard living . . . we was able to live there pretty content."

Packer didn't say why he and the others felt impelled to leave the camp in spite of Ouray's warnings. He only said, "We made up our minds a few of us to go hunt for the agency. We bundled up two blankets and cooking utensils. . . . We had seven days' grub for one man."

Then, in the hush of the courtroom, he began to relate the story that everyone in the courtroom had been waiting to hear, the Man-Eater's own account of the ghastly ordeal that had ended in the death, butchery, and cannibalization of his five companions.

+ + +

After just a few days of wandering in the snow, the six men were already down to their last pint of flour. Packer recalled, "We boiled snow water and made a thickened gravy or mush. After we had eat our grub it was snowing and storming so, we couldn't see any distance. The wind was sweeping the snow so deep that we couldn't follow the gulches. We followed the ridges. We had an idea that the Los Pinos Agency was laying off under the Rocky Mountains, and all under the ridge we could see the valley. We argued with each other and all came to that conclusion.

"We plowed the Rocky Mountains, followed the ridge up across, and kept on. After the little pint of flour was eat, George Noon give up his moccasins made of goatskin. We roasted them and eat them. We pulled the hair off and eat them—that was our supper. We soon used up our matches. We carried our fire in a coffee pot. Old Man Swan carried this fire on account of keeping his hands warm. He was getting worn out, poor and sick. He would travel on behind and we broke the trail. When I tired out, another man stepped in and walked ahead.

"About four or five days after we eat George Noon's moccasins, Bell gave up his. We eat up these moccasins. There was a little cranky word right there. Bell begun to get cranky. After we eat Bell's moccasins, sitting by the fire, George Noon, I believe it was, got up, walked around the fire and stepped on Bell's foot. Bell cussed him, said he was tired and didn't intend to be tramped to death. Old Man Swan cautioned him not to talk that way when on such a trip. That was the first cranky word in the outfit.

"The next morning, without breakfast or anything, we kept on. The second day from the day we eat Bell's moccasins, we found a patch of rosebuds. We devoured the rosebuds. From that time after we eat the rosebuds, we camped down near a big tree. We built a fire at the root of some tall trees. From the time we eat Bell's moccasins till we found these rosebuds was five or six days. Then I give up my moccasins. That was right on top of the ridge, near the top of the Rocky Mountains. Camped all night.

"Bell was getting cranky. He was a stout, red-faced, redheaded man. His starvation was worrying him worse than the rest of us. He was growling all the time—was cussing all the time because he was a fool in leaving a country where there was plenty and coming there to starve to death.

"We were all about gone, and our last dying words were that we wanted salt. We burned the hair off my moccasins and cooked and eat them. We started on again, traveled over and down the ridge. George Noon was leading and broke through the snow that deep. Took hold of him and pulled him out. The wind was blowing. We didn't know where the agency was. It was snowing hard all the time. You couldn't see any distance. We came to the conclusion to follow the ridge. Followed it one day and we came to the conclusion we was liable to freeze to death and we had better find a shelter. We did find shelter and camped on this side of the main ridge.

"I don't know how many days we were on the ridge. Swan by this time had give out and had hard work to keep from freezing to death. We had been praying, shouting, crying, everything. Bell never spoke, hadn't said a word for two or three days, looked wild. Swan prayed, I tried to pray. Miller and Noon prayed. Humphrey prayed. We all prayed—prayed and cried for salt.

"When we came down the hill into the place where these men were found, we had been eating everything we get our hands on in the shape of food. We chewed pine gum, but it would make us weak. Keeping our mouths open, the air would get in and we would swallow it. After coming down on the side of the hill, we camped at a big pine root. That night we had our prayer meeting. Everything we could think of, we would wish for. But the whole wish was for salt.

"The next day, we came up to what you call a lake. We camped there. We found some buds. Miller gave them the name Eder buds but we couldn't eat them. The next morning, Miller was on the lead, breaking the trail where we left this lake. We got on the ice. We seen water and thought we might find some fish. The water was only that deep, the rest was slime and mud. George Noon was the lighter man, so he ventured out. We tried to but couldn't find anything.

"We traveled how far below this lake I don't know. The snow was deep. We camped at a good place where the timber was thick. It was a good shelter for us to camp. We found some willow buds and some cottonwood buds. Right there we give up to die. Swan was gone in entirely. Swan was an old man, entirely gone. Said he couldn't go any further. Bell didn't speak a word. When we camped there that night, we gave up. I don't say I was a strong man. We all give up, were crying, praying. Old Man Swan was the poorest man in the outfit—was clean gone, said he couldn't go any further. That settled it—we couldn't go any further. We couldn't leave him there.

"I told him that I would go up the hill, maybe I could see where the agency was. When I volunteered to go, Old Man Swan begged me to go. The boys prayed for me to go, said they would have a good fire and see if they could find some rosebuds.

"As I went up the mountain from there, I found a patch of rosebuds—about a pint of rosebuds on the bushes. If I hadn't found these rosebuds, I would have froze to death because I was cold and hungry and very weak. I took a light gun as a walking stick and expected to see some game to kill—always on our guard for game. When I found these rosebuds, they braced me up. Way up there was timber and snow, nothing but timber and snow. Couldn't see down the stream. Came back on the same trail. It commenced to snow going down the hill. When I came back into camp, it was pretty near night.

"Bell was kneeling near the fire. It was dark, very dark, the bushes were very thick in the shelter from the storm. As I came in on the trail, I got as far to the fire as from here to that bench. Bell grabbed his hatchet and made for me. I asked what was the matter. I was standing on the trail. I fell down on the snow. Bell had his hatchet up this way. He didn't say anything. I never thought, I took aim. No, I didn't take aim but I shot him. As he came forward, I struck him with the edge of the hatchet. It struck him right that way and cut through. I hollered to the party. Nobody answered me so I stood looking at Bell for a little while. I went to the fire and let the hatchet lay here. It was storming then—snowing hard. I saw the fix the rest of the men were in."

At this point in his testimony, Packer—like Preston Nutter before him—was given a half dozen law books and asked to indicate the relative position of the bodies.

"This is Swan, that was our camp fire," said Packer, laying the volumes, one at a time, on the floorboards. "Here was Noon's and Miller's, just them two. I calculate this was Miller's. He was hit on the back of the head three times, I believe, with a hatchet. Bell owned this hatchet, only when we would use it for cutting wood. That was the only weapon Bell had, besides the gun. Swan—I think it was Swan, one of these men—had two licks. One man had a cut on his breast bone. That same night, I took blankets and covered every man up, and I sat by the fire. Kindling up the fire. I sat there all night long. The pieces of meat Bell laid there was laying there yet."

Packer paused for an instant. When he spoke again, his voice was solemn. "Gentlemen, right there is my last feeling. The next morning, I eat this piece of meat. That is what hurt me, eating this meat, and it had hurt me for nine years. I was not responsible for what I eat, I couldn't help it. Right there I had no feeling. I had no fear of freezing. I just was happy. Right there I cut that piece of meat—boiled it in a tin cup and eat a little."

Packer offered virtually no details about the grim period that followed, when he camped beside the corpses of his slaughtered companions and subsisted on their flesh. His entire account of that period consisted of a few vague, disjointed sentences, as though he had lived the experience in a dream. Whether he was being deliberately evasive or accurately conveying his mental state at the time is impossible to say.

Packer continued, "I laid down and slept. I took sick and sat up against a tree. I put a pole across, set up pieces of bark and two pieces of pine. Right there I lived in that stupid position. I don't know how long I was in that fix. I felt perfectly happy and contented. I didn't think of freezing, didn't think of the agency, never thought of nothing only sleep. The meat was a little salty. I had always been praying for salt. In the course of time, I don't know how long, fear came back again. I wanted to leave there. When I waked up, I wanted to leave. I thought of the men, thought of everything. I wanted to go. I did go. I started. I wanted to go out. I came back. I went down the stream. Didn't take any provisions. I took a coffee pot with fire. I came back both times and exactly how long I stayed there living this way—I told you that it begun to thaw sometime in March, because I came out the last of March. It began to thaw crossing on the snow. I tried again. Before I tried to go, I came back and cut some flesh off these dead bodies and cooked it. I had a stick to cook it on. I have nothing but the butcher's skinning knife to cut it with."

Without saying that he had rummaged through the dead men's clothing, he confessed to taking their money and professed remorse: "I seen Bell's pocket book. I opened it and found a fifty-dollar greenback. I took it. That was wrong, I admit that. Had got twenty dollars more off the others. I put that in my pocket. If there was any more, I left it on the ground."

Next came his trip to the agency, an arduous journey through snow so deep he sometimes sank in up to his neck. Packer recalled, "It was almost too deep to get out. I took the dead limbs of trees and tied them together with strings made with my blanket to make snow shoes for my feet, but I couldn't make it, so I had to take them off. I didn't travel very far in a day. I had brought this coffee pot with coals and some meat in a cartridge sack. Whenever there was any rosebuds, I would eat them with my meat. Every patch of rosebuds I came to I would eat. I don't know how many days of traveling before I had lost everything, but at the last camp, I know I eat rosebuds and three pieces of meat. That was three quarters of a mile from the agency, though I didn't know it at the time."

Packer had little to say about his arrival at the agency, though he mentioned twice that he had sold his gun to Major Downer for ten dollars, which "made [him] a hundred dollars in greenbacks." His account of his time in Saguache was an increasingly embittered attack on Larry Dolan: "Larry Dolan kept this saloon. He knowed how I suffered. I didn't tell him nothing and this man Larry Dolan bought oysters and all kinds of canned fruit. We batched there and I slept with Dolan. When I wanted a drink, I went to the bar and got it whether I paid for it or not. Larry used to go out and leave me tending his bar. I boarded at the other house and eat some of my meals there. Eat there when Larry didn't fetch in canned oysters.

"I was there six days with Larry Dolan when the General drove up, he drove up on the seventh day. Now that evening, the seventh, I was in Larry Dolan's saloon and Larry wanted some money changed. The silver wasn't in the country. It was all greenbacks. He gave me a greenback of a ten-dollar bill and asked me to take it to Otto Mears and get some change. It was a very light color. General Adams was standing at the counter. Mears said, 'That bill has been in this house before and it is a counterfeit.' General Adams said it was a good imitation of a counterfeit. I think the bill was faded. I took the bill back and he gave me another—I took that back and got it changed. Larry Dolan, he commenced to talk about counterfeit money. I told Larry Dolan there was one time when Colorado was flooded with counterfeit money. The Denver papers and other papers said it was money made in Chicago. Larry Dolan said he would get this counterfeit money, as he had a good chance to pass it. Pretty soon I went to bed. Nobody in the house. The next morning I started for the agency. I left Larry Dolan there. Larry swore right here in this court that I had a fifty dollar gold note, and further he swore that he didn't know what a gold note was. Yesterday, after swearing I had the fifty dollar gold note, he swore I had a pocketbook. I had a memorandum book with a pocket in this side. That is what I came over and showed in there. I bought that in Utah. That was my pocketbook that Larry Dolan swore to.

"He swore I lost $37 at Freeze-out in his house. Larry Dolan swore I was a soft snap and he was taking me in. He swore that I offered to loan him from three to four hundred dollars. Dolan was a stranger to me, and you bet Packer was too smart to lend money to a stranger. I say Packer never played a game of Freeze-out poker in Larry Dolan's house. I never played a game of Freeze-out and lost $37, which Larry Dolan swore to. I am going to prove to you by my deputy sheriff what Larry Dolan said, what passed between him and me at the jail. I was going to call on him for a witness until he swore here and I had no use for him. Larry Dolan knows what I stated. My pocketbook was never—Larry Dolan spent more money with me than I did with him. I took a drink of my free will. I tended bar for him when he was out. I had no occasion for spending $37 at Freeze-out for whiskey. I hope I am not that big a fool."

By this point, Packer was so worked up he was almost spluttering. Attempting to get him back on narrative track, attorney Mills asked him to "resume your journey to Saguache." Packer, however—oblivious to the impression he was making on his listeners—stubbornly refused to be swayed. "I have listened to twenty-one witnesses and I have listened patiently," he declared, "and you can cross-examine me after I have got through." He then plowed ahead with his increasingly disjointed tale.

"Well, we went to the agency. I followed General Adams' wagon. Everybody wanted me to tell about it, what I had been through and where the other boys was. They got me confused, and really I didn't know what I did tell. I told anything that came into my mind. I made the first statement. I told a lie, I acknowledge. But I did tell the truth when I told them I had killed Bell.

"They come to the conclusion that I must take them back. Nutter was one and Lauter was another. We packed up the horses and started right up this gulch across that way from the agency. I showed Nutter my coffee pot, showed him where I had some live coals in it, and showed him my camp. They didn't find nothing when they searched around. The snow was only in spots, I could show him right where I got the rosebuds. We had no snow. How many days I don't know. We stopped so many days at these rosebud places and so many camps. The last camp was this Quaken Asp grove. I told them they would have to climb that hill. The next morning we started up this mountain. We had a horse, a packhorse and had trouble getting him up and down. He was a big, clumsy horse. We started to follow the ridge. In a short distance I would have shown them my other campfire. The next they went—that horse— there was snow. They would go to the right. Of course I knowed they were going just right out of the way, which they wouldn't do if they had followed my trail. I didn't say anything more. We went till we came to the creek. On the banks of the creek, we tied the horse. They asked me if I didn't recognize it. How could I recognize it when I hadn't been there before? I said it must be a higher stream. No growling on the way. They asked me if I could recognize the mountain. I couldn't because I hadn't been there before. I told them that was my trail. They thought Packer was lying. They got mad but didn't say anything to me. The next morning, they started back to the agency."

In recounting the return to the agency, Packer scoffed at Herman Lauter's testimony, mocking the very notion that such a pitiful being could have overpowered him in a physical confrontation.

"On the way back—don't you remember that constable swearing right here on the witness stand that I drew a knife on him and he grabbed my arm and took it away from me? He said I was going to murder him. Do you think that man or any other man could take a knife away from me? Is there any two men here in this room that could do it? No, I would cut both his hands off before he could take that knife. To think that one little Dutchman could take a knife away from me! No, sir."

His account of his escape from the Saguache jail was jumbled to the point of incoherence.

"After we got to Saguache, it was the duty of the sheriff to tell the next sheriff that I was a desperate man. They put a boy over me for a guard. I guess I could have tossed that boy like a ball. He slept that night in the back end of Mears' house. Next morning, Mears said, 'You are a fool, you ought to skip if there is a chance you get.' My guard was on the outside, and that is what Mears said to me, and he said I had a draft. I don't know whether I told Mears that I was going to skip or not. Mr. Mears didn't advise no more, but they thought I was going to skip and they put a pair of shackles on my legs.

"These men who talked of my being a desperate character left me there with Amos Wall. We did something, though we hadn't much to do. We built a pole fence. There was the tools, axes, planes, and other tools. I could have knocked Amos Wall in the head. There was butcher knives and a pistol of Wall's. We would catch black birds, cut pieces of newspaper, put over their heads and let them fly away. During this time, Amos Wall had a colt that was sick. It was about two years old and expected to die.

"Men kept coming to me and saying, 'Why don't you bust your shackles all to hell and skip, get them off and go?' At last a man came to me, fetching me some whiskey and this horse for $20 after they put me in irons. This bottle of whiskey was a pint of whiskey in a flat flask. I don't know if I told him, Amos Wall. I tried the key. I have no doubt that I tried to get him away so I could try and cut my shackles. This man said to me that Amos Wall was going to be gone, and right there I would find a sack of grub. I don't know whether Amos Wall was indicated—implicated— in that or not, but it looked rather suspicious.

"I went to sleep and slept I don't know how long. I waked up and dressed myself. It was pretty near morning. I came near sleeping too late, and right there sat my sack of grub, boiled ham and beef. As I went to the stream, I pulled off my shoes and went into a hole up to my breast. It was breaking day and I came out. I had a notion to go back to jail and put my irons on again. There were some high Chico brush, some call it greasewood. I laid down, stayed there that day and slept. Just after dark, I went right across the country. I went right in and didn't see anybody and went over the Arkansas and travelled the next day eating my lunch."

After leveling a few more words at the perfidy of his supposed friend Larry Dolan, Packer finally reached the end of his seemingly interminable speech. "Now gentlemen," he said, "that is the whole story of it. Now I am going to quit. It isn't interesting what I have done from that on."[3]

26.

GRILLED

After a few perfunctory questions from his defense attorney, Packer was subjected to a relentless cross-examination by District Attorney Bell, who hammered away at every detail of the confession that had been entered into evidence.

He began by asking about the supplies Packer's party had taken with them when they left Ouray's camp. "You say you had but seven days' provision for one man?"

"About that," said Packer. "We understood that the agency was but a little ways."

"How many men did you have in that party?" asked Bell.

"Six," said Packer.

"Then you were out of grub on the second day?" asked Bell.

"No sir," Packer said. "We limited ourselves. Some days we made half the flour do us."

"How did it come that you started out with so little grub?"

"Some men had no grub," Packer replied. "I and Swan and Miller had some grub."

"Can you give the number of days that you were out from Ouray when you first discovered that the provisions were short?"

"We were out three days, four days probably. Then we commenced to limit ourselves of grub."

Bell considered this reply for a moment before saying, "Then you had more than grub enough to last one man seven days."

"We might have had more than that," Packer grudgingly conceded.

Having shaken Packer's story, Bell immediately pressed his advantage. "You say again there were six men in that party, that you were out four days before you discovered the grub was limited. You had provisions for six men for four days. Would not that be equal to one man for twenty-four days?"

"I told you I did not know," Packer snapped. "When we started, I did not know some men didn't have no grub. We was out four days when the grub got short."

Bell would not let the matter go. "You persist in saying that you had provisions for one man for seven days only?"

"I don't know just how much," said Packer. I told you, about seven days' provision for one man."

"And yet six men had sufficiency for four days?" Bell said with a note of wonder.

"I did not say we had a sufficiency," Packer answered. "I said on the fourth day, the grub was give out."

"But you say you had enough for six men for four days before you discovered that the grub was out?"

"I did not say we had plenty of grub," Packer angrily replied. Then, with heavy sarcasm, he added, "What amount of grub would *you* eat in three or four days?"

Eager to keep his client from being provoked into insolence, Aaron Heims interjected, "Just answer the questions, Mr. Packer."

Bell instantly resumed his line of questioning. "Give us the exact date when you discovered the shortness in your provisions."

"That date I told you I could not give you," said Packer.

"Well, give us the number of days you were out from the Uncompahgre."

Here Heims spoke up again, this time appealing to Judge Gerry. "He has answered this question three or four times, your honor."

"He has not made that as clear as he can," came Gerry's reply.

When Bell posed the question again, Packer answered, "Three or four days."

"You say you only started with provisions for one man for seven days and you discovered the shortness when you were out three days?"

"Yes."

"Then six men ate of those provisions to their satisfaction for three days?"

"Yes, I suppose."

"For three days they had a sufficiency?"

"Yes, they had enough to eat," said Packer, who had assumed an air of nonchalance.

"Then you had at least provisions for one man for eighteen days?"

Packer shrugged. "I don't know about that one man for eighteen days. I know all grub was gone in three or four days."

By this point, it seemed clear that the district attorney was attempting to do more than puncture holes in Packer's confession. He was trying to prove that the six men had more to subsist on than Packer claimed. Packer's defense, after all, was that Shannon Bell, driven mad by hunger, had slaughtered the others for food. If the prosecutor could show that Bell hadn't been in the throes of starvation, however, then Packer's story fell apart.

Pressing ahead with his interrogation, the district attorney asked, "How many provisions did you have on the third day when you discovered the deficiency?"

"At the end of the third day," said Packer, "we had a little dab of flour altogether. Swan had flour and Miller had flour."

"How much?"

"I don't know," Packer said. "Some men had no meat, some had no flour."

"How long did you expect to be on this journey to the agency?"

"I calculated to make the trip, as near as I can remember, in five or six days."

"You say some had meat and some had flour," said Bell. "What day after your departure was the provisions exhausted?"

"In the first place, as I stated before, I answered that question," said Packer, his studied composure beginning to crack. "We eat only two meals a day. Breakfast and supper. And when we found our grub was running out, we got down to one meal a day. About the ninth day we was out of flour and everything."

"Which gave out first," asked Bell, "the bread or the meat?"

"Our meat ran out first," said Packer.

"How long first?"

"I don't know how long."

"Give us your best judgment."

"My best judgment wouldn't be worth a cent," Packer retorted.

"Do you think it was three days?" asked Bell.

"Yes, sir," said Packer, "because we lived on flour entirely."

"Do you think it was five days?" asked Bell.

"Yes," said Packer, seemingly unaware that he had been caught in a glaring contradiction. "After that, the meat was gone and we lived on flour."

Bell paused, as though to give the jury a moment to register Packer's conflicting replies. Then—continuing his inquiry into precisely what, when, and how much the men had eaten—he asked, "How long did you go after eating your last flour until you got other provisions, that is, your moccasins?"

"After we had eat our little dab of flour," Packer said, "we travelled three or four days before George Noon gave up his moccasins. He was the first to think of it."

"Did you all partake of the moccasins?"

"Yes. They were high," said Packer. Bending over, he held a finger to one ankle. "They laced up to here. Mine was the longest. Came to there," he said, raising the finger halfway up his calf.

"Did the eating of the moccasins gratify you?"

"It was something near what we relished," said Packer. "Salt."

"After eating the moccasins of Noon, how long before you had the next meal?"

"Bell gave up his moccasins three or four days after," Packer said.

"How long was it between the eating of Bell's moccasins and yours?"

"Between Bell's moccasins and mine must have been five days," said Packer. "But between those we found some rosebuds. That was what put our moccasins so far off."

"Were these the last moccasins in the crowd, these of yours?"

Packer acknowledged they were.

Bell had now come to what he called "the culminating of this affair"—the slaying of the five prospectors and the consumption of their bodies, events that Packer had made only cursory mention of during his own protracted statement. "How long had you been in your camp below the lake," he asked, "before Bell and the balance of the party were killed?"

"We camped there at night," said Packer, "and the next morning the boys give out. Swan give out entirely."

"Do you know how long you stayed there?"

"No," said Packer.

"Have you no judgment?"

"I think I must have stayed there at least—no, I can't say. All I can tell is I laid there some time, you bet I did."

Abruptly Bell asked, "From whose body did you take the meat?"

"The first was Miller's," said Packer. "It was the chunk Bell had cut. He had cut it from the top of the leg."

"Where did you find that meat when you got into camp which Bell had cut from Miller?"

"I found it right at the fire, roasting, and when I went to the fire, Bell had his back to it."

"When," asked the district attorney, "did you first taste of a piece of the meat?"

"There in the pines," Packer said.

Bell rephrased the question: "How long had you been in camp before you eat the meat?"

"That night I killed Bell, I didn't eat any meat."

"Why did you not eat some of this flesh when you first killed Bell?" asked the district attorney.

"The thought of eating my fellow man, that's what was the matter," Packer exclaimed. "Then it seems as though after I did it that everything was happy. I tell you I was beside myself! I thought of nothing."

"You say you saw Bell stooping over the fire when you returned from the ridge?"

"Stooping or kneeling," said Packer. "I couldn't say which."

During his testimony, Packer had provided almost no details about his fatal confrontation with Shannon Bell. Now, the district attorney asked him to "tell us just that occurred, how the killing of Bell took place."

"As I stated, I came in from the ridge," Packer began. He then pointed to Preston Nutter, who was seated about ten feet away from the dock. "I got within about as far as from here to Mr. Nutter, or not as close. It was dark in here, and snowing at the time I come up. Bell came after me with a hatchet." Raising a finger to his forehead, Packer touched a spot above his right eye. "As Bell was coming, I shot him in here."

"After shooting him, what did you do?"

"I struck him with the hatchet."

"What did he do when first shot?"

"He fell forward," said Packer.

"What did he do with the hatchet?"

"It fell forward with him."

"Do you know how to account for that act?" asked Bell.

"My shooting him?"

"Yes, and striking him with the hatchet."

"I can't say why I grabbed the hatchet and hit him. If it was today, I would probably knock him down with the gun. But it was done so quick."

"He was a large man?" asked Bell.

"Yes," said Packer. "Bigger than I am, though not taller."

"He was a clumsy man?" Bell asked.

"I didn't have any occasion to test him," Packer said dryly.[1]

+ + +

It was noon by now, and the court recessed for lunch. When it reconvened at two o'clock, the district attorney returned to the slaying of his namesake.

"You say when shot, Bell fell forward?" he asked.

"Yes, sir."

"How deep was the snow?"

"Probably eighteen inches. It was thicker than under the trees."

"At what place in the head did you strike him?"

Once again, Packer pointed to the spot above his right eye. "In this side of the head on the forehead," said Packer. "More off to the side than the center."

"About how far above the right eye?"

"I didn't measure" was Packer's sardonic reply.

Keeping his own voice even, Bell continued, "How long after he had fallen before you struck him with the ax or hatchet?"

"Only an instant," said Packer. "I just grabbed it in a flash and struck him here in this part of the head."

"When he fell, did he speak?"

"No, sir. I think when the hatchet struck him, he couldn't speak."

"Did he make any effort to get up?"

"Yes, he straightened out."

"Did he rise up?"

"No, he didn't have time to rise up."

"Did he fall on his face?"

"Yes, sir."

"Did he hold his head up?"

Though he was doing himself no favors with the jury—who would take a dim view of his open disdain for the district attorney—Packer couldn't refrain from crude sarcasm. "I didn't ask him," he said.

"How deep did you cut him?"

"I told you, I struck him in the forehead as he fell."

"Before he struck the snow or afterwards?"

"He had fallen on the snow when I grabbed the hatchet and hit him."

"He was wholly defenseless, was he?" Bell asked in a neutral tone.

Packer answered without hesitation. "Yes," he said, with no apparent sense that he was blithely admitting to having brained a "wholly defenseless" man with a hatchet. "I think the shot would have killed him if I hadn't struck him with the hatchet."

Evidently "hoping to confuse the defendant and thereby elicit information not otherwise obtainable," Bell continued to bombard Packer with rapid-fire questions.[2] What had he done with the hatchet? How much money had he taken from Swan's body? From Humphrey's? From Miller's? Were there other effects among the men's clothing? How many days had they all been traveling before they first "struck snow"? Why had Packer told a lie when "first questioned about this affair?"

As he had throughout his testimony, Packer sometimes replied with a flippancy that struck observers as grossly inappropriate to the occasion. At one point, for example, Bell asked if Packer and the others had seen "any signs of game" at all during their journey.

"Nothing but snow," said Packer.

"Not even a chipmunk?" asked Bell.

"It wasn't the time for chipmunks," said Packer. "They would have had a hard time unless they had snow shoes."

Before letting Packer go, Bell brought the subject back to the specifics of the five murders. Asked again about the layout of the bodies, Packer claimed that, before leaving the camp, he had rearranged all five corpses—"swung the boys in together," as he put it—and covered them with blankets. That was the position in which Preston Nutter and the others had found them months later.

"Now, Mr. Packer," asked Bell in conclusion, "how do you account for the death of these parties in the orderly manner with no signs of a struggle about them?"

"I think that Bell raised with that hatchet and struck this man the butcher, who started to run, and he ran after him and knocked him down," said Packer. "It would not take much to kill a man, they were nearly dead anyway, and it wouldn't take much more to kill a man. Some of the wounds were deep. Some of their brains showed."[3]

Packer was then dismissed. From the time he had begun his statement that morning until the moment he left the stand, roughly six hours had passed.

+ + +

Before the defense rested its case, Preston Nutter was recalled to the stand. Once sworn and seated, he was asked if he had examined the bodies when he "found them in August 1874."

"Yes," said Nutter.

"Do you recollect seeing a bone which belonged to any of the bodies?" asked attorney Heims.

"I saw several bones there," answered Nutter. "The bodies at that time were almost skeletons."

Had he seen "a bone separate from the rest of the bodies?" asked Heims.

When Nutter confirmed that he had, Heims asked if "there was evidence of a gunshot wound there."

"There was a bone lying close to one of the bodies then," said Nutter. "At one end it ran down to a sharp point four inches wide, run up at the other end, barely as thick as a man's wrist and about that long and a little hole through it, but the hole was round, though it didn't look like a plain smooth shot."

"Was it more like a gunshot wound than anything else?" asked Heims, clearly trying to corroborate Packer's account of having shot Shannon Bell in self-defense.

"Yes, sir," said Nutter.

The defense had seemingly scored a point. Cross-examination by prosecuting attorney J. Warner Mills, however, swiftly undercut it.

"I will ask you to state to the jury," said Mills, "what portion of that bone this hole was you spoke of."

"About half way between the two ends of the bone," said Nutter.

"You are tolerably well acquainted with the bones of the human body?"

"No, sir, I don't say that I am."

"This was not the back bone?"

"No, certainly not."

"Was it large enough for or larger than the bone of the arm?"

"Maybe large enough for a man's arm," Nutter allowed.

"But if it was the bone of the arm or leg, that wound was at a place where it could not be fatal?" asked Mills.

"Certainly not," said Nutter. "I have hunted considerably, and there is a sharp bone which resembles the sharp part of this bone in animals, but I don't know as I ever saw a bone of that kind from a human."

"Just take the trunk of a human body composed simply of ribs, spinal column—this was none of those bones?" asked Mills.

Nutter was emphatic. "No, sir."

"Would this bone indicate a gunshot wound that had taken effect by virtue of the bullet coming through the belly, as testified by the witness?"

"I should think not," said Nutter.

Under redirect examination, Aaron Heims attempted to undo the damage of this testimony by asking how Nutter could tell from this bone that the bullet hadn't passed through the belly.

"From what I know of a person's body," Nutter replied, "I am satisfied that it didn't."

"You are not an expert?" said Heims.

"No," answered Nutter, "not at all."

"You have no knowledge of the bones of a human body?"

Non sequitur though it was, Nutter's reply could hardly fail to have a chilling effect on his listeners. "I saw more bones there," he said, "than I ever saw in my life belonging to the human race."[4]

With that, the defense rested.

+ + +

Following Judge Gerry's instructions to the jury, District Attorney Bell began his summation, which was interrupted at six o'clock, when court was adjourned until the next morning.

Describing Packer's performance on the stand that day, the *Silver World* assailed the defendant for his "thinly disguised falsehoods and occasional displays of his native fiendish spirit."[5] Packer, however, left the courthouse convinced that he had persuaded the jury of his innocence. So confident was he of an acquittal that, later that evening, in conversation with his jailer, he commented on the "large attendance of ladies" at the trial and remarked that, once set free, "he thought he could easily marry a Lake City woman."[6]

27.

THE SENTENCE

Though a complete transcript of the testimony presented at Alfred Packer's 1883 trial exists, it does not include the closing statements of either the defense or the prosecution. Newspaper accounts of these summations are sketchy. It appears that Aaron Heims stressed the "purely circumstantial" nature of the case and argued "that the circumstances indicative of guilt were equally consistent with those of innocence."[1]

The closing arguments of the prosecution—begun by District Attorney Bell late Wednesday afternoon and completed by his cocounsel, J. Warner Mills, the following day—strove to weave the many "strands of circumstances pointing to guilt into one rope," a rope that would ultimately end up around Packer's neck. Mills in particular would be praised in the local press for his "masterly effort." By the time he brought his remarks to a close on Thursday afternoon, April 12, "the conclusion was irresistible"—in the estimation of the reporter for the *Silver World*—that Packer was guilty of "the fiendish crime of deliberately, and with diabolical premeditation, having piloted his five unsuspecting victims into the defiles of these mountains and, while they slept, murdered them in cold blood for their money."[2]

It was close to seven in the evening when the jurors received the case and were escorted to their hotel for supper. After finishing their meal, the twelve men took their first ballot, which—as the newspapers later reported—"resulted in eleven to one for conviction." The lone holdout finally came around at five minutes past ten. At the opening of court at nine o'clock the next morning, Friday, April 13, they delivered their verdict: "guilty of premeditated murder."[3]

After polling the twelve jurors, Heims requested a recess to prepare various motions. When court reconvened several hours later, he moved for a new trial on a dozen different grounds, arguing, among other points, that "the jury had no power to render such a verdict, that the verdict did not sustain the indictment, that the court had no jurisdiction to hear the case, and that the jury had not been drawn according to law." When his motion was denied, he announced his "intention to appeal the verdict to the Colorado Supreme Court and if necessary to the United States Supreme Court."[4]

It was already late afternoon when the prisoner was finally directed to stand and face Judge Gerry. As Packer got to his feet, the spectators, too, arose from their chairs and noisily pressed toward the front of the courtroom. Gerry banged his gavel and ordered silence. Immediately, wrote one on-scene observer, "quiet reigned. The people were almost motionless, the ladies moved uneasily, all were breathlessly waiting."[5]

His voice charged with emotion, Gerry asked, "Alfred Packer, have you any reason to or cause to show the Court why the sentence of death should not be pronounced upon you?"

Packer's bitter reply rang out in the hushed courtroom: "I don't feel I am guilty of the act I am charged with."

"What is your age?" asked Gerry.

"Thirty-four," lied Packer, who was seven months shy of his fortieth birthday.

"Is your correct name Alfred Packer, or is it assumed?" Gerry asked.

"My correct name is Alfred Packer. I had it tattooed on my arm when I was thirteen," Packer replied—another flagrant falsehood, since Packer's tattoo bore the name and number of the infantry he had joined at nineteen.

"Have you any family, wife or children?"

"I have not."[6]

Judge Gerry took a moment to consult the sheaf of papers in his hands. Then, in his sonorous, southern-accented voice, he commenced to read.

+ + +

Of the various legends connected to the Packer case, the most enduring concerns Judge Gerry's sentence. According to the apocryphal version, Gerry—worked into a state of such acute indignation that steam was virtually spewing from his ears—pointed a trembling, accusatory finger at the prisoner and, speaking in the twangy frontier dialect of a Mark Twain character, thundered, "Stand up, ye voracious man-eatin' son-of-a-bitch, stand up! There was seven Dimmycrats in Hinsdale County, and ye ate five of them, goddamn ye! I sentence ye t'be hanged by the neck until ye're dead, dead, DEAD, as a warnin' ag'in reducin' the Dimmycratic population of th' state! I'd sentence ye to hell but the statutes forbid it!"[7]

In truth, Gerry's sentence was the diametrical opposite of this cartoonish condemnation, a high-flown oration that struck many observers as a supremely affecting display of judicial eloquence: "one of the finest written documents of this character ever heard" in a courtroom, as the *Silver World* gushed.[8]

"It becomes my duty, as the judge of this court, to enforce the verdict of the jury, rendered in your case, and impose upon you the judgment which the law fixes as the punishment of the crime you have committed," Gerry began. "It is a solemn, painful duty to perform. I would to God the cup might pass from me. You have had a fair and impartial trial. You have been faithfully and earnestly defended by able counsel. The presiding judge of this court, upon his oath and conscience, has labored to be honest and impartial in the trial of your case, and in all doubtful questions you have had the benefit of the doubt.

"A jury of twelve honest citizens of the county have sat in judgment on your case and upon their oaths they find you guilty of willful and premeditated murder—a murder revolting in all its details.

"In 1874, you, in company of five companions, passed through this beautiful mountain valley where stands the town of Lake City. At that time the hand of man had not marred the beauties of nature. The picture was fresh from the hands of the Great Artist who created it. You and your companions camped at the base of a grand old mountain, in sight of the place you now stand, on the banks of a stream as pure and beautiful as was ever traced by the finger of God upon the bosom of the earth. Your every surrounding was calculated to impress upon your heart and nature the omnipotence of the Deity and the helplessness of your own feeble life. In this goodly favored spot you conceived your murderous designs.

"You and your victims had a weary march, and when the shadows of the mountain fell upon your little party and night drew her sable curtain around you, your unsuspecting victims lay down on the ground and were soon lost in the sleep of the weary; and when thus sweetly unconscious of danger from any quarter, and particularly from you, their trusted companion, you cruelly and brutally slew them all. Whether your murderous hand was guided by the misty light of the moon or the flickering blaze of the campfire, you only can tell. No eye saw the bloody deed performed; no ear save your own caught the groans of your dying victims. You then and there robbed the living of life and then robbed the dead of the reward of honest toil which they had accumulated: at least, so say the jury.

"To other sickening details of your crime I will not refer. Silence is kindness. I do not say things to harrow your soul, for I know you have drunk the cup of bitterness to its very dregs, and wherever you have gone the sting of your conscience and the goadings of remorse have been an avenging Nemesis which have followed your every turn in life and painted afresh for your contemplation the picture of the past.

"I say these things to impress upon your mind the awful solemnity of your situation and the impending doom which you cannot avert. *'Be not deceived. God is not mocked, for whatsoever a man soweth, that shall he also reap.'* You, Alfred Packer, sowed the wind; you must now reap the whirlwind.

"Society cannot forgive you for the crime you have committed. It enforces the old Mosaic law of a life for a life, and your life must be taken as the penalty of your crime. I am but the instrument of society to impose the punishment which the law provides. While society cannot forgive, it will forget. As the days come and go and the years of our pilgrimage roll by, the memory of you and your crime will fade from the minds of men.

"With God it is different. He will not forget, but will forgive. He pardoned the dying thief on the cross. He is the same God today as then—a God of love and mercy, of long suffering and kind forbearance: a God who tempers the wind to the shorn lamb and promises rest to all the weary and heartbroken children of men; and it is to this God I commend you.

"Close your ears to the blandishments of hope. Listen not to the flattering promises of life, but prepare for the dread certainty of death. Prepare to meet thy God; prepare to meet the spirits of thy murdered victims; prepare to meet thy aged father and mother, of whom you have spoken, and who still love you as their dear boy.

"For nine long years you have been a wanderer on the face of the earth, bowed and broken in spirit: no home, no loves, no ties to bind you to the earth. You have been, indeed, a poor, pitiable waif of human-ity. I hope and pray that in the spirit land to which you are so fast and surely drifting, you will find that peace and rest for your weary spirit which this world cannot give."

According to the reporter for the *Rocky Mountain News*, Gerry delivered this peroration "with a feeling of tenderness unmistakable in its tone, every word falling on the ear like the tolling of a bell. Several times the judge almost gave way to his feelings." Now, "before delivering the final fatal words," his emotions almost overcame him and "his utter-ance failed for a painful period."[9]

"Alfred Packer," he declared after regaining his composure, "the judgment of this court is that you be removed from hence to the jail of Hinsdale County and there confined until the 19th day of May, A.D. 1883, and that on said 19th day of May, 1883, you be taken from thence by the sheriff of Hinsdale County to a place of execution prepared for this purpose, at some point within the corporate limits of the town of Lake City, in the said county of Hinsdale, and between the hours of 10 A.M. and 3 P.M. of said day, you, then and there, by said sheriff, be hung by the neck until you are dead, dead, dead, and may God have mercy upon your soul."[10]

+ + +

Throughout most of this "impressive delivery," Packer maintained a stoic demeanor, keeping his feelings in check even at Gerry's overwrought and cloying description of the circumstances of the crime, which made it sound as if Packer and his companions were hikers out on a delightful camping trip in a "beautiful mountain valley" instead of a group of desperately debilitated men driven half-mad by starvation in a savage wintry wasteland. Only twice did Packer display any emotion. He "broke down and sobbed like a child" when Gerry made reference to Packer's "aged father and mother." And when the death sentence was finally pronounced, Packer's face grew dark with fury. Denouncing Otto Mears and Larry Dolan as liars, he loudly "threatened them with bodily harm if he ever got the chance."

Aaron Heims quickly leaned toward his client and ordered him to hush. Then the condemned man was hustled away to the Lake City jail.[11]

28.

REACTIONS

On Saturday, April 14, less than twenty-four hours after Packer was con-demned, the *Lake City Silver World* ran an editorial by publisher Henry C. Olney that was remarkable for its tone of smug self-congratulation. "It was one of the fairest criminal trials on record," Olney boasted. "The prisoner was given every opportunity to prove his innocence and the benefit of every doubt which could possibly be made to favor him."

Evidently it did not occur to Olney that, under the American system of jurisprudence, the defendant is not required to prove his innocence; he is presumed to be innocent. It is the job of the prosecution to establish beyond a reasonable doubt the defendant's guilt. While acknowledging that "the evidence [against Packer] was almost entirely circumstantial," Olney insisted that those circumstances "pointed directly, conclusively, and unquestionably to the certain guilt of the accused." The "verdict of the jury and the sentence of the judge were just," insisted Olney, "and must be approved by everyone who heard or may read the evidence. No other verdict was possible."[1]

In point of fact, a number of Olney's peers in the Colorado press believed otherwise. Of the dissenting voices, perhaps the most caustic was that of J. C. Fincher, publisher of the *Breckenridge Daily Journal*. In Fincher's view, Packer's trial, far from being among "the fairest . . . on record," was a travesty. The prosecution's theory—that a man "should willingly go into the jaws of death, risk starvation, death by frost and save himself only by the most revolting of food" in order "to commit a wholesale murder for a few dollars"—was "too absurd to receive the universal sanction given it." By contrast, Packer's "own story was consistent and natural. . . . Any one who will read Packer's testimony and try to imagine himself in his place will realize that the story bears the evidence of truth."

To be sure, Fincher opined, Packer erred "in not making a clean breast of the whole transaction when he first came to the agency." But "with frozen feet, a famished body, and an almost dethroned reason, his physical and mental demoralization at that time was well calculated to unman him." His "sufferings were well calculated to weaken him mentally and physically, so that he would fear to tell the whole story of his sufferings"—a fact that "ought to have been considered favorably by the jury." And while it was true that he "did wrong in rifling bodies and appropriating the spoils of his dead companions," that transgression was "not a capital crime." While there was "much about the man that is uncanny and revolting," wrote Fincher, "men are not hanged for such matters by law."

His harshest words were reserved for Judge Gerry, assailing his presentencing speech as a "tirade of abuse against the prisoner." Gerry's "assertion that [Packer] had had a fair trial" was little more than "a gratuitous insult." Indeed, Packer should never have been tried in Lake City at all, since a "jury selected from a community which had almost openly declared its disposition to lynch him could not give a prisoner an impartial trial such as law contemplates.

"For the sake of Colorado's fair fame," Fincher concluded, "we hope this verdict will be reversed."[2]

Other newspapers echoed Fincher's sentiments. In the *Grand Junction News*, editor Edwin Price challenged Olney's assertion that "no other verdict was possible." With more competent representation—so Price believed—Packer would never have been convicted. "A first-class criminal lawyer would have cleared him," he opined. The Lake City jurors, predisposed against Packer, may have been persuaded by the prosecution's case. But in the minds of other, less biased citizens of the state, Price stated, "there will always be a doubt." Price also minced no words in his denunciation of Judge Gerry, whose "senseless declamation" exhibited "utter disregard of Packer's rights as a human being." By needlessly tortur[ing] the poor wretch whom he had in his grasp," Price fumed, "Gerry made an ass of himself, and took the most objectionable means to do it."[3]

Even more critical of the trial's outcome was the *Pueblo Chieftain*. Like Price, its editors believed that, had Packer "been tried anywhere else except Lake City," the "chances are five to one that . . . he would have been acquitted." While acknowledging that "Packer was no doubt a murderer," the *Chieftain* argued that his crimes were committed under "mitigating circumstances." Packer "was insane when the murder was committed," the paper declared. "Few men are in their right minds after starving four or five days or longer, and when hunger attacks a man he will generally eat anything he can procure. Thirst will drive a man insane, why not hunger?"

Like J. C. Fincher and Edwin Price, the editors of the *Pueblo Chieftain* were particularly scathing about "the manner in which Judge Gerry saw fit to sentence" Packer:

> It is certainly not the duty of a judge on the bench to make a spread-eagle Fourth of July oration in sentencing a man for murder, no matter whether that man be a cold-blooded mur- derer, a lunatic, or a ghoul. It is not pleasant for a man to be sentenced to be hanged, and while it may and undoubtedly is the prerogative of the judge to lengthen or shorten his speech of sentence, we do not consider it necessary or genteel or human to make that speech any longer than is necessary to state the law and declare the sentence. When a judge on the bench departs from this simple rule, he certainly assumes more than the law asks and belittles himself in the minds of an unprejudiced people.[4]

Finding his hometown under assault from these quarters, Olney leapt to its defense, firing back in an editorial headlined "Far Fetched Sympathy." The "frigid fact" of the matter, he insisted, was that Packer had "received as impartial a trial in Lake City as could have been granted in any court in Christendom. . . . The insinuation that this community demanded the blood of Alfred Packer, guilty or innocent" was a gross insult, prompted by pure "venom." Brushing off the *Chieftain's* main criticism, Olney proclaimed that "the mitigating circumstance of hunger was clearly shown to have been a fabrication, false and fallacious as it was unreasonable"—a remarkable statement in light of both Packer's consistent and convincing testimony and the undisputed fact that O. D. Loutsenhizer's party had come close to perishing of starvation while making the same journey. For Olney, Packer's "known criminal career since [his escape from jail] confirm[ed] the wisdom and justice of the verdict"—another jaw-dropping assertion, since the manifold murders attributed to Packer were nothing more than sheer rumor and, in any case, he was not on trial for any alleged crimes committed in the nine years between his jailbreak and capture.

As for the criticisms of Judge Gerry's sentence, they were "unworthy the dignity of a passing reply," Olney sniffed.

The increasingly embattled Olney found himself even more fiercely on the defensive when the *Denver Republican* published an interview with Louis H. Eddy, the court stenographer who had been brought from Denver to transcribe the trial testimony. Asked if "the excitement was very great at that time" among the Lake City populace, Eddy affirmed that, when Packer was first transferred from Gunnison to Lake City for the start of his trial, "the street through which the stage enters the little city" was crammed with a "wild crowd," evidently bent on a lynching. "It is quite likely," said Eddy, "that Packer would not have been in court to receive a sentence of death had not this crowd been disappointed."

Decrying this statement as a "gross, outrageous falsehood and slander," Olney countered, "Not a solitary citizen gathered at the end of the street to . . . molest the prisoner. As law-abiding citizens, there was here a united sentiment demanding a fair hearing and an impartial trial. . . . There was no excitement farther than a natural curiosity to see the prisoner." As for Eddy, his "insinuation that [Packer] would have been lynched without a trial" was—in Olney's ridiculing words—"a gratuitous evolution of a nervous sterile brain and a vivid imagination unaccustomed to mountain scenery."

As confirmation that Eddy's charge was an infamous lie—"baselessly unjust, reckless and unreliable"—Olney reported that, when shown a copy of the *Republican* and "the statements regarding his alleged danger from a mob," Packer himself reacted with outrage: "He became much excited and very indignant, and characterized the statement in severest terms."[5]

Packer may have agreed with Olney on this score, but—immured in the Lake City jail with his execution looming—he remained deeply embittered about the outcome of the trial. "If it was for the killing of Bell that he was convicted and to be hung, he would not complain," an article reported. "But still adhering to the story of his innocence of the crime for which he was tried, he says it is a terrible injustice to suffer for what he is not guilty of."[6]

29.

UNHUNG

When the good citizens of Lake City avenged the murder of Sheriff E. N. Campbell in April 1882, they lynched the two perpetrators, George Betts and James Browning, from the Ocean Wave Bridge, just north of town. For the scheduled execution of Alfred Packer—the first legal hanging in the nine-year history of Hinsdale County—an actual gallows would be required. Joseph S. Roatcap, owner of a local sawmill, supplied the raw material for the scaffold—over two thousand feet of lumber at a cost of thirty-five dollars per thousand feet. A professional noose, fashioned with a double loop, was special-ordered from Denver. Formal invitations were distributed to the lucky few, requesting their presence at the hanging of the celebrity prisoner, whose name—in accordance with his preferred pronunciation and misspelled arm tattoo—was printed as "Alferd Packer."[1]

As the designated day approached, the *Lake City Silver World* kept its readers abreast of developments. On the last day of April, so the paper reported, a drunken miner, arrested for disorderly conduct and hauled off to the jailhouse in the middle of the night, began shouting, "I ain't going to sleep in no jail with a man-eater! Packer the man-eater is in that cell, and I'm damned if I'm going to stay here!" Awakened from his slumbers, Packer purportedly yelled back, "Dry up there, goddamn you, or I'll chew you up!"[2]

A few days later, on Thursday, May 3, Packer was visited by the Reverend Father Quinn, who found the prisoner "sociable but not penitent. He says he is ready for his fate," Quinn told editor Henry C. Olney. "He doesn't care." That same week, Olney himself came by the jail and confirmed that Packer "seemed in good spirits. Said his appetite was good; that he ate all the food given him; slept well and was comfortable. Said he would rather hang than go to Cañon" (i.e., the state penitentiary at Cañon City).

With the scheduled hanging just two weeks away, Sheriff Clair Smith announced that it would be held "in the secluded gulch or cañon just east of town." An enormous crowd from "all over the San Juan" was expected to attend. "Packer will cross the range next Saturday about midday," Olney informed his readers in the newspaper's May 12 edition. "Sheriff Smith will commence constructing the scaffold the day after tomorrow."[3]

By the time this story was published, however, Packer's lawyer, Aaron Heims, had already taken steps to keep his client from the gallows. Armed with a typed transcript of the trial, he had traveled to Denver by stagecoach and train, arriving on the very morning—Friday, May 11, 1883—that Chief Justice W. E. Beck of the state supreme court handed down a decision with immediate repercussions for Packer's case.

On May 23, 1880, during a cattle roundup in Weld County, Colorado, a cowboy named Albert Garvey shot and killed his trail boss, George Wolf. He quickly found himself in the hands of vigilantes, who—after preparing to string him up from the nearest tree—were persuaded to turn him over to the authorities. Tried in November 1881, he was found guilty of murder and sentenced to life in the state penitentiary.[4]

In appealing the verdict, Garvey's lawyers made the same argument to the Colorado Supreme Court that Heims made to Judge Gerry at the start of Packer's trial: namely, that in May 1881—when state legislators repealed the murder law of 1870 and enacted a new one—they had failed to include a "savings clause." As a result—so Garvey's counsel maintained—there was no operative statute under which their client (or anyone else) could be tried for a murder committed between 1870 and 1881.

On Friday, May 11, 1883, Chief Justice Beck, agreeing with Garvey's lawyers, reversed the conviction and granted the defendant a new trial. After quickly reviewing Beck's opinion, Heims immediately applied for and was granted a stay of execution for his own client. Packer's formal appeal, so the chief justice ruled, would be taken up at a future term of the supreme court.[5]

The judge's decision in hand, Heims hurried to the telegraph office and dispatched a message to Sheriff Smith, informing him of the stay. Fearing that the people of Lake City, thwarted in their vengeance, might take the law into their own hands, Heims directed Smith to put an extra guard on the jail. "If Packer is lynched," Heims warned, "I will spend ten years of my life and all the money I can get to ferret out and punish the perpetrators."[6]

Heims had reason to worry. According to the *Gunnison Review*, "an organized plan was afoot to remove [Packer] from the jail and lynch him." Michael J. Gavsick, editor of the *Leadville Herald Democrat*, went so far as to urge the residents of Lake City to rectify the "egregious blundering of Colorado's legislative lawmakers":

> It cost Hinsdale county $4,343.77 to convict Al Packer, and now the Supreme Court says he cannot be punished because the thick-headed legislature of 1881 repealed the old murder law. If the Hinsdale county people don't hang the cannibal and two or three members of that Legislature, they're no good.

In the *Silver World*, Henry Olney insisted that the "peaceful law-abiding citizens" of Lake City had no intention of resorting to lynch law. Even as he made this claim, however, he acknowledged that Sheriff Smith himself would not be averse to seeing Packer "swing from the scaffold or even the [Ocean Wave] bridge."[7]

Much as Smith might have wished to see Packer meet the same fate as Betts and Browning, he was duty bound to protect his charge from vigilante violence. On Wednesday, May 16—in accordance with an order from the probate court of Hinsdale County—Smith, under cover of the night, removed the manacled prisoner from the Lake City jail. "As if to illustrate the irony of cheated justice," the *Silver World* reported, "Packer was led across the Ocean Wave bridge, where a team and buggy awaited." The "unhung fiend" (as the paper now called him) was then driven back to Gunnison, fifty-five miles away, and immured in its imposing brick jailhouse to await his appeal.[8]

30.

THE GREAT AMERICAN ANTHROPOPHAGINIAN

In 1845, an enterprising American journalist named George Wilkes came up with an ingenious idea for cashing in on his countrymen's insatiable appetite for violent diversion. He would publish a newspaper that eliminated all extraneous subjects—like world affairs and national politics—and concentrated mainly on sensational crime. The result was the *National Police Gazette*, a forerunner of the unabashedly lurid tabloids that would proliferate in the twentieth century.

Though the *National Police Gazette* eventually evolved into a "sporting paper" with a heavy emphasis on gossip, celebrity scandal, and athletics (especially boxing), it never stopped dishing up horror and gore. "Shot Her through the Head," "Assaulted Him with a Razor," "Killed by Her Lover," and "The Murder of Mary Wertheimer's Baby" were the headlines of a single typical issue. Additional titillation was provided by the many beautifully rendered woodcut illustrations, whose "technical detail in the period before the photograph came in," writes one scholar, "was a wonder of journalism."[1]

On March 31, 1883, shortly before the start of Packer's trial, the *National Police Gazette* published a prominent story on the case. "A Man Eater," ran the headline, "Lurid Romance of the Wilderness and Its Ghastly Sequel—a Party of Gold Seekers Assassinated and Eaten by Their Guide, Who Confesses the Crime." Based on a dispatch from Denver, the article reported that, after nine years, "one of the greatest murder mysteries of the frontier was cleared up with the capture of the murderer at Fort Fetterman, Wyoming Territory." The article went on to recount how "Packha" (as Packer's name was misspelled) slew his companions "to obtain their money and, running out of food, ate their flesh. After having committed the deed, he constructed a brush house and apparently resided there. Between it and the bodies there was a trail which he often traveled to gloat over his deed or cut a meal of human flesh." Accompanying the piece was a portrait of the Man-Eater, based on the same souvenir photograph that the *Lake City Silver World* had offered for sale.[2]

Several weeks later, in early May, an item appeared in the *Albion New Era*, the local newspaper of Albion, Indiana, a small town in Noble County in the northeast corner of the state. "Some time ago, we noticed the fact that a man named Alfred Packer was on trial in Colorado for murdering his companions in the mountains, and that he was driven to it by starvation and self-defense," the article began. It then went on to report a surprising development. Residing in the neighboring county of LaGrange was "a gentleman named Packer" who had "a son in the west named Alfred." The elder Packer had recently been browsing through the March 31 issue of the *National Police Gazette* when he came upon "a portrait of the criminal" and was "struck with its resemblance to his long lost son." The "probability of the culprit being of his own flesh and blood," the article concluded, had left the old man "greatly agitated."[3]

Twenty years after Alfred Packer left home, his family finally knew what had become of him.

+ + +

At the emotionally fraught climax of his controversial sentence, Judge Gerry had admonished the condemned man: "Prepare to meet thy God, prepare to meet the spirits of thy murdered victims, prepare to meet thy aged father and mother of whom you have spoken." Clearly, Packer had led the world to believe that his parents were dead. Whether Packer believed this himself or thought he might garner some sympathy by presenting himself as an orphan is impossible to say. In any event, the world learned the truth when, just days after the trial ended, a letter, postmarked LaGrange, Indiana, arrived for Sheriff Smith. Its writer was

Melissa Fought, who identified herself as Packer's sister. "She states that their venerable parents are still living," the *Silver World* reported. "The lady writes a touching letter. The sheriff gave the letter to Packer. He said she was not his sister, but finally admitted she was. . . . He burned the letter."[4]

Weeks later, Fought tried again. By then, another lawman was in charge of watching over Packer: a laconic, sharp-shooting, steely-eyed frontiersman named Cyrus Wells Shores.

+ + +

Recounted in a memoir that remained unpublished until the early 1960s, Shores's life was every bit as eventful as that of far better-known contemporaries. Born in Michigan in 1844, he set out for the West by steamboat at the age of twenty-two and, in succeeding years, worked as a bullwhacker in Montana, a hunter and trapper in Wyoming, a freight hauler in Colorado, and a cowboy on the Chisholm Trail, before embarking on his career as a lawman. Along the way he crossed paths with Wild Bill Hickok; befriended the legendary outlaw Tom Horn; fought Indians; survived cattle stampedes; and tangled with rustlers, robbers, gunslingers, and desperadoes of every stripe. In later years— having gained fame as "the best thief catcher West of the Missouri"—he participated in the manhunt for Butch Cassidy's Wild Bunch. Following his death, one Colorado newspaper paid him what was clearly considered the ultimate tribute in that time and place: "It has been said that he did more than any other white man to make western Colorado a fit place for white people to live."[5]

+ + +

At the time he received Melissa Fought's letter in early 1884, "Doc"— as Shores was known from childhood onward—had been the sheriff of Gunnison County for just a few months. "It was part of my job to check the incoming and outgoing mail of the prisoners," he explained in his memoir.[6] After reviewing the letter, he turned it over to Packer.

This time, Packer did not burn the letter; he stuck it in an envelope and returned it to the sender with no response.

Nothing if not persistent, Melissa sent Shores another letter, whose crude, barely literate spelling only heightens the pathos of her plea:

> Mr Shore, Dear Sir
> I rote you some time ago, and received no answer you gave my letter to my Brother, and he put it in an invelop and sent it back to me, without riting a word. My Fother wants to here why he is kep so long in jail, was he let go, and arrested again please tell me, so i can tell Fother and Mother they are old, and wants to here from ther boy, why is Alfred so rough about riting to me, I have pled i have beged of him to rite to me, he rites to one man here that aint in the family at all and we dont get to heare from him. My Fother and Mother feels terable about Alfred, and why dont he rite good letters home to them, dont show this to him, but please rite yourself to me and tell me all.
> Malissa Fought
> Lagrange
> Lagrange Co
> Indiana

Eventually, Packer did respond to his sister, composing what Shores described as one of "the most depraved letters I have ever seen. Among other things, he accused her of neglecting him, and threatened to kill her when he was released from prison." Shores dispatched the letter to Melissa with an accompanying note. Some time later, she replied with another piteous missive:

> Mr Shore, Dear sir
>
> I received your short but kind letter and many thanks to you for riting it, as my poor unfornate Brother is in your care, i feal as though you was the one to rite to, when he is set free dont fail to let me know as soon as possible, why is it they hold him so long in jail here so long, i am afraid if he does get out, they will mob

him, what a life to live and to think of, please dont show him my letter for he is despert against me because i rote and found out that he was in jail, i felt it my deauty to know about him, and my Fother always wants to hear from him, when Alfred did rite to me, he rote so unkind and maid such terable threats to me, i could not read them to my Fother and Mother and if you please rite me once and a while i will pay you for all yar truble.[7]

Melissa Fought wasn't the only person to find herself on the receiving end of Packer's threats. General Charles Adams stated:

While confined in the jail at Gunnison awaiting his second trial . . . Packer often and repeatedly threatened the lives of the witnesses who testified in his case, and of Judge Gerry who had sentenced him, declaring in a paroxysm of rage not only that he would become free to kill us, mentioning particularly the witnesses Dolan, Mears and myself but that he would also take dire vengeance on our families. In my case, he stated that he would come to my home at Manitou directly after he got out of prison, would set my house on fire, and if I left the house would shoot me and any member of my family down like dogs, and would yet have the pleasure of eating a piece of my flesh.[8]

To Sheriff Shores, such savage outbursts were proof of Packer's "persecution complex." "Of all the prisoners that I held in my custody during my eight years as sheriff," Shores later recalled, "Packer was the only one in whom I failed to find at least a few good qualities. He was slow-witted, cowardly, vicious, and a natural bully. He seemed to want to dominate the other prisoners."[9]

Not everyone viewed Packer in such a hostile light. Shores's own wife, Alice, thought that, on the whole, "he behaved very well" and "kept his cage very clean." She agreed with her husband, however, that he expected the other prisoners to treat him like "the boss of the jail."[10]

One prisoner who refused to be cowed by Packer was a hard case named Virgil Prentiss, a.k.a. Virgil Wilson, convicted of shooting his schoolteacher brother with a Winchester rifle, beating in his skull with a hammer, then throwing the corpse down an abandoned well. Wilson, as one local historian writes, "was too tough for the Man-Eater and was one of the few prisoners that Packer left alone." Later, however, when Wilson was taken to Montrose for trial, "the cowardly Packer, who didn't dare say anything to antagonize Prentiss to his face, wrote him a number of iniquitous letters, calling him a lot of obscene names and threatening to kill him if their paths ever crossed again." Sheriff Shores, who checked all of Packer's correspondence, found the letters so appalling— "the worst that could be written"—that he never mailed them. He would hold on to them for years, believing that the time might eventually arrive when they would serve as irrefutable proof of Packer's irredeemable villainy.[11]

+ + +

However bitterly he resented the local citizenry that had (so he insisted) wrongly condemned him, Packer was happy to profit from their continuing fascination with him. Men and women eager to get a glimpse of the notorious Man-Eater were regular visitors to the jail, and Packer kept himself well stocked with souvenirs that he would sell for modest sums: photographic portraits and handcrafted watch fobs and other gewgaws—some of a surprising delicacy—he fashioned from dyed and braided horsehair.[12]

Among his visitors was Alice Polk Hill, a "literary lady of note" (as the newspapers described her), later to be honored as Colorado's first poet laureate on the basis of her maudlin newspaper verse.[13] In 1884, the Kentucky-born Hill traveled to Gunnison to interview Packer. Not long afterward, she published *Tales of the Colorado Pioneers*, an informal history of her adopted state that proved to be a regional bestseller. Two of its chapters are devoted to the man she refers to (using the most jaw-breaking synonym for "cannibal" in the language) as "The Great American Anthropophaginian."

Much of her section on Packer quotes Mrs. Charles Adams, who, after encountering Hill on a train ride from Pueblo to Colorado Springs, spent the trip regaling her companion with her recollections of the Man-Eater. Mrs. Adams, who first met Packer over breakfast at Otto

Mears's house in Saguache and—by all accounts—found him a fascinating figure at the time, now claimed that, from the first, "there was something about his countenance that convinced me he was a murderer." So "great was my mistrust of him," she confided, that, on the trip back to the Los Pinos Indian Agency from Saguache, she "did not feel comfortable when he fell behind for fear of being shot."[14]

Hill's own impressions of Packer, whom she interviewed in his cell, were in line with Mrs. Adams's. Though conceding that his "features are not wholly bad . . . his nose is straight; his brow broad and suggestive of intellect"—she could perceive his degenerate character at a glance. "Anyone possessing even a moderate knowledge of human nature would say he belonged naturally to the criminal class," she declared. The very way he moved gave her the shivers. "He walks," she observed, "like one . . . creeping upon a victim." In response to Hill's request, he related his familiar story with "vivid but rude eloquence." When he finished, he seemed overcome with emotion. "Oh God, if I could have died then, I should have been spared nine years of misery," she quotes him as saying. "Those who have never been without their three meals do not know how to pity me."

To Hill, Packer seemed at his most human at that moment. Even then, however, there was a palpable air of the monstrous about him—"a shade," as she put it, "of uncanny horror."[15]

Indulging in what she clearly regarded as a clever bit of wordplay, Hill concluded by observing that "Packer is not yet hung, up to the time of this writing, but *his case is hanging* in the Supreme Court of this State, where it is likely to bide the law's delay for a long time yet." However feeble the pun, her prediction proved accurate. The supreme court would not rule on Packer's appeal until the fall of 1885. While awaiting the ruling, local newspapers fretted that the Man-Eater might yet wiggle free. "It is expected that, in accordance with the decision on the Garvey and other cases, the verdict of the jury which convicted Packer will be reversed," wrote the editor of the *Golden (CO) Transcript*. "It may be that there is a technical crook through which Mr. Packer's attorneys may drag him from the clutches of the law, and he will go out into the world unconvicted." Should Packer "be set free," the editor ominously concluded, "it is doubtful whether the people of the San Juan country would allow [him] a very long lease on life."[16]

Just a few months before those words were written, the people of the San Juan country had perpetrated a particularly remorseless act of frontier justice. In October 1883, a motherless ten-year-old girl named Mary Rose Matthews—who had been consigned to a Denver orphanage by her reprobate father—was placed under the care of a farming couple, Michael and Margaret Cuddigan, residents of the town of Ouray. Three months later, the child died under mysterious circumstances. Responding to rumors that she had been subjected to severe physical abuse, the county coroner exhumed her body and discovered unmistakable signs that Matthews had suffered "barbarous and inhuman cruelty" at her caretakers' hands. The Cuddigans were promptly arrested for her murder and confined in town at the Delmonico Hotel. Five days later, however, a mob of masked vigilantes stormed the hotel, overpowered the guards, and dragged the prisoners out of town, where the pair was strung up, Michael Cuddigan from the ridgepole of a cabin, his seven-months-pregnant wife from a tree across the road. Though some Colorado newspapers condemned the act, others had high praise for the vigilantes, declaring that "they had done themselves and their county proud" and even proposing that "each member of the mob be given a gold medal."[17]

According to one chronicler of the Packer case, "a wave of uneasiness swept though the jail" when news of the double lynching reached Gunnison.[18] In the end, however, the citizens of the San Juan country made no attempt to circumvent the law in Packer's case. The "Great American Anthropophaginian" would live to have another day in court.

31.

THE GREELY EXPEDITION

At the very time that Hill's book was rolling off the presses, the American public was riveted by a new story of cannibalism, first reported on the front page of the *New York Times*.

Three years earlier, in the summer of 1881, a twenty-five-man team led by Lieutenant Adolphus Greely of the Army Signal Corps had set out for the Arctic on a mission to establish a base camp for meteorological observation. Arrived on the shores of Lady Franklin Bay, six hundred miles south of the North Pole, they constructed their outpost—which they christened Fort Conger—and set about collecting masses of scientific data.

After the long, pitch-dark winter, the men—most of whom had never been subjected to the rigors of Arctic existence before—eagerly anticipated the arrival of a scheduled relief ship, bringing fresh food and news from home. It never arrived. When a second supply ship failed to come to their aid the following summer, Greely ordered that the camp be abandoned.

Loaded into five small boats, the men made a torturous journey through the ice-choked sea, finally ending up on Cape Sabine, 250 miles south of their departure point. Huddled in a makeshift camp, Greely and his team underwent an agonizing eight-month ordeal, their remaining rations so meager that they were reduced to eating boot soles, candle wax, and bird droppings. Before long, they began to perish of exposure and starvation. One man, a private named Henry, was executed after repeatedly pilfering food. Another, Jens Edwards, drowned in the frigid water while attempting to harpoon a seal. By May 1884, the survivors were too weak to bury the dead. When a rescue party finally reached their camp in June, only Greely and six other members of the expedition were still clinging to life. One of them, Corporal Joseph Ellison, died on the homeward journey after surgeons amputated both of his frostbitten legs. At his death, he weighed seventy-eight pounds.[1]

Greely and the other survivors—along with their rescuers—received a boisterous welcome upon their return to the United States. Arrived in Portsmouth, New Hampshire, they were greeted by cheering throngs, marching bands, and buildings draped with banners reading "Welcome to Our Arctic Heroes!" Following a grand procession along the central thoroughfare—lined with thousands of jubilant spectators—they were honored at a celebratory dinner by various dignitaries.[2] The public adulation continued for a little more than a week. Everything changed on Tuesday, August 12, when the *New York Times* ran a front-page story headlined "Horrors of Cape Sabine."

"When the vessels of the Greely relief expedition reached St. John's," the article began, "the world was told that only six members of the Greely colony were living. One had been drowned, one had died on the way home, and seventeen, it was said, had perished miserably of starvation. This was a shocking story, but today there must be told a story more appalling. When their food gave out, the unfortunate members of the colony, shivering and starving in their little tent . . . were led by the horrible necessity to become cannibals." Far from being a case of heroic endurance in the face of unimaginable hardship, the true story of the Greely expedition turned out to be "the most dreadful and repulsive in the long annals of arctic exploration."

The revelation by the *Times* that the starving survivors had subsisted on the flesh of their dead comrades "unleashed a wave of articles by other newspapers anxious to exploit popular interest in the macabre details of the scandal."[3] At the instigation of the *Rochester Post Express*, whose editor offered to finance the exhumation, the body of one of Greely's officers, Frederick Kislingbury, was disinterred on August 14. The emaciated corpse presented a ghastly sight. "The skeleton was shrunken," the paper reported. "There was little if any flesh on the arms

and legs, and the body from the throat down was denuded of its skin.
. . . Upon the right side of the breast, between the ribs, appeared two
gaping wounds. . . . When the remains were turned over on one side, the
skinless back and shoulder blades presented the same sickening specta-
cle as the front."

Following the autopsy, the examining physicians concluded that
"the flesh had been cut by someone who understood the use of a knife.
It was not hacked at all. For instance, we could see how it had been cut
around the wrist and removed in a systematic manner. All the solid
portions of the body had been taken off in this manner." The report left
little doubt that, following Kislingbury's death from starvation, his body
"had been eaten by his comrades."[4]

A few days later, another body—that of Private William Whistler—
was removed from its grave in a small country churchyard near Delphi,
Indiana. "The body was wrapped in a cotton waste, around which was
a hemp cord," reported the *New York Times*. "Displacing these, a blanket was found next to the body. When this blanket was removed, the
ghastly sight of a mere skeleton was seen":

> There was nothing of the body left, save the head and trunk. All the
> flesh had been cut from the limbs. The arms, legs, and shoulders
> were bare bones. . . . It was particularly noticeable that the bones
> were picked entirely clean; not a vestige of flesh is left on them. The
> back has nothing on it. In fact, the only things left of the man are his
> head, breast, intestines, and the left hand and foot. The appearance
> would show that an expert had done the cutting of the flesh.

Whistler's elderly grandmother was among the fourteen witnesses
present at the grave site. Interviewed by the *Times*' reporter following
the exhumation, she merely shook her head sadly and said, "Poor boy.
He was a good lad, but it is better that he has been eaten by his comrades
than that he should have eaten of them."[5]

Throughout the late summer of 1884, these and similarly gruesome
accounts fed the public's appetite for morbid titillation. For Coloradans,
however, even the cannibalistic horrors of Cape Sabine couldn't match
the atrocities of their own homegrown monster. "The ill-starred Greely

expedition afforded no such episode of utter depravity as the deliberate butchery of five men that their bodies might furnish food," declared one Denver newspaper. "The crime of Alfred Packer . . . will long remain unique among the horrors of criminal records."[6]

Part Three

THE PRISONER

32.

PRELIMINARIES

Periodically during Packer's prolonged incarceration in the Gunnison jail, the *Lake City Silver World* gave editorial voice to the gravest concern of the Hinsdale County public: that Packer's conviction would eventually be nullified, thanks to "the humiliating stupidity . . . of our legislative law-makers."[1] In October 1885—two and a half years after Judge Gerry pronounced his sentence—that fear was realized when the state supreme court finally handed down its decision. Citing the Garvey case as a precedent, Chief Justice Beck ruled that, since the "sections of the Criminal Code which authorized and prescribed the punishment for murder were repealed by the legislature without a savings clause," the "judgment [in Packer's case] must be reversed."[2]

Though defense attorney Heims could claim a victory on this score, another part of his appeal failed to persuade the supreme court. Heims had contended that, under the principle of double jeopardy, his client could not be retried for the killings and must therefore be "unconditionally discharged." Rejecting this argument, Beck maintained that, since the proceedings against Packer were now deemed to have been illegal, he was "never in jeopardy on account of his crime." Denying the motion to set Packer free, Beck declared that the state was entitled to try Packer again, albeit on the lesser charge of manslaughter.[3]

For reasons still unexplained, nearly another year would pass before Packer was brought to trial. In the interim, his new defense attorney—Aaron Heims's one-time law partner, Thomas C. Brown—applied for a change of venue.

In his formal petition, submitted to Judge Gerry on March 9, 1885, Brown argued that the people of Hinsdale County, "almost without exception," were convinced that Packer had killed his five companions "not only . . . for their money but from a craving and vicious desire for human flesh and blood." As a result, they were so "incensed and prejudiced" against him that "it would be difficult if not impossible to find a single person in said county who has not a fixed opinion that the petitioner is guilty." According to Brown, "prejudice against him was so bitter" that, in the weeks leading up to the trial, "threats were frequently made openly and publicly by inhabitants of Hinsdale County that they would hang petitioner, law or no law." Once the trial was concluded, "the officers of the law . . . deemed it absolutely necessary to remove the petitioner to the county jail in Gunnison County in order to prevent his being mobbed and murdered at the hands of the inhabitants of Hinsdale County."

There was also the matter of Judge Gerry's own bias, an issue that Brown was at pains to address in exceedingly tactful, not to say fawning, terms:

> And petitioner further states that, while he regards your Honor as an upright and conscientious judge, he fears and verily believes that you are prejudiced against him and that he cannot for that reason have a fair trial before you as judge of said court because he says that at the time of his trial and for many years prior thereto, you were a resident of Hinsdale County and had then and now have many friends and acquaintances among the inhabitants, and petitioner verily believes that it would have been almost, if not quite, impossible for you to not, in some respect and to some extent, share in the prejudice and belief of petitioner's guilt existing on the part of your neighbors, friends and acquaintances, and petitioner verily believes that you regard him as guilty of the offenses charged, and while petitioner believes that your honor would endeavor conscientiously to give him a fair and impartial trial, being mindful of the frailty of one man, however just, honest and conscientious, he

fears that your prejudice, if such you have, might unbeknown to you swerve or bias your judgment upon some important questions involving the petitioner's rights.[4]

After considering Brown's arguments, Gerry announced his decision. Owing to "the prejudice of the inhabitants of Hinsdale County" (Gerry himself included), the motion was granted. Packer's second trial would be held at the district court of Gunnison County, and a different judge would "be procured to hear and try the said case in said Gunnison County."[5]

Following a four-month delay, Packer was arraigned on Saturday, July 31, 1886, before the new judge, William Harrison. Charged with manslaughter in the deaths of Israel Swan, Shannon Wilson Bell, James Humphrey, Frank Miller, and George Noon, the defendant entered a plea of not guilty. Bail was set at $10,000—$2,000 for each of the five cases—a sum Packer couldn't possibly raise, roughly equivalent to a quarter million dollars today. This time, legal matters would move with unaccustomed speed. He was returned to his steel cell in the city jail to await his trial, scheduled to begin on Monday, August 2, just two days away.[6]

33.

SECOND TRIAL

Sometime in the summer of 1886, a woman residing in Georgia murdered a young child, devoured part of the corpse, and preserved the rest for future consumption. When this atrocity was discovered, the perpetrator's neighbors took revenge on her by burying her alive.

This sensationally lurid crime—surpassing in sheer ghastliness the most grotesque imaginings of Edgar Allan Poe—was reported on the front page of the Monday, August 2, 1886, issue of the *Gunnison-Review Press*. For the same racist reason, however, that, even today, the horrific murder of a child in the inner city ghetto will receive far less media attention than an analogous crime in white suburbia, the newspaper's entire coverage consisted of a single sentence: "A Georgia negress killed a four-year-old child and made a stew of a portion of his flesh which she served upon the table, and pickled the remainder; the discovery of the latter led to a confession of her guilt, whereupon the negroes buried her alive."[1]

By contrast, the start of Alfred Packer's second trial was trumpeted by a bold headline and accorded the bulk of the front page.

The proceedings moved swiftly. By late morning of day one, the jury had been selected and sworn and the first witness, Preston Nutter, called. The testimony itself was, by and large, a replay of the original. Once again, Nutter told of the prospecting party's journey from Utah, their stay at Chief Ouray's camp, the departure of Packer and his five companions for the government cattle camp, Packer's initial confession at the Los Pinos Agency, the search for the missing men, and the subsequent identification of their bodies.

This time, however, Nutter added a few damning details clearly meant to discredit Packer's story. Packer's insistence that he and the others had been driven mad by starvation was surely a lie, since—so Nutter maintained—"deer, antelope, rabbits and grouse were plentiful" in the area. There were also "plenty of beaver in the lake and they could have been easily caught," especially by someone like Packer, "who always said that he had been an old beaver trapper and been employed by the Hudson Bay Company in the north." Asked about a particular bone found at the dead men's camp, Nutter unhesitatingly identified it as "the shoulder of a deer," further undercutting Packer's claim that the men had been reduced to foraging for snails and eating their own moccasins.[2]

Other witnesses who offered more-or-less verbatim recaps of their original testimony were George Tracy, James "Larry" Dolan, O. D. Loutsenhizer, and General Adams. Hezekiah Musgrave had also been expected to take the stand. Unfortunately, as District Attorney Herschel M. Hogg learned shortly before the trial commenced, Hessie had been "killed in a snowslide" the previous winter.[3]

+ + +

On the morning of Tuesday, August 3—day two of the proceedings—the prosecution rested its case. Up to that point, the trial had been a perfunctory affair, so utterly devoid of drama that, for the *Gunnison Review-Press*, the highlight had been the testimony of civil engineer H. W. Plumb, whose "elegant and correct drawings of the [Lake Fork] country," gushed the newspaper, "were splendid works of art and prove him a master of his profession."[4] Then, shortly before eleven in the morning, defense attorney Thomas C. Brown called Alfred Packer to the stand.

The years behind bars had taken an obvious toll on the prisoner. "He looked pale," reported the correspondent for the *New York Times*, "his cheeks were hollow, and his eyes sunken." Standing in his shirtsleeves in front of the courtroom, "waving his mutilated hand" and speaking "in an excited manner," he held forth for more than two hours, delivering a harangue so wild and disjointed that it made his rambling oration at his previous trial seem like a model of judicial eloquence.[5]

Though the world had heard the story before, this latest recital struck the *Times'* reporter as "excitedly interesting and horrible," particularly when Packer arrived at its ghastly climax.

"We must have been in the mountains several weeks after we run out of food," Packer recounted. "Bell first give up his moccasins and we made a meal of those. I next give up mine, and then the others. The men were getting desperate. Bell was getting crazy. His eyes bulged from his head. The men cried for salt. They didn't ask for food, only salt, salt."

After making camp by the shores of the big lake, "we saw a game trail up the mountains. It was agreed that I should go on the trail, as I was the strongest. Next morning, I took the Winchester rifle and went. I left the men crazy with hunger. Found a bunch of rose bushes but no game. When I got back in the evening, I saw Bell bending over the fire, cooking some meat. I spoke some words to him, and he rose up and started for me with a hatchet. I run back down the bluff but I fell, and while down I shot at him through the side as he come at me. He fell and the hatchet dropped by me. I snatched it up and threw it at him and it struck him in the head. I went back up to the camp and found that the rest of them were dead. The meat Bell was cooking was flesh from Humphrey's leg. I stayed in the camp the rest of that night.

"I then made my camp off a short distance," continued Packer. "Stayed there possibly fifteen days. I was crazy with hunger and cut the flesh from Bell's leg and boiled it in a tin cup and ate it. My stomach was empty, and I vomited it up. After that, I frequently ate the meat. Several times I tried to get out of the country. I'd climb the mountain but didn't see no way out, so I'd return to camp and cut the flesh from the legs of the dead men and eat it."

As he had at the previous trial, Packer acknowledged his guilt in only one regard. "I am accused of robbing the dead," he said. "Yes, I did rob the dead when I cut flesh from the bodies. Here is where I done wrong. I robbed the dead, but I knew the money would do them no good. I am willing to take the blame for that."[6]

Having reached the end of his lengthy statement, Packer seated himself in the witness chair for his cross-examination. For the next several hours, he underwent a relentless grilling by District Attorney Mills, whose "cunning questions" so unsettled the defendant that, as the newspapers reported, Packer periodically exploded in rage, unleashing "a fearful tirade of abuse" at Mills, the jury members at his first trial, and particularly at Judge Gerry, whom he denounced "in the most wicked terms known to the English language."

Once, when his own attorney tried to calm him down, Packer turned to him and shouted, "You shut up, I'm on the stand now!" At another point, he became so violently agitated that Sheriff Shores was "obliged to take hold of him" and physically subdue him. In the opinion of the *New York Times*, Packer was "the most remarkable witness that was ever placed on the stand in this country. He would abide by no rule. . . . He proved incorrigible, inconsistent, irrepressible, and violent, and he was finally excused, pale and trembling, yet defiant."[7]

Packer's furious outbursts on the witness stand might have been seen as the natural expression of an innocent man venting his outrage and frustration at a terrible miscarriage of justice. To those who witnessed it, however, it merely confirmed the prevailing view of him as a fiend. At those moments during the cross-examination when he lost control and half rose from his seat, his fists clenched and face contorted, "he looked the demon that he has been pictured, and his conduct caused a chill to pass over the audience."[8]

34.

VERDICT

Closing arguments began on Wednesday, August 4. Four hours were allotted, two each for the prosecution and defense. No transcript of these statements exists, though the local press hailed District Attorney Mills's "closing peroration" as "a brilliant display of oratory . . . one of the best ever made before a Gunnison jury." Everyone present, even the defendant, was "visibly affected. For the first time Packer was seen to quail."[1]

At four in the afternoon, after receiving Judge Harrison's instructions, the jury retired to deliberate. Packer himself felt sure of the outcome. He had no doubt, he told Sheriff Shores, that he would "get it in the neck."[2]

+ + +

A few days earlier, a local man going by the name of Hugh McCabe was arrested for murder. It was not the first homicide committed by McCabe, whose actual name was Thomas Hurley. In August 1875, Hurley—then a member of the Molly Maguires, the secret society of Irish American miners that terrorized the Pennsylvania coal fields in the mid to late 1800s—had shot and killed a bartender, Gomer James. With the Pinkertons hot on his trail, he had fled Pennsylvania, leading a knockabout life under various aliases before ending up in Colorado, where he'd adopted the name McCabe and found work in the Baldwin coal mine, not far from Gunnison.[3]

Following a prize fight held at the mining camp on the evening of August 2 and attended by somewhere between fifty and a hundred spectators, a miner named Luke Curran got into an altercation with McCabe and ended up dead, his belly slit open with the long-bladed knife McCabe used to cut his plug tobacco. Arrested and taken to Gunnison, McCabe was arraigned at the city hall at the very time that the Packer jury was beginning its deliberations in the courthouse.[4]

Sheriff Shores was about to lead Packer back to the jail to await the jury's decision when a messenger burst into the courtroom and informed him that an enraged mob, intent on lynching McCabe, was gathering outside the city hall. "I immediately rushed Packer back to the jail, which was only about a hundred feet from the courthouse," Shores recalled in his memoir. In his haste, he stuck Packer in a cell with four other prisoners, who were none too happy about the prospect of spending the night with the Man-Eater. Shores then hurried over to the city hall.[5]

Elbowing through the crowd, he made his way into the building, where his deputy, Sam Harper, was keeping watch over McCabe. With one hand grasping McCabe by the arm and the other clutching his six-shooter, Shores led his prisoner through the rabble and over to the jail, threatening to shoot the first man who interfered.

"Although there were the usual threats," Shores recalled, "the crowd got out of our way and no serious efforts were made to detain us. Upon reaching the jail, I locked McCabe in the cell where I usually kept Packer. Harper and I then hastened back to the courthouse with Packer. The jury had not yet appeared but they were expected at any moment and the court room was filled to capacity with curious spectators."[6]

+ + +

The jury needed just two and a half hours to reach a unanimous decision. Like their counterparts at the first trial, they were convinced by the testimony of Preston Nutter and other prosecution witnesses that Packer had deliberately "misled the party to the secluded spot where the crimes were committed"; that "all the victims had been struck with the hatchet while asleep"; that "Bell, upon being hit, jumped up and started to run, whereupon Packer shot him and then finished him with hatchet blows"; and that Packer's "sole motive in committing the crime was robbery." They also discounted Packer's claim that he and the others had been crazed with starvation, since "some of the jurors knew from their own experience that, despite the heavy winter in 1874, game was not scarce in the region"—indeed, that it was "alive with snow-shoe rabbits, birds and beaver."[7]

Shortly before seven in the evening, the jurors sent word that they had arrived at a verdict. A buzz of excitement spread throughout the courtroom. Suddenly, Sheriff Shores became aware of a "muffled roar, like the sound of a sudden wind," coming from the direction of the jail. "Fearing that a mob might be storming the jail," he rushed from the courtroom. He was halfway down the stairs when he nearly collided with his jailer.

"It's McCabe!" cried the jailer. "He's slit his throat!"

Running to the jail, Shores found McCabe "lying on his stomach in the front part of his cell. Blood was streaming across the floor in all directions. I grabbed the fallen man by the shoulder and turned him on his side. Although accustomed to sights of violence, I shuddered as I looked down at his grotesquely dangling head, which was nearly severed from his body. Blood was spurting from a deep gash which extended nearly from ear to ear. His jugular vein had been cut, and he had bled to death within only a few minutes."

The noise Shores had heard in the courtroom came from the other prisoners, who had set up a horrified shout when they saw the blood gushing from McCabe's gaping throat.

How McCabe had managed to kill himself was a mystery, since he'd been thoroughly searched at the time of his arrest. Shores found his answer when he searched the cell. On a high metal shelf lay the straight razor that Packer—the cell's usual resident—had used that morning to shave himself. Its blade was slick with blood.[8]

+ + +

Shores was still inside the cell waiting for the coroner to arrive when, up in the courtroom, jury foreman S. S. Duree handed in the written verdict: guilty of voluntary manslaughter in each of the five cases.

The verdict was read aloud to the packed courtroom. Then, with a bang of the gavel, Judge Harrison adjourned the trial until the following morning, when sentence would be pronounced.[9]

+ + +

To the disappointment of the dozens of spectators who flocked to the courthouse first thing the next morning, Thursday, August 5, Judge Harrison sent word that his arrival would be delayed until two in the afternoon. Packer himself expressed his frustration, declaring that he "wanted the suspense ended." Before being returned to his cell, he approached District Attorney Mills and, to show he harbored no hard feelings toward the prosecutor, presented him with one of the braided horsehair watch fobs he spent his time making in jail.[10]

When the trial reconvened that afternoon, Judge Harrison, dispensing with preliminaries, immediately ordered Packer to rise. "Mr. Packer," he intoned, "you have been convicted of the crime of voluntary manslaughter on five indictments. If you have anything to say before sentence is passed upon you, you can now do so."

Confirming that he had, in fact, prepared a statement, Packer took a drink of water and proceeded to deliver another of his inimitable speeches, this one—as the *Rocky Mountain News* grudgingly acknowledged—"rather a manly" acceptance of his fate.[11]

"I will not say that I have not had a fair and impartial trial," he declared, speaking directly to the jurors, "for I could not have obtained a jury in the state of Colorado that could have given me a fairer and more impartial trial than I had. If I had been on the jury and such evidence had been produced, I would have done the same thing. There is a chain of evidence against me that I cannot wipe out. I hold no malice to the jury. I am going to my long home. I expect to get forty years and I don't want to live to see the end of it."

Next, he turned and—"adopting the curious habit of referring to himself repeatedly in the third person"[12]—addressed the spectators:

"I do not want the Gunnison people to think that I hold any malice towards them. They have been good to me during the last thirteen years that I have been here in jail, and I do not want them to think that Packer harbors anything against them, for Packer has had a fair and impartial trial here in Gunnison.

"I want to say that Mr. Mills has done his duty and prosecuted me as a lawyer, which was perfectly right," he continued, with a nod toward the district attorney. "He knows I do not hold any malice against him. He has only seen that I had a good, square prosecution and no more. He has not abused me and I bear no ill will towards him.

"Now I want to say one thing," said Packer, speaking directly to the spectators. "My counsel has done the very best they could do for me. But this is a mysterious case. It is a mystery to me. I can't wipe out the evidence against me, although I know there is something wrong about it. In later years, it will be cleared up, for there has never been a case where a man has been sentenced unjustly that sooner or later it was not cleared up. I had one hope, and that was that sometime I would be able to hold up before the people of Colorado that I am not guilty of the murder of the four men. I killed Bell. I admit it, and have done so all along. But he is the only man I killed. As I said before, the old mystery will be cleared up in the course of time. Some of the old witnesses will die, and if they don't die suddenly, they will—on their deathbeds—throw lots of light on this matter, and then you will see that Packer was innocent.

"I don't expect to live to hear this, but don't understand by that that I intend to commit suicide. I want to live, but I am going to the penitentiary, and once there, I will be dead to the world.

"Now Judge," he concluded, turning back to the bench, "I expect a sentence of forty years. You must give it to me under the circumstances, but won't you do this? Won't you sentence me to forty years for the killing of Bell? Don't say anything about the others. Just give me all for one man."

"I would like to if I could, Mr. Packer," said Harrison, "but the law will not permit it."[13]

In stark contrast to the much-maligned Judge Gerry, Harrison refrained from high-flown speechifying. In solemn tones, he simply pronounced the sentence: a "continuous term of forty years," composed of five consecutive terms of eight years for the voluntary manslaughter of each victim.

Though he knew it was coming, Packer seemed visibly affected by the sentence. He hung his head and murmured, "Forty years." He had reason to be shaken. At the time, it was "the longest term ever imposed by an American judge."[14]

Even so, there were some who felt he had gotten off easy. The next day's headline of the *Rocky Mountain News* read:

**Packer, the Man Eater, after Thirteen
Years Receives a Punishment
Inadequate to His Crimes**[15]

35.

CAÑON CITY

Prior to 1868, Colorado law officers had no place to incarcerate convicted criminals besides their town jails, many of those little more than flimsy log or adobe cabins. "A sentence in Colorado Territory doesn't mean a damn thing," one pioneer sheriff complained. "We don't have a place to put them after the judges pass sentence. The only sentence that can be carried out is hanging. A jail conviction amounts to an acquittal."[1]

In July 1868—"concerned with the lawlessness of the region"—the United States Congress appropriated $40,000 for the construction of a prison in the Colorado Territory, its exact location to be left entirely up to the territorial legislature. Thomas Macon, a member of the legislature and resident of Cañon City, was eager to see the prison built in his town. The previous year, Macon had supported Denver in its successful bid to be named territorial capital over its rival, the city of Golden. His vote earned him enough backing from grateful colleagues to have Cañon City selected as the prison site.[2]

Land for the prison was donated by an early settler to the area, Jonathan Draper. Over the next two years, a two-story building constructed of native stone rose in the middle of the twenty-five-acre site. In addition to its forty cells—each measuring six by eight feet and equipped with nothing more than a cot and "honey bucket"—the prison featured a kitchen, a shower room, and a guard office. In its early years of operation, the entire staff consisted of four daytime guards and two night guards, each earning a salary of $25 a month for seven-day workweeks, along with the warden, who was paid the relatively princely sum of $208 per quarter.

By June 1871, the prison was ready for business, though it would be another few months before it received its first prisoner, one John Shepler, convicted of larceny. By the end of the year, Shepler had been joined by twenty-three other inmates, all male.[3] The first female convict—Mary Salanden, sentenced to three years for manslaughter—would be admitted in March 1873. By then, every cell in the prison was occupied.

Prison garb for the men consisted of white woolen suits, described by one visiting journalist as "handsomely adorned with black stripes." When inmates walked as a group outside their living quarters, they were required to march single file in lockstep under the watchful eye of a guard, each prisoner holding on to the shoulders of the man in front of him. During the day, they were put to work making shoes, manufacturing bricks, quarrying limestone, and building roads. Punishment, not rehabilitation, was the point. Those who defied the rules were subjected to the usual draconian measures: immured for month-long stretches in a lightless hole, shackled to a ball and chain, flogged with a cat-o'-nine-tails, or strapped facedown over a sawhorse and beaten with a wooden paddle.

To deter a growing number of escapes—the first of which took place just a few weeks after the prison opened—a wall, enclosing four and a half acres, was erected in 1875. Shortly after Colorado gained statehood in 1876, the Cañon City prison officially became the state penitentiary and funds were allocated for its enlargement. Even with the construction of additional cellhouses, the penitentiary—which, by 1877, was receiving new inmates at an average rate of fifty per year—suffered from chronic overcrowding.

Among those consigned to the Cañon City pen in the first decade of its existence was George Witherell, described by one chronicler of the Old West as a "moronic murderer." In September 1871, a rancher named William Underwood, residing on Big Dry Creek about twenty miles from Denver, came upon a human hand poking out of a pile of sand and rocks. Dismounting from his pony, he proceeded to uncover the decomposed remains of a man quickly identified as S. H. Wall, a local sheepman who had gone missing some days earlier.

At virtually the same time that Underwood was making his gruesome discovery, another rancher, Ira Palmer, encountered Witherell, who was driving a large herd of sheep across the prairie. Knowing the twenty-four-year-old Witherell to be a "ne'er-do-well who hardly ever had more than two bits in his jeans," Palmer "smelled something rotten." In reply to Palmer's queries, Witherell explained that he had purchased the 350 head of sheep from Wall for $400 and that Wall had subsequently "left the territory." The story only heightened Palmer's suspicions. The going price for sheep at the time was $1.25 a head. Wall, who was well known among his neighbors as a hardnosed businessman, was scarcely the type to sell his animals at a discount.

Promptly arrested and convicted, Witherell was sentenced to a life of hard labor in December 1871. Described by a contemporary reporter as a "cunning . . . brute" who "will kill at any time for the mere sake of killing . . . one of the class of men you would naturally hate to meet on a lonely road"—he became the newly built prison's most infamous inmate—a distinction he would retain until 1886, when Alfred Packer came to Cañon City.[4]

+ + +

Handcuffed to a cattle thief named Fred Myers, Packer arrived at Cañon City by train on Friday, August 6, accompanied by Sheriff Doc Shores. Taken directly to the prison, he was assigned his permanent convict number—1389—then subjected to the standard admissions process: stripped of his clothing, scrubbed in the shower room, and shorn of his long hair and whiskers.

The following morning, prior to his departure, Shores showed up at the prison and obtained permission from the warden to interview Packer privately. "I wanted to talk with him about other prisoners I had in jail," Shores would recall.

At his first glimpse of the freshly barbered prisoner, however, Shores was so taken aback that he "could hardly think of anything to say to him." An apparent believer in the then-popular pseudoscience of phrenology—which held that an individual's character traits could be read from the topography of his skull—Shores was shocked by "the brutal shape of [Packer's] head . . . that [Shores] had never noticed before when he was wearing his hair long." To Shores, the startling sight offered incontrovertible scientific proof of what he had long ago concluded about Packer. "There was no question," he declared, "but that this man was a born murderer."[5]

36.

CONVICT NUMBER 1389

Contrary to Packer's prediction at the close of his trial that, once shut up in prison, he would be "dead to the world," he continued to be an object of fascination to the public. With no restrictions placed on the number of visitors he was permitted, he attracted "a constant stream of the curious." Many of those who came to gape at "Colorado's Nationally Known No. 1 Prisoner" (as he was dubbed in the press) left with a handsome souvenir: a belt, bridle, or watch fob fashioned from dyed and braided horsehair, a gracefully carved wooden cane, or one of the other incongruously elegant products of the Man-Eater's "talented hands." Packer did a tidy business selling these items, though occasionally he bestowed one as a gift. Even today, visitors to Lake City can marvel at one of his creations on display at the Hinsdale County Museum: a magnificent Victorian dollhouse, standing four feet high, that he built for the warden's daughter.[1]

Packer's epileptic seizures, which continued to afflict him on a regular basis, rendered him unfit for the hard manual labor to which he had been condemned. In lieu of other, more arduous jobs, he was permitted to tend to the prison gardens and shrubbery, eventually becoming a skilled florist who "took pleasure in giving away bouquets of his blooms" to visitors.[2]

In June 1890, the United States Congress passed the Dependent and Disability Pension Act, providing stipends for all Civil War veterans who had served in the Union army for at least ninety days and were no longer able to perform manual labor. No sooner had the new law gone into effect than Packer began the application process. Retaining a pair of Washington, DC, attorneys—Charles and William B. King—to assist with the paperwork, he obtained copies of his military and medical records from the War Department and sent letters to various acquaintances from his past, seeking written affidavits attesting to his condition. Among those he contacted was a fellow named George Collins, an old friend from his days in Deadwood, South Dakota. Collins responded with a letter affirming that, during the time of their acquaintance, Packer—then attempting to earn a living as a shoemaker—"was able to do about ½ the labor of an able bodied man."

After undergoing an examination by the county coroner, Dr. Frank P. Blake—who expressed his professional opinion that the prisoner was "mentally unsound as a result of epilepsy"—Packer filed his application in late 1890. In it, he claimed—falsely—that he had been "in good, sound physical health" until enlisting in the army, and that he had developed epilepsy as the direct result of a bout of typhoid fever contracted while performing "constant, prolonged, and unnecessary guard duty" at Camp Douglas in 1862. Eventually his application was approved and he began receiving a monthly pension of twenty-five dollars.[3]

Between his pension and the earnings from his handicrafts, Packer would never lack for funds. By all accounts, he was openhanded with his money, "granting loans to departing prisoners to tide them over until they could re-establish themselves in the outside world. . . . Periodically he made contributions to help defray the legal expenses of those fellow prisoners still waging a fight for freedom."[4]

It was the fight for his own freedom, however, that would consume him in the decade to come.

+ + +

Over the years, news items about the Man-Eater continued to appear with some regularity. When midwestern reporters discovered that newspaper publisher DeAlton Rheubottom—owner of the *Middlebury Independent*—had been a playmate of Packer's during their childhoods in LaGrange, Indiana, the story became widely publicized news.[5] At about the same time, various papers ran a sensational story headlined "Told of a 'Lost Mine.'" Several years earlier—so the article reported—Packer, convinced he was dying, summoned a Cañon City physician, J. W. Dawson, and asked if "there was a chance of recovery." Informed "that there was not, he requested the doctor to give him some paper, upon which he drew a diagram of the Uncompahgre mining district and designated a certain spot and called it the 'Lost Mine,' in which he said there were millions.

"'If it had not been for the discovery of that spot,' Packer told the doctor, 'I would not be here, and my chums would be alive.'"

Though Packer would say no more, he asked for pen and paper and put the story into a letter, requesting "that it should remain sealed until he was dead." Contrary to Dawson's prognosis, however, "Packer did not die, and the hypothesis is that he stated in that letter that lots were drawn when the party were starving as to which men should die, and that he and Bell were the only survivors when they discovered the 'Lost Mine,' and that he slew Bell so that he would have the riches."[6]

Given the public's undiminished appetite for any scrap of news about Packer's prison life, it was, perhaps, only a matter of time before one of these stories caught the eye of a Denver barber named Duane C. Hatch. In 1875, Hatch, then a fifteen-year-old orphan, had made his way west to the Wyoming Territory, where he was befriended by an older fellow going by the name of John Swartze. The two worked side by side as cowhands for several years until they drifted apart. During the time they herded cattle together, Swartze had served as a surrogate father to the lonely boy, and Hatch had never forgotten the kindness the older man had shown him.

Recognizing now that "Swartze" was actually the notorious Alfred Packer, Hatch promptly paid a visit to the Cañon City penitentiary, where he and his former benefactor had an emotional reunion. From that point on, Hatch would dedicate himself tirelessly to winning Packer's release.[7]

In December 1892, as the first of the Man-Eater's five consecutive eight-year terms neared its end, Hatch—supplementing Packer's funds with some of his own—retained the services of Denver attorney John R. Smith on behalf of his friend. "One of the luminaries of the Colorado bar," Smith promptly filed a petition with the state supreme court, seeking his client's immediate release from prison.[8]

According to Smith's brief, Packer was the victim of a "monstrous . . . injustice." Though there were "five different indictments of manslaughter for the killing of five different persons," Packer was given only a single trial before one jury. To Smith, this consolidation of the five indictments was "plainly a mere travesty of justice." Had Packer been tried separately for each indictment, the verdicts might well have varied. One jury, for example, might have found him guilty beyond a reasonable doubt for the killing of Shannon Wilson Bell, while—owing to the highly circumstantial evidence in the case—a different jury might have acquitted him of the death of Israel Swan or any of the other victims.

By the same token, the cumulative sentence imposed by the judge had "no precedent in the long history of criminal jurisprudence." Since Packer had been found guilty in a single consolidated case, he could only be sentenced—so Smith maintained—to "the highest punishment which could be imposed on one conviction of manslaughter." That punishment was eight years, which Packer was on the brink of having served. Indeed, "by reason of his good behavior and strict observance of the rules and regulations of the state penitentiary," Packer had earned reduced time for good behavior and should properly have been "discharged on the 6th day March, 1891."[9]

The mere possibility that Packer might be set free sent the local press into fits of indignation. "Alfred Packer, known in Colorado as the Man-Eater from his habit of dining upon his associates, desires to leave the penitentiary, the diet there not agreeing with him," wrote the wisecracking editor of one Boulder paper. "A lawyer has found what seems to be the necessary technicality. It is hoped that the lawyer will not succeed, but if he should, the only just recompense would be to fatten him and feed him to his carnivorous client."[10]

The *Rocky Mountain News*, in the meantime, disseminated scare stories about Packer's possible reversion to his cannibalistic ways:

Now that the Man-Eater stands a fair chance of again breathing the air, a free man, thrills of fear are said to be chasing themselves down the spinal columns of at least a half-dozen persons who bore prominent parts in the conviction of Packer. Dreadful threats, made by Packer at the time, are remembered, and it is not only feared but openly expressed by friends of Packer's alleged prosecutors that the Man-Eater may repeat his horrible act of fifteen years ago.

Packer is known to be especially vindictive toward Otto Mears, General Adams, and James Dolan, as it was largely upon their testimony that he was found guilty. In the open court he declared that if he ever survived his imprisonment he would surely kill and eat the three persons named. He also had a cannibalistic feeling toward Preston Nutter.

A gentleman who was present at the first trial of Packer stated yesterday that in his opinion it would be highly dangerous to give Packer his liberty. "The man is crazy," said he, "and has a mania for killing and eating persons who have crossed his path. If I had incurred Packer's ill feeling, I would never feel safe a moment if he were at large."[11]

In the end, Mears and the other supposed objects of Packer's cannibalistic vengeance had nothing to fear. Six months after Packer's lawyer filed his petition, the Colorado Supreme Court issued its decision, rejecting Smith's arguments. "In our opinion," wrote Chief Justice Charles D. Hayt, "the authority of the district court to inflict successive penalties for the several convictions should be upheld."[12] As of June 1893, Alfred Packer still faced another thirty years behind bars.

37.

THE INSANITY COMMISSION

In the wake of the supreme court's decision, sensational rumors about Packer's mental condition began appearing in the press. According to these stories, the bitter dashing of his hopes had caused him to become mentally unhinged. From a model prisoner with a spotless record, he had turned into a "raving maniac." His "taste for human meat [has] revived," one Denver paper claimed, "and he threatens to make food of fellow prisoners and guards at the Cañon City Penitentiary"—to "eat everyone in sight and on sight." "What few docile traits he formerly exhibited have all disappeared," another reported. He had become "a dangerous lunatic with an unnatural lust for human flesh, determined to whet his appetite on any piece of man's anatomy on which he could fasten his teeth."[1]

While these stories were nothing more than the sort of luridly titillating fantasies that would soon become the stock-in-trade of twentieth-century tabloid journalism, Packer's behavior had, in fact, become increasingly erratic in recent months. Believing that he might be better off in the state insane asylum at Pueblo, Warden Frank A. McLister urged Governor Davis Hanson Waite to appoint a commission to "inquire into the mental condition of Prisoner Packer." Within days, three physicians had been selected for the task: P. R. Thombs, superintendent of the state insane asylum; Frank P. Blake, the Fremont County coroner who had examined the prisoner several years earlier when Packer applied for a government pension; and Eugene Grissom of Denver.

A graduate of the University of Pennsylvania medical school, Grissom served with distinction in the Civil War before returning to his native state of North Carolina to practice medicine. Following two terms in the state legislature, he was made head of the North Carolina Insane Asylum in Raleigh, beginning a twenty-one-year tenure that would earn him a reputation as one of the nation's leading alienists. A frequent contributor to leading medical journals, he also found time to serve as the first vice president of the American Medical Society, the president of the Association of Medical Superintendents of American Institutions for the Insane (later the American Psychiatric Association), a member of the state board of agriculture, surgeon general of the state guard, and a trustee of the University of North Carolina. His brilliant career was abruptly derailed in June 1889, when he was accused of having taken "indecent liberties" with female attendants and of "gross mistreatment" of his patients. Though acquitted at the climax of a sensational three-week trial, his reputation suffered irreparable damage. Resigning under public pressure, he moved out west to start a new life and settled in Denver, where he resumed his medical practice.[2]

Accompanied by a reporter for the *Denver Republican*, Grissom and the other two members of the Commission de Lunatico Inquirendo (as it was formally known) arrived at Warden McLister's house on the penitentiary grounds shortly after noon on Wednesday, August 16. After a brief consultation about procedure, they summoned a string of witnesses, beginning with the prison chaplain, the Reverend Dr. L. J. Hall.

Though he had known Packer for years, Hall had spent relatively little time in his company. "He never came to me for religious counsel," the minister testified, "and I do not know that he has any religious inclinations." During their infrequent encounters, Hall had observed no signs of mental disorder in Packer, beyond an occasional "lack of continuity of thought." Among his other duties, Hall was responsible for reading all the mail written and received by the inmates, and it was "only ... from the prisoner's letters to others" that he knew Packer "suffered from epilepsy."

D. H. Bruce, the deputy warden, offered much the same testimony. Packer's "mind seemed to be all right, except when he was seized with epileptic attack," Bruce told the commissioners. At those times, "he seemed to understand what was said to him but was unable to answer clearly." Beyond that, Bruce "had seen no evidence of insanity."

Next to be interviewed was prison guard S. A. T. Tyo. During the five years he had known the prisoner, Tyo had often witnessed Packer's seizures. "I have seen him fall many times," said the guard. "Frequently of late several times in one day. He generally knows when the heavy ones are coming and gets into his cell. It used to be that he got over them very soon, but in the last year or two the effects have been noticeable for two weeks sometimes. He hears what you say and seems to understand, but try him and you'll find he does not." Though Packer "would be irritable and cross and exhibit a bad temper" following one of these attacks, he had "never shown a disposition to assault anyone" or displayed any other signs of the homicidal impulses attributed to him by the sensationalizing press.

J. W. Dawson, the prison physician, agreed that Packer's "attacks had grown more frequent and violent within the past year." During these seizures, "the prisoner fell down in fits and . . . bit his tongue and lips." In the intervals between these attacks, Dawson explained, Packer "talked ordinary sense but not so clearly as formerly. The day after one of his fits, he had acted so strangely in the dining room that he had to be taken back to his cell. He did not manifest a disposition to commit any violent act but looked wild and did not appear to comprehend what was said to him." Dawson "did not consider the prisoner a lunatic but thought his mind was not as strong as it was two years ago, or even one year ago." It was Dawson who had advised the warden to ask for a commission of inquiry, believing that Packer might "have a better chance to recover in the state asylum."

Warden McLister himself was the last witness to testify. Though he had received occasional complaints about Packer from inmates who "were afraid he would injure himself or someone else" during one of his "fits," the warden "had never heard him make any threats against other prisoners or any of the officers." True, Packer had told the warden that he sometimes felt "like cleaning out this prison or tearing it down." But he had been perfectly calm when he said it, and for a man faced with forty years of confinement, such a sentiment seemed understandable.

Like every other official who had appeared that day, McLister declared that he "had no reason for believing the prisoner demented."

Having concluded their questioning of the various officials, the commissioners informed McLister that they wished to interview the prisoner himself. As the warden went off to fetch Packer, the three physicians began discussing the case. Grissom, author of a highly regarded pamphlet on epilepsy, *The Borderland of Insanity*, did most of the talking.

"People sometimes become crazy from the effects of epilepsy," Grissom remarked to his colleagues, "but epilepsy is not insanity. After all, Napoleon was an epileptic and so was Caesar, but we don't consider them crazy."

Their conversation was interrupted by the sound of rapidly approaching footsteps. Suddenly, the screen door banged open and Warden McLister entered with a stoop-shouldered man wearing striped convict garb. Inscribed in indelible black ink on the breast of his jacket was the number "1389."

"How are you, Mr. Packer?" Dr. Grissom said pleasantly. "Have a seat."

Without a word, Packer lowered himself into the chair facing the three physicians, crossed his long legs, and folded his hands on his lap.

"How are you feeling?" asked Dr. Thombs.

"Pretty lively," said Packer.

To the reporter for the *Republican*, Packer's upbeat assertion was belied by his appearance. Far from looking "pretty lively," Packer seemed as if he wasn't "long for this world":

> He is gaunt and his pale blue eyes, sunk deep in his head, are surrounded by pink circles. His high cheek bones are accentuated by the flesh tightly drawn over a narrow, pointed jaw and chin. The forehead is broad and moderately high, the nose sharp and straight. His hair is still black, but the top of his head is bald and from the rear a heavy bunch is combed forward in a neat twist so as to completely cover the denuded scalp. The hair on the sides, too, is brushed with the same nattiness, and even in convict stripes the man shows a desire to look as presentable

as possible. He wears a slightly straggly, drooping moustache covering his mouth. . . . A long, black goatee hangs from his chin. The hands are bony but not large, and from the left the first joints of both the index and little fingers are missing.[3]

After some small talk about Packer's military service, which put him at ease—"limbered [him] up from his stiff attitude," as the newsman reported—he was asked about his epilepsy. He explained that, against the advice of the prison physician, Dr. Dawson—who (with good cause) distrusted the unidentified ingredients in the nostrum—he had been relying on a patent medicine, Towns' Epilepsy Treatment, that seemed to be doing him "much good."[4] Blood used to gush from his nose during one of his fits, he explained, "and didn't do so anymore." The medicine also helped him sleep so well that he could no longer manage without a shot of it at bedtime.

After examining Packer's eyes to see "if there was any unusual dilation," Dr. Grissom leaned back in his seat. "Mr. Packer," he said, "we want you to tell us the story of your trouble. Begin at the beginning, do not linger on details, but tell us all about your trip in the mountains."

Packer, who was keenly aware of the reporter's presence, was reluctant at first. "I don't want to talk for the newspapers," he said in bitter tones. "They have been hounding me for years. Whenever my case comes up they have big headlines: 'Packer the Cannibal,' 'Packer the Man-Eater.' My big mistake was admitting to anything at all. Hundreds of people have told me that my experience wasn't unusual, that starving men have eaten each other on the ocean and when lost in the mountains or on the prairie. Look at the Donner Party. Men were eating their own wives! Now they tell me that many survivors moved to California, raised families, and became rich."

Assured that anything he said would remain confidential, Packer finally relented. Though the story was familiar to his listeners, none of them had heard it from Packer's own lips, and they sat spellbound during his recital.

When Packer was done, the physicians thanked him and explained that they would soon be submitting their report to the governor.

"I don't care particularly whether I'm transferred to the asylum or not, though I suppose I'd just as soon stay here in the penitentiary," said Packer as he made ready to leave. "I just don't want the world thinking that Packer is insane."[5]

+ + +

Three days later, on August 19, the commission submitted its results. Handwritten on Colorado State Penitentiary letterhead—featuring a handsome engraving of the main prison building framed by towering peaks—the eight-page report summarized the testimony of the various interviewees. On the basis of its "thorough and deliberate" examination of Packer, the commission found "that while his power of concentration is not strong, his memory is unimpaired and that his statements agree with those formerly given by him. . . . The conclusion of the commission is that epilepsy has not yet so weakened the mind of Alfred Packer as to constitute insanity."[6] Convict Number 1389 would remain in Cañon City.

+ + +

Ironically, it was not Packer but one of his examining physicians, Dr. Eugene Grissom, who would end up in the state insane asylum. The scandal that had driven him from his longtime home in North Carolina—and that he blamed on political enemies—left a permanently festering wound. Even at the time of the insanity commission, Grissom had become a morphine addict. Two years later, in 1895, he attempted suicide by swallowing chloroform and was committed to the asylum in Pueblo. Released after six years, he moved to Washington, DC, to live with his son. Not long afterward, early on the morning of July 27, 1902, he stepped onto the front porch, removed a revolver from his pocket, pressed the muzzle to his temple, and pulled the trigger.[7]

38.

UNFORGIVEN

For the rest of the decade, as the nineteenth century drew to its close, Packer made unceasing efforts to win his freedom. In the third week of August 1893—just days after the insanity commission submitted its report to Governor Waite—Packer's lawyer, John R. Smith, sent a letter to one of the examining physicians, Frank P. Blake. What, asked Smith, was Blake's professional opinion "concerning the health of Alfred Packer and probable effect upon his mind of continued confinement"?

Blake replied at once. "My opinion as a medical man," he wrote in a letter dated August 24, "is that under continued confinement . . . his epilepsy will grow worse and he will become entirely demented—if he lives long enough. I do not think he can live very long in prison, [as] they have no separate hospital for such cases."

Confirming the findings of the committee, Blake explained that, while Packer was not technically insane, he was "of unsound mind as a result of epilepsy." Like other victims of encroaching dementia, Packer could recall the past "in minute detail" but had a severely impaired short-term memory: he was "not capable of keeping his mind on matters at hand in a continual effort," as Blake put it.

Blake minced no words in his concluding sentence: "On the whole, I think it would be a humane act to exercise clemency in his case and that it is barbarous to continue keeping him as he is."[1]

Armed with this letter and its emphatic plea for clemency, Smith had his client file an application for a pardon on September 2, 1893.

The state board of pardons was still deliberating the matter eight months later when it heard from an individual vehemently opposed to Packer's release: General Charles Adams.

In a thirteen-page handwritten letter composed on May 31, 1894, Adams—then residing in Manitou Springs, where he was engaged in various business ventures, including silver mining and the bottling of local mineral water—recapitulated the details of Packer's "peculiarly obnoxious" crimes. He then described the "dire vengeance" the Man-Eater had sworn against those who had testified against him at his 1883 trial. Adams wrote, "[Packer vowed] to come to my home at Manitou directly after he got out of prison . . . set my house on fire, and [as] I left the house . . . shoot me and any member of my family down like dogs. Is such a man fit to be turned loose upon the community do you think, gentlemen?"

Still, it was not Packer's threats of retributive violence that troubled Adams most deeply. It was the hideously degraded existence he foresaw for the Man-Eater should the latter be set free:

> He says he has no friends to go to, he has no employment open to him, he has no money to support himself in idleness. According to his own statement he has been a cannibal, he has eaten human flesh. All good people will shrink from such a man, men will not employ him when that becomes known. I have heard that Packer intends to show himself as the "Great Colorado Cannibal" and in that way make a living. Will it be to the credit of this state to let such a thing happen? And will it be to the comfort of Packer himself, subject as he is to epileptic fits, partial aberration of the mind, and general crankism, to live in constant excitement on a stage and make an exhibition of himself? It seems to me, gentlemen, if you give him liberty . . . you deliberately send him into the world to exhibit himself as a cannibal, or you send him to poverty, to want, or to further crime.

Adams insisted that, in objecting to a possible pardon, he only had Packer's best interests at heart. "I have not been this man's enemy," he asserted. "I know I have saved his life twice, and I would fain save him from himself. . . . With nothing to look forward to, no friends, always to be held in abhorrence by his fellow men, I consider Packer worse punished by being granted his liberty than he was when a virtual life sentence was pronounced upon him."

Even so, Adams concluded his lengthy letter not with an expression of sympathy for the Man-Eater but with a dark threat of his own: "In conclusion, I beg to repeat my protest against the release of this man and will say that I shall hold the State of Colorado responsible, if by reason of such unwarranted release, harm shall befall me or mine."[2]

+ + +

A hearing on Packer's case was scheduled by the state board of pardons for early July. Shortly before the designated date, John R. Smith suffered an accident and, laid up in bed with his injuries, was unable to attend.

Informed that General Adams had filed a protest, Smith sent a letter to the board, assuring them that "any personal fear of General Adams" regarding Packer was "wholly without foundation." His client's prison record was one "of unvarying excellence and obedience," as attested by "many of the former wardens of the penitentiary."

Smith reminded the board of the opinion Dr. Blake had conveyed in his letter: that is, that "continual imprisonment, without any hope in the future relief from this most unusual sentence, the longest sentence ever imposed in Colorado, must end in the prisoner's death in a comparatively short period." Smith concluded with a plea that, should the board not see fit to grant an outright pardon, "at the least there should be a commutation of sentence to some definite number of years more proportionate to the statutory punishment of the offense of which he was convicted, and which holds out to him the hope of freedom in the not distant future."

It had been over twenty years since "this offense was committed, if at all," wrote Smith, and Packer had "been in confinement, in one form or another, for about fifteen years of that time." Smith continued, "A commutation to fifteen years would release him sometime in 1895 and would, I believe, cause the ends of justice in this case to have been more than satisfied."[3]

Smith's appeal fell on deaf ears. The following day, July 6, 1894, Packer's application for pardon was refused. Though no record exists of General Adams's reaction, it seems safe to assume that he breathed a sigh of relief, given his expressed concerns over his personal welfare should Packer be released.

+ + +

One year later, on Monday, August 19, 1895, Denver was the scene of a historic disaster. Sometime around midnight, the Gumry Hotel, located in the middle of the 1700 block of Lawrence Street, was destroyed in an explosion so massive that residents of the neighborhood initially believed that their city had been hit by a major earthquake. The force of the blast brought down the entire rear half of the five-story building, reducing it to an enormous heap of timber, brick, plaster, splintered furnishings, floorboards, and other debris that quickly burst into flames.

Firefighters rushing to the scene managed to rescue most of the guests trapped in front-facing rooms, though they struggled in vain to save others. While attempting to douse the conflagration at the rear of the building, firemen heard the agonized voice of a man crying out that he was burning and begging them to keep playing the water over the spot where he lay trapped. They eventually managed to reach the man, a contractor from Omaha named James Murphy, whose legs were pinned beneath a heavy beam. "After almost herculean effort," reported the *San Francisco Chronicle*, "with the dense smoke blinding the firemen's eyes, Murphy's left leg was released." At that moment, however, a sheet of flame erupted from the debris, driving the rescuers back. Murphy cried out in desperation, offering $1,000 to anyone who would free him and pleading with them to chop off his leg. A second later, the west wall of the building collapsed, burying him under tons of ruin.

"No words can portray the scene around the ruins," the *Chronicle* wrote. "Women and children, maddened by terrible suspense, hurried to and fro in anxious inquiry concerning loved ones that are missing. Strong men, hard at work amid the ruins, quaked at the sickening smell of roasting flesh and turned pallid countenance from the scene. Never before has such absolute wreckage and ruin devastated any portion of the state."[4]

Some of the recovered victims were disfigured beyond recognition. "A large amount of debris had fallen on it, mashing it flat," the *Denver Evening Post* reported, describing one of the first bodies removed from the ruins. "The head also was flat and the eyeballs laid out upon the cheek bones. The entrails protruded from several places and hung down like ropes from the temporary stretcher, and the stench that arose made many of the workmen ill."[5]

Though the former governor of Colorado, John L. Routt, opined that the hotel had been deliberately dynamited by enemies of its owner, Peter Gumry, the cause, as an investigation ultimately showed, was a poorly tended boiler. Primary blame was laid on the building's irresponsible young engineer, Hellmuth Loescher, who, on the night of the calamity, had reportedly gotten "drunk during his watch and neglected to keep sufficient water in the boiler, then flooded it with cold water, causing the explosion." A coroner's jury also fixed responsibility on the building's owner and manager, Peter Gumry, and his son-in-law Robert C. Greiner, blaming them for employing Loescher in the first place— "an engineer whose habits were dissipated and unreliable, and whose experience did not justify them in placing him in such a responsible position."[6]

While Loescher was arrested on charges of manslaughter and criminal negligence, Gumry and Greiner, as the *Evening Post* observed, had "passed beyond accountability to any human tribunal," both having been killed in the explosion. Altogether twenty-two people perished in what the nation's newspapers termed "one of the most awful disasters of the century."[7] A number of victims were so deeply buried beneath the tons of rubble that it took gangs of laborers several days to retrieve them. Among the last of the bodies to be recovered was that of the hotel's most eminent guest, who had been staying in Room 11 in the rear of the building, directly over the boiler: General Charles Adams.[8]

39.

THIRD CONFESSION

On Tuesday, August 20, 1895—while workmen continued to dig through the rubble for the remains of General Adams and the other still-missing victims of the Gumry disaster—James P. Daily walked out the front gate of the Cañon City penitentiary a free man.

An inveterate scam artist, Daily had been incarcerated since November 1893, when he'd received a two-year sentence for passing bad checks. With his con man's eye for a potential mark, he had quickly set his sights on Packer, who was squirreling away every penny he earned to bankroll his next bid for freedom. Portraying himself as a "man with much influence in the state, particularly with politicians having a pull" with the governor, Daily persuaded Packer to turn over $75 of the $125 he had managed to save, promising that, upon his release, he would use the money to get a petition for Packer's release into the hands of his "state house friends [who] would lay it before the governor."

Daily headed straight for Denver following his parole. After whoring, drinking, and gambling away the $75 within a couple of weeks, he wrote a letter to Packer, explaining that he had managed to gather 4,000 signatures on the petition. This number was not enough, however, but if Packer "would send on that other $50, 2,000 or 3,000 more signatures would be speedily added," at which point Daily's political connections would "turn their 'pull' loose in the state's executive."

The desperate Packer promptly forwarded the remainder "of his slowly earned hoard." That was the last he heard of Daily. When it gradually became clear to him that he been the victim of a "bunco game," he informed Warden John Cleghorn, who notified Denver chief of police Goulding. Daily was promptly tracked down and rearrested. By then, however, all of Packer's money was gone.[1]

+ + +

Two years passed before Packer made another bid for freedom. He did so at the urging of his devoted friend Duane Hatch, who paid a visit to Cañon City in July 1897 and was shocked by the physical condition of his former benefactor. "I could not keep the tears from my eyes when I saw Packer in the penitentiary," Hatch told a reporter following his trip. "He is weak and broken. The report that he bears ill feeling against any of the persons who were responsible for his conviction is false. He forgives them all."[2]

Intent on obtaining what the duplicitous Daily had failed to deliver—a petition on Packer's behalf signed by thousands of sympathizers—Hatch asked his friend to prepare a statement that could be circulated among potential supporters. Packer promptly complied, composing a lengthy handwritten document notably more literate than any of his earlier accounts—a testament to the long hours of reading and letter-writing he had put in during his years of incarceration. While sticking to the general outline of his now-familiar narrative, this letter—which came to be known as his third confession—differed in crucial respects from his previous statements, omitting certain potentially incriminating details and understating the extent of his cannibalism.

Addressing Hatch as "my kind friend," Packer begins by suggesting that the twenty-one-man expedition from Salt Lake City was doomed from the start. "Deficient in supplies for the entire journey," they had run out of food long before arriving at their destination. By the time they reached the Green River at the head of the Colorado, they had been subsisting on horse feed for nearly a week. "Thus early in our journey," writes Packer, "we were already suffering most terrible pangs of hunger."

They were saved from starvation by the sudden appearance of "Chief Ouray and a band of fifty Indians," who invited them to lodge at their camp until the mountains became passable. In about one week,

however, "a man by the name of Loutsenhizer and four others" started
for the Los Pinos Agency by foot. With "no other provisions beyond
what each man carried," they quickly ran out of food.

Refuting those witnesses at both his trials who claimed that, even in
winter, the land was teeming with game, Packer points to the desperate
plight of the Loutsenheizer party, who were soon "fainting" with hunger. Indeed—so Packer now claims—they were on the brink of resorting to cannibalism. With their provisions gone and no game to be found
in the snow-choked wilderness, "these five men concluded to cast lots
to see who should be food for the others." Only a fortuitous occurrence
saved them from this "tragical fate": "Just at this time a coyote was seen
which was immediately killed. . . . And as this party neared the cattle
camp where Gunnison now stands Loutsenhizer saw a cow fast in the
snow and he crawled up to her and shot her with his revolver."

Having established the perilous nature of the journey from Ouray's
camp to Los Pinos, Packer goes on to describe the terrible experience of
his own six-man party:

> After nine days our provisions were entirely exhausted. The
> snow being deep we were compelled to keep on top of the divide
> in order to travel at all. . . . Our matches had all been used and
> we were carrying our fire in an old coffee-pot. Three or four
> days after our provisions were all consumed we took our moc-
> casins which were made of rawhide and cooked them and of
> course ate them. Our suffering at this time was most intense—
> in fact the inexperienced cannot imagine it. . . . In places the
> snow had blown away from patches of wild-rose bushes and we
> were gathering buds from these bushes, stewing them and eat-
> ing them. On following these divides we soon gained the top of
> the Rocky Mountains and the snow being blown away from the
> top of the mountains and our feet encased in pieces of blankets
> we were able to travel along steadily. Now my friend, can you
> imagine our condition, on the top of the mountains with no liv-
> ing thing to kill for food, and not even any of those rose bushes?

"Starvation had fastened its deathly talons upon us and was slowly but most tortuously driving us into a state of imbecility," writes Packer, pulling out the rhetorical stops. Of them all, it was Shannon Wilson Bell—"the strongest and most able bodied man of our party"—who completely "succumbed to the power of mental derangement and was causing the party to become very much afraid of him."

Unable to determine from their vantage point "whether [they] had passed the Agency," they "came down off the mountain," descending "to the Lake Fork of the Gunnison River."

In describing what happened next—his lethal encounter with Bell—Packer makes several significant alterations to his previous versions. He makes no mention, for example, of grabbing Bell's hatchet and delivering the coup de grâce to his assailant's skull. Nor does he describe in any detail the savage wounds inflicted on the other four victims:

> On the morning [after coming to the lake] I ascended the mountain for the purpose of ascertaining if there were any visible signs of civilization on the opposite side. The snow being very deep it required the entire day to make this trip and return. As I neared the camp on my return . . . I saw no one but Bell. I spoke to him. He raised his head and there, with the look of a terrible maniac, his eyes glaring and burning fearfully, he grabbed a hatchet and started for me, whereupon I raised my Winchester and shot him. The report from my rifle did not arouse the camp. So I hastened to the camp-fire and found my comrades dead.

Most striking is his revised account of his cannibalism. In previous statements, he freely admitted to having dined on meat carved from the corpses of his dead companions for the entire sixty days of his ordeal. Now, however, he claims to remember only his initial sampling of human flesh, a mere taste that made him violently ill:

> In looking about I saw a piece of flesh on the fire which Bell had cut from Miller's leg. I took the flesh from the fire and lay it to one side. After which I covered the bodies of my dead

comrades. I remained here with them during the night. In the morning I moved about one thousand yards below, where there was a grove of pine trees. I distinctly remember of taking a piece of flesh and boiling it in a tin cup. I also know that I became sick and suffered a powerful emission.

The ensuing weeks passed in a nightmarish blur. "Can you imagine my situation?" Packer writes in anguished tones. "My comrades dead and I left alone, surrounded by the midnight horrors of starvation, as well as those of utter isolation? My body weak and my mind acted upon in such an awful manner that the greatest wonder is that I ever returned to a rational condition." Though conceding that he "must have eaten some of the flesh" during that time, he insists that he survived largely on stewed rosebuds—a fact he discovered with the coming of warm weather and the clearing of his mental faculties: "My mind was a total blank for a considerable period of time. When my mind returned, I found by my tracks that I had been visiting around the adjacent territory seeking rose-buds which I apparently found, for I noticed that by force of habit I had been stewing them in my tin cup."

His description of his journey from the lakeside camp to the Indian agency also differs dramatically from his earlier accounts. In his second confession, made to General Adams following his arrest in Wyoming, Packer told of roasting a chunk of "human meat" before setting out on his trek, packing it in a bag, and eating it "a little at a time" until he reached his destination. In his letter to Hatch, however, he presents a radically different picture, claiming that, when spring arrived, he happened to stumble upon the agency while wandering "around seeking rose-buds for food."

Packer ends his letter with a heart-tugging appeal that, in an age that wallowed in rank sentimentality, was clearly meant to wring a sympathetic tear from tenderhearted readers:

Now my kind friend, in conclusion permit me to say that I am today as ever before a member of the human family, although isolated and away from that which is dear to the heart of every man. Am I the villainous wretch which some have asserted me to be? No man can be more heartily sorry for the acts of 24 years ago than I. I am more a victim of circumstances than of atrocious designs. No human being living can say that in cold blood or evil intent I murdered my companions upon that awful occasion. What could be the object of my taking their life in a wanton manner? I bear no malice toward any living man, even though I may feel that I have been unjustly dealt with. . . .

In this the darkest hour of my earthly existence, I feel as I have long felt that I would have been far better off had my execution taken place years ago, and I might now be with those companions, whose ghosts I assure you do not haunt me. For as the soul has existence beyond this mortal life, each and every one of those unfortunate men know that I am innocent. As it is there is some unexplainable power which refrains my hand from freeing my soul. Hence all the brightness in the firmament of my earthly future is centered in the hope that I may eventually be given an opportunity of proving to the world that I am "less black than has been painted." And to all my kind friends, I can but reiterate that my heart today as before abounds with thankful gratitude for your many expressions of good will. I should like to be set at liberty under the banner of a pardon, but if that should not be deemed best I would gladly avail myself of the opportunity that a commute would give of showing that I came into existence under circumstances similar to that of others and that I still possess the desire to live and do right. O! My friend! Were it not for the flame of hope which forever burns within the human heart, life would certainly be beyond endurance.[3]

+ + +

On August 7, 1897, the *Rocky Mountain News* reprinted Packer's third confession in its entirety. "Pathetic Letter from the Saguache Man-eater, Imploring Commiseration of the Board of Pardons for a Crime Unparalleled in the History of Colorado," read the subhead. Public reaction was everything that Duane Hatch could have hoped for when

he passed the letter on to the paper. In the days and weeks that followed the publication of Packer's letter, Hatch gathered statements
from dozens of eminent citizens, including prison superintendent R.
E. Lults, former chief of police David J. Cook, and Justice of the Peace
Charles A. Chapman. All conveyed the identical sentiment: that Packer
(as Chapman wrote) had been "punished *more* than he deserved" and
"should be pardoned on the evidence given."[4]

In the meantime, Packer and his lawyer prepared a formal petition,
addressed to both the governor of Colorado and the board of pardons.
Submitted on September 22, it requested a pardon based on five consid-
erations: (1) that Packer was "innocent of the charge of manslaughter";
(2) that "his conviction was largely the result of prejudice aroused by
the feeling against him"; (3) that, having "been broken down by a long
imprisonment of upwards of three years before his trial," he "was mentally in such a condition that by his language and manner at his trial he
[unintentionally] prejudiced his cause"; (4) that the testimony against
him was "wholly circumstantial"; and (5) that his sentence was "wholly
unreasonable and excessive upon a conviction of manslaughter." The
petition concluded by requesting that, "if a full pardon is refused, the
sentence should be commuted to a term of years."[5]

+ + +

The passage of nearly a quarter century since the terrible events of 1874
had clearly softened the judgment of many of Packer's contemporaries.
With the advent of the twentieth century less than three years away,
Coloradans had begun to romanticize their harsh frontier past. Colored
by "nostalgia for the early days of prospecting, when men battled the
elements,"[6] Packer's deeds were increasingly viewed not as the atrocities
of a "human hyena" but as the justifiable acts of a man in the midst of
the most desperate circumstances.

"His victims and himself were starving to death," the *Denver Times*
editorialized. "That a man in such condition becomes temporarily
insane is well known to every physician—death by starvation or by
thirst being always preceded by mental aberration, and when a party of
two or more are dying of thirst or starvation, the natural instinct acting

on each is . . . to save life by cannibalism." For Packer to have been sentenced to "imprisonment for a term of years beyond the life of a generation" was "revolting to every instinct of humanity," the paper argued. "It is a cruel and unusual punishment. The circumstances of this case, as strange as a story of fiction, present the strongest possible appeal to the consideration of the Board of Pardons."[7]

Still, though the public mood was shifting in his favor, powerful voices continued to be raised against Packer's release. Both Judge Melville Gerry—now practicing law in Telluride—and former district attorney Herschel M. Hogg wrote letters to the board of pardons, asserting their belief that the killings of Bell, Miller, Swan, Noon, and Humphrey were "willful and premeditated murders" perpetrated "in cold blood" by Packer.[8]

One week after Packer's latest confession appeared in the *Rocky Mountain News*, a letter arrived at the office of Governor Alva Adams. Its author, Sam Phillips of Leavenworth, Kansas, was the father of young Harry Phillips, whose murder in 1882 was one of the many unsolved crimes attributed to Packer at the time of the latter's arrest. Having received a copy of the *Rocky Mountain News* from a Colorado acquaintance, Phillips, as he wrote, wanted both the governor and the state board of pardons to "know all the facts against" Packer.

In the fall of 1882, Phillips recounted, his son—"only 20 years old and known to be strictly temperate and reliable"—had left Billings, Montana, with $700 in cash after selling three hundred cattle. Before heading home, he decided to visit his uncle, F. M. Phillips, a "prominent stock man" in Laramie, Wyoming. Along the way, Harry met up with a stranger, and the two traveled together as far as Buffalo, Wyoming, where they camped a short distance from town on the banks of a stream called Clear Creek.

That evening, Harry and his companion went into town for something to eat. While there, the other man grew "rather boisterous and attracted much attention." Harry, according to witnesses, "appeared to be much put out" by his companion's behavior "and tried to quiet the fellow." Eventually, the pair returned to their camp.

Sometime around midnight, several people in town heard a pistol shot coming from the direction of Clear Creek. "The next morning,"

Phillips wrote, "these people found my son . . . with a bullet hole through his head showing he had been shot while asleep." Harry's pockets had been emptied and his pinto pony stolen. The young man was buried where his body had been found.

When Harry failed to arrive at his uncle's ranch, "an investigation was made." Two weeks later, Harry's father arrived in Buffalo. His son's corpse was exhumed and "identified . . . without trouble." Two lawmen—Sheriff Canton of Johnson County and Detective A. M. Sparhawk—immediately set out in search of the killer "and traced him as going towards the mining camp where Packer was caught." Brought to Cheyenne, Packer had his photograph taken. The picture was "sent to Buffalo, and all who saw [Harry] and his companion swore he was the same man.

"Pardon me for taking your time with this but the death of a good son urges a father to act," Phillips concluded. "I hope your board will consider this crime I accuse him of well before releasing him."[9]

How much weight the board of pardons gave to Phillips's letter is unknown. What is certain is that on December 3, 1897, Packer's petition for pardon was refused.[10]

+ + +

One month later, on January 1, 1898, the editor of the *Denver Times*—who had written so eloquently in support of a pardon—received a letter from Packer. Distinguished (like his letter to Hatch) by its fussily formal style and frequently mawkish tone, it was reprinted on the newspaper's front page beneath the headline "Touching Letter from the Man Whom the Pardon Board Refused to Free."

"Being stranded upon the shores of either misfortune or an adverse fatality is not sufficient to make me insensible to the kindnesses bestowed upon me from any and all sources," the letter begins. After offering his heartfelt thanks for "the kind efforts that have been made in [his] behalf," Packer insists that, while he "knows not why [his] application was rejected," he bears no "malice or ill-feeling toward the board":

I feel proud that my present mental condition is such that I can truthfully say that I entertain no grudge or ill-will toward any. For many years have I been confined in this "palace of sighs," and whatever I may have gained or lost thereby, I have at least learned to know myself. And while I had expected favorable action from the board, still, when the adverse and fatal news reached me I did not accept it in anger, scorn, or derision. But I think I displayed as much of the spirit of equanimity as it was possible for one in my situation to do.

Indulging in a rhetorical flight that gets tangled in a web of mixed metaphor, he declares that, from his extensive reading while in prison, he "finds that no man has always been free from a surrounding horizon that had every appearance of engulfing him in a flood of oblivion and of dark and bitter despair." He himself, however—so he assures his readers—has no intention of succumbing to despair. While "personally sorry that circumstances have not been favorable to me, yet I shall endure to the end, doing my best to be a man. I try not to surrender to the feeling of despondency."

As for his future, Packer holds completely self-contradictory views. On the one hand, he expresses the "hope that even yet, at some time far or near, the people will feel constrained to grant me the priceless boon of liberty." On the other, he flatly declares that "the adverse action of the state board of pardons convinces me that it would be futile to longer entertain any earthly hope of physical liberty.

"The flame of hope," he writes, "is completely extinguished."[11]

Part Four

LIBERATOR

40.

POLLY

Considering the prominence she enjoyed over the span of a colorful twenty-five-year career, certain basic facts about Leonel Ross Campbell are inexplicably hard to pin down. Some biographers claim that she was born in Kentucky, others in Mississippi.[1] All agree, however, that she was born in 1857 and raised in Southern gentility, the pampered daughter of a plantation owner.

Strong willed and rebellious from her earliest years, she was shipped off to a Saint Louis boarding school at the age of thirteen. If her parents hoped that institutional life would help tame their headstrong daughter, they were soon disabused. At fifteen—already a statuesque blond beauty—she donned a black velvet dress, scaled the wall of the school, and eloped with one George Anthony, the son of a Kansas railroad tycoon.

Within a week of their marriage, Nell (as she was called) found herself living in Mexico City, where her husband had a commission to oversee construction of the Mexican Central Railroad. Despite her relatively comfortable circumstances—she and George lived in a richly appointed private railroad car and were frequent guests at the palace of President Porfirio Díaz—Nell quickly tired of both Mexico and her spouse.

Two years after their wedding, she abandoned her husband and headed for New York City, where she managed to wangle a job at Pulitzer's *New York World* for a weekly salary of six dollars. In emulation of her journalistic role model, the pioneering woman journalist

Elizabeth Jane Cochrane, a.k.a. "Nellie Bly," she adopted the pen name Polly Pry, by which she would thereafter be known to the world.[2] Her early stories—particularly one about a suspicious fire at a Greek Orthodox church—so impressed editor John Cockerill that he made her the paper's Latin America correspondent and dispatched her to Panama, where early surveys for a proposed canal were in the works.

In 1892, Pry's family moved to Colorado, seeking a more salubrious climate for two of her brothers, who suffered from tuberculosis. Precisely how Pry herself came to relocate to Denver is unclear, though the usual (if unsubstantiated) story is that while traveling west by train for a family visit, she met fellow passenger Frederick Bonfils, co-owner, with Harry Tammen, of the *Denver Evening Post*.[3]

+ + +

Born in Baltimore in 1856, Harry Heye Tammen had been fending for himself since the age of eight, when—not wishing to be a burden on his newly widowed mother—he quit school for good and left home to make his own way in the world. After working for a time in a print shop, he took a job with an outfit that sold patented rubber doorknobs. Fed up with the life of a peddler—"a tough game" that he "didn't much care for"—he answered a newspaper ad for a bartender. First in Philadelphia, then in Chicago, he worked in a series of saloons, becoming so adept in the fine art of mixology that, by the time he was twenty, he was manning the bar of the famed Palmer House Hotel.[4]

Describing himself with characteristically charming bombast as "the best booze-juggler in the world," he was lured to Denver in 1880 by the manager of the recently opened Windsor, the city's most opulent hotel. It was during his time there that Tammen came up with the scheme that would lead to his first great success.

Since coming to Colorado, Tammen had begun to collect rocks as a hobby, buying unusual bits of ore and other mineral specimens from the miners who came in to drink. To display his growing collection, he had a cabinet built in the corner of the barroom. When tourists, eager to bring home a Rocky Mountain souvenir, began offering to purchase samples of his pyrite and feldspar and petrified wood, Tammen—an all-American go-getter with "a generous dash of Phineas T. Barnum" in him—was seized with an inspiration.[5]

Packaging assortments of stones in cigar boxes, he began to sell them for twenty-five cents apiece. The items proved so popular that he soon quit bartending and became a dealer in western curios, initially operating out of a cluttered shop on the ground floor of the Windsor Hotel. Besides his rock collections—now boxed in polished hardwood cases and priced at $2.95 for the deluxe set of forty-eight specimens—he sold everything from Pueblo Indian pottery to Zuni war clubs, collectible silver spoons to antelope-horn letter openers, scenic postcards to souvenir photo albums, mounted tarantulas to stuffed buffalo heads. He also did a booming mail-order business, offering a dizzying variety of western tchotchkes, like his horseshoe-shaped "Hoof Clock," "Pike's Peak Agate Paperweight," and gem-encrusted "Rocky Mountain Mineral Inkstand."[6]

Within a few years, Tammen's personal fortune was estimated at $150,000—close to four million in today's dollars. He lost everything, however, in the Panic of 1893, the country's worst financial crisis before the stock market crash of 1929. Never one to be discouraged by a small setback like bankruptcy, Tammen set his sights on a new enterprise: newspaper publishing. At the time, the owners of the *Denver Evening Post*, an eight-page daily with a meager circulation of just 4,000, were looking to unload their struggling little paper. The asking price was $12,500. Eager to purchase the paper but lacking the funds, Tammen cast about for a well-to-do partner. He soon found one in Frederick Gilmer Bonfils.

The diametrical opposite in both looks and temperament of the ebullient, roly-poly, frequently disheveled Tammen, Bonfils—taciturn, "leanly athletic," and a snappy dresser who "looked like a handsome gambler"—was born in eastern Missouri, son of a Corsican judge who claimed kinship with Napoléon Bonaparte. Before finding success in the newspaper business, he had a notably checkered career. Failing to graduate from West Point after three years at the military academy, he worked successively as a New York City bank clerk, an insurance salesman in his hometown of Troy, a mathematics teacher in Cañon

City, Colorado, a newspaper reporter back in Troy, and a clerk for the Missouri state legislature.[7]

He eventually struck it rich in a couple of highly dubious ventures, first as a land speculator in Oklahoma, then as the operator of a crooked lottery in Kansas City, Kansas. By the time his lottery scam was closed down by authorities, he had acquired a considerable fortune. It was then that he encountered the brash, fast-talking Tammen, who persuaded Bonfils—who was deeply skeptical at first—to partner in the acquisition of the *Evening Post*. "You've got money, I've got brains," Tammen declared, "and there's the bargain of a lifetime waiting for us in Denver."[8]

At the time they took it over, the *Evening Post* was losing $600 a week. Employing the sensationalizing tactics pioneered by Joseph Pulitzer and William Randolph Hearst, the new owners swiftly transformed the "piddling little paper" (in Tammen's words) into the city's most popular daily.[9]

With their showmen's grasp of the public's perennial taste for the lurid, they packed their front pages with stories of crime, scandal, and gossip, headlined in screaming banners printed in flaming red ink. "A dogfight on a Denver street is more important than a war in Europe" was Bonfils's credo, while Tammen instructed his editors to model their stories on crowd-pleasing entertainment: "You've seen a vaudeville show, haven't you? It's got every sort of act—laughs, tears, wonder, thrills, melodrama, tragedy, comedy, love and hate. That's what I want you to give our readers!"[10]

Billing itself as "The People's Champion," the *Post* also launched innumerable crusades against the "vested interests," running blistering attacks on "the community's largest utilities, most of its public officials ... its preachers, and almost everyone else in positions of power."[11] When local coal companies increased their prices, Bonfils and Tammen—declaring war on the "coal trust"—leased their own mine and began selling coal to the public at a steep discount.

Entering the coal business was only one of the myriad stunts pulled by the brazen pair. To boost circulation, they sponsored countless carnivalesque promotions, including "cross-country roller-skating contests, ladies' wrestling matches, high-wire acts over Denver's business district, outdoor concerts, kite-flying contests, competitions to name the new elephant in the city zoo, and hundreds of other events, an average of about one a week."[12]

Within a few years the *Post* had become the largest paper in the state. Bonfils and Tammen, on their way to being multimillionaires, moved their operation into a handsome new building on the corner of Sixteenth and Curtis Streets. The walls of their private office were painted the same flaming color as their now-notorious headlines. They referred to the office as "The Red Room." Others called it "The Bucket of Blood."[13]

+ + +

By the time Pry and her new acquaintance arrived in Denver, Bonfils had offered her a job. Equal parts sob sister, gossip columnist, and fearless muckraker, she quickly became one of the paper's most popular— and controversial—reporters. Mixing maudlin human interest stories, chatty observations on the social scene, and blistering attacks on the powers-that-be, she won a large and devoted following, while incurring the wrath of her many political targets. On any given day, readers of her column might be treated to the heartrending story of an orphan newsboy who sacrificed his life saving a baby from a building fire, an account of a sumptuous banquet attended by members of Denver's "smart set," or a scathing portrait of once-mighty politicians who, through their own mendacity and greed, had been "plunged into the fiery furnace of notoriety" and reduced to "mere burnt-out cinders."[14]

In the manner of her idol, Nellie Bly, she also established a reputation as a daring investigative reporter, exposing the appalling conditions in various public institutions. One of her earliest pieces for the *Post* was a lengthy article headlined "Polly Pry Tells of Some of the Horrors of Our State Insane Asylums." She followed this up with shocking accounts of mismanagement, corruption, and abuse at the Girls' Industrial School, the State Children's Home, and the Fort Lewis Indian School (where, as she discovered, girls as young as eight were subject to the sexual predations of male staff members).[15]

In May 1899, Polly embarked on a new crusade—an investigation into conditions at state penal institutions. Her first stop was Cañon City.

41.

THE PALACE OF SIGHS

She arrived shortly before noon on Saturday, May 13, via the Denver & Rio Grande Western Railroad—"The Scenic Line of the World," as it billed itself. Disembarking from her Pullman, she was met by Warden Hoyt, who greeted her warmly before leading her to his carriage. On the drive to his home, she was struck by the beautiful cream-white stone of the prison buildings. Hoyt pointed out the mountain in the near distance where the stone had been quarried. She could see a great gloomy cleft in the mountain: the entrance, Hoyt explained, to the Royal Gorge—"the Grand Canyon of the Arkansas River," from which the town had derived its name.[1]

Waiting to welcome her at the warden's residence was his twelve-year-old daughter, Ruth, and the family servant, Casey, "a good-looking darky," as Pry described him, "with smiling face and shining teeth," who relieved her of her carpetbag, brought her a glass of spring water, and assured her "that he would be at [her] order during [her] stay." It was all "very pleasant, charming, idyllic," she wrote—a stark contrast to the grim scenes she was about to observe.

Her initial tour of the prison lasted three hours. Hoyt led the way through the various buildings. Though much of the prison impressed her as immaculately clean, she found the kitchens so lacking in "sanitary plumbing" as to be "a menace to the health of the inmates." The bathhouses, barbershops, and soap factory were likewise in "wretched shape." She was also dismayed by the severe overcrowding: nearly six hundred inmates crammed into 450 tiny cells.

The sights she observed on that first afternoon filled her with melancholy: the "drawn white face" of the teenaged prisoner who regarded her with "despairing blue eyes"; the ceaseless pacing of the elderly convict who had gone "mad as a March hare" and now spent his days patrolling his cell "with meaningless gestures and vacant unseeing eyes"; the hollow look of the middle-aged inmate, convicted of a crime he swore he didn't commit, whose voice, when he spoke, "was like a dead thing—soulless and terrible." Some of the inmates glared at her with open hostility—"fierce glances that would have slain if they could." Her mere presence was a bitter reminder of the outside world from which they were exiled. As she passed by their cells, she could feel the resentment emanating from the "silent, striped-clad figures" within.

Walking past the prison bakery, she spotted a broad-shouldered man, standing with folded arms beside the enormous ovens. He wore a mustache and goatee, and his sooty black hair was arranged in what a later generation would call a comb-over: "parted low down on one side and brushed forward and then around in a curious circular way." His lips were curled in a cynical smile, and his eyes seemed to glitter with insolence. Instinctively, she felt "that those eyes had seen strange things in their time."

Seeing the number on his jacket, she asked Warden Hoyt, "Who is Convict 1389?"

"Alfred Packer," he said. "Would you like to talk to him?"

"Ah!" she exclaimed. "Is that the man? Yes, I want to hear his story. But not today. I am too tired."

+ + +

Pry was treated to a memorable meal at the warden's home that evening. She had, of course, been a guest at many fine dinners, though never one prepared by a convicted murderer—"an affable creature who killed a man but roasts a leg of lamb so perfectly that you forgive him," as Pry chirped. Their waiter—"irreproachable" in his manners—was a "grand larceny man," dapperly dressed in a white servant's jacket over his striped prisoner's shirt. Seated across from an open window, Pry could see the warden's lawn being tended by a pair of gardeners—both, as her host explained, notorious burglars.

Dinner conversation focused largely on Hoyt's penal philosophy, particularly his rejection of some of the more extreme forms of punishment employed by his predecessors. He was especially proud of having "abolished the use of dark cells": the practice of immuring inmates in lightless solitary cages for extended stretches and feeding them nothing but bread and water. Not only was the method inhumane, Hoyt explained as he sipped his after-dinner brandy, it was extremely inefficient.

"It took weeks to break some of the toughest men," he explained, "and some we could not break at all." Far more effective was a session on what he euphemistically called the "spanking machine"—the device known to inmates as "The Old Gray Mare," the specially constructed wooden sawhorse over which the victim was bent facedown and subjected to a prolonged flogging. Just recently, Hoyt boasted, "six men threw down their tools and swore they wouldn't work another minute. They were marched in to the spanking machine and in just half an hour they were all back at work."

Pry was deeply impressed by her host, "a big, whole-souled man with good, practical common sense," as she later described him. "If I am ever sent up to prison," she wrote, "I hope it will be to Cañon City, and while Mr. Hoyt is warden!"

+ + +

The next morning—Sunday, May 15—Pry visited the chapel, where, accompanied by an orchestra of three violins, a zither, a piano, and a cornet, a choir of twenty-two men guilty "of every crime under the sun" offered a stirring rendition of the old hymn "Room for Jesus":

Have you any room for Jesus,
He who bore your load of sin?
As He knocks and asks admission,
Sinner, will you let Him in?

Following the service, Warden Hoyt led her to his office, where she took a seat while he went off to fetch the inmate she was especially eager to interview. A short time later, Alfred Packer walked in.

Pry's initial impressions of him were decidedly mixed. On the one hand, she was impressed with his still-imposing physique. "He must, as a young man, have been magnificently built," she reported. "His form is straight, his great shoulders and broad back without the slightest droop." At the same time she was struck by his "absolutely repellent manner and perfect lack of magnetism." "His skin is a chalky, unpleasant white, and his goatee and mustache are a dead, listless black, his thin hair is the same sable hue, and his hand, which he offered me, slipped from mine like a lifeless thing," Pry wrote.

When he learned that Pry was a writer for the *Post*, Packer's lips curled into a "cynical sneer." In a voice "hard and bitter," he informed her that he had nothing to say. He was tired of being maligned and misquoted—of being interviewed by reporters who "came, asked for him, offered to help him, talked about what they would do, and then went away and wrote reams of slush. They never did him any good; in fact, the lies written of him had been of great harm—they prejudiced the people against him."

Assuring him that she had "neither the desire nor intention to misrepresent him," Pry insisted that she simply wanted to "hear the truth" from his own lips. Though Packer remained skeptical, his "burning desire to be believed in" proved "too strong for him. Once loosened, the words tumbled over themselves, the flood gates were down."

For the next hour, Pry was "inundated with a perfect torrent, first bitter denunciation of the world—the great world that had treated him so badly—then scathing rebuke of the members of the bar and other interested persons who had taken his money and made no effort to help him, furious scorn for his own family who had left him to fight his battles alone, and finally the tale of that awful journey which had ended in the tragedy which had brought him to this place without hope."

Though Packer was clearly "not a man of particular education, or in any way superior intellect," his recitation was so gripping that Pry was transfixed by it. By the end of it, she was firmly convinced that if she could make her readers "see the man as I saw him," they "would believe his story, as I do."

+ + +

Pry's account of her visit to the penitentiary—published under the headline "Polly Pry Serves a Brief Term at Cañon City" and occupying a full page and a half of the paper—appeared the following Sunday, May 21. Though a good portion of the article is given over to "the strange and pathetic sights she saw" (in the words of the subhead) along with Warden Hoyt's praiseworthy management of the "great penal institution," nearly half is devoted to the case of Alfred Packer.

To convey the horrors of Packer's ordeal, Pry—who had turned out the occasional potboiler for the New York City publishing firm Street & Smith during her years with the *World*—employs her most melodramatic style. Not long after leaving Ouray's camp, she writes, Packer and his companions found themselves in desperate straits, "their lips cracked and bleeding, their clothing in rags, and their eyes bloodshot and red from the glare":

> For days and days the wretched men had trailed along the frightful mountain passes, through deep gulches, past yawning chasms, and up almost inaccessible heights. The snow was everywhere. They waded to their armpits in the shifting mass. They walked on frozen places, fell through the icy crust and dragged each other out of unknown depths, and always, gnawing hunger tugged at their vitals, and bitter cold froze the marrow in their bones. One began to wander in his mind, and his eyes took a wild and wolfish glare. . . . They stumbled on until, weak, exhausted, starved and frozen, they came to a place where a grove of tall pines grew so close together that, underneath them, the ground was almost clear, and there they found fallen timber and made a great fire, and took their moccasins from their feet, cut them in strips, boiled and ate them, just to relieve for a little their awful hunger.[2]

To bring a sense of vivid immediacy to the next part of the tale, Pry abandons all pretense of journalistic objectivity, using all the novelistic tricks at her disposal to dramatize Packer's plight. Having volunteered to scale "the great peak that towered above them" to "see if there were any signs of the place they sought," Packer set out in the morning with "his feet wrapped in rags":

> This man—starved, emaciated, weak, his feet bleeding inside the frozen rags, his Winchester fastened to his back as he climbed painfully up and up and up that rocky height, clinging with hands and feet and lithe body, falling, sliding, exhausted with weakness, pausing to rest and again and again struggling on, never giving up, unconquerable, dogged, determined. And at last, the summit. He falls, and with heaving chest and bursting eyeballs, grovels on the rocks in his efforts to get his breath. And then he feels the falling flakes—it snows again, and below him is blotted out. Incredible injustice! He crouches close to the sheltering rocks. How cold it is. The wind has a thousand biting lashes and each one cuts through his rags and leaves its mark upon his quivering body. Hours he waits, but the snow still falls and rolling black clouds float down below him. He realizes hell. He knows the torture of the damned, and he repudiates God.

Then comes the terrifying climax of the tale, rendered, like the previous sections, in the overheated style of a lurid dime novel:

> He does not know how he got down. . . . It was late in the day when he approached the camp and saw a man bending over the fire. He called and the man at the fire dropped something from his hand, grabbed a hatchet and rushed at him. The light of reason had fled from the man's blazing eyes, and his lips curled back from his teeth as he gave vent to a frightful cry.
>
> He started to run, stumbled, fell, and, recovering himself, swung his Winchester up and fired. The man fell dead. He bent above him. It was Bell, poor fellow, gone completely mad! It was strange none of the other boys came. He gathered up his fallen

rifle and went on, and then he saw a sight which almost blinded him. Close to the fire lay two of the men, killed as they slept, their heads split open, and farther away, lying on his face, the third who had evidently tried to get away. And this one's clothing was torn, and a piece of flesh had been cut from his thigh.

He shivered and went back to the fire, where he crouched a long time and then he saw the piece of flesh the poor maniac had been roasting, and he grabbed it up and held it over the fire and took a bite of it. And then how sick he was. His empty stomach rejected the hideous offering, and he lay for hours sick unto death. . . . It was days before he could bring himself to try more of that meat, but finally he did eat the remainder of the cooked meat, and it gave him new strength. Then one morning, he went to where he had left Bell and dug down into the snow and with his knife opened the clothing and cut a piece out of the thigh and went back and cooked it, cutting it into tiny bits and boiling it. This he put in a bag, and then he ate, took up his gun, and started he knew not where.

+ + +

Pry's article had begun much like her pieces on the state insane asylum and the Girls' Industrial Home: as an inside look at a public institution whose workings were hidden from general view. It ended, however, on an unexpected note: not with an outraged call for reform but with a heartfelt plea for clemency. Two years earlier, Colorado—"out of her great heart," as Pry put it—had abolished the death penalty.[3] "How, then," she cried,

can she justify herself for the persecution and detention of this man who has suffered unbelievable hardships and expiated a thousand times over the crime of which he was accused and of which there is no proof? He was given forty years—think of it! For manslaughter—not for murder—he was never accused of murder—forty years! Is it possible that no member of the board of pardons in this great state, from the governor down, has the courage and humanity to investigate this case and try to right what looks like a monstrous wrong?

Polly Pry had traveled to Cañon City looking for an attention-grabbing story and had come away with a cause. And Alfred Packer had found a champion.

42.

CRUSADER

A few days after Pry's Sunday feature appeared, John Deeble, treasurer of Montrose County, sent a letter to the *Post*, taking strong objection to Pry's sympathetic portrayal of Packer. Suggesting that her article was little more than "sentimental gush," he reiterated the arguments made by the prosecution at Packer's first trial, comparing the Man-Eater to a "tiger from an African jungle" who, "ax in hand," had crept up on his peacefully sleeping companions and "almost severed their heads from their bodies." As for Packer's claim that he and the others had been half-mad from hunger, Deeble scoffed at the notion, describing the scene of the crime as a "lovely little park" that "abounded in game such as deer, antelope, rabbits, grouse, quail, etc." Deeble himself, so he claimed, had "lived for years and mined within half a mile from" the murder site. "My horse would feed outdoors all winter, and there was scarcely ever snow enough for sleighing," he wrote.[1]

Pry's response was swift and scathing. She reminded her readers that "for a week prior to the meeting with Chief Ouray," the twenty-one prospectors "had been compelled to subsist on horse feed," that Loutsenhizer's party had only avoided starvation because of their providential encounter with a coyote, and that Packer and his companions were reduced to eating their own moccasins. "Does Mr. Deeble think it likely that six men of nerve enough to undertake [such] a winter journey . . . would take the shoes from their feet and make a meal of them if there had been deer and quail and grouse and all those other luxuries he so glibly writes about within their reach?

"Mr. Deeble says there is no snow in Colorado mountains," she continued in her most withering tone, "that the winter breezes are gentle zephyrs, balmy and warm, and that he hardly ever saw enough snow to take a sleigh ride." The truth, as anyone who truly knew that part of the state, was radically different:

> I talked the other day with a gentleman who had been compelled to take a trip out into those same mountains this year in February, about the time of year those men were trying to make their way over those inhospitable heights, and he told me that the little town he visited was buried under the snow from a depth of from ten to fifteen feet, that they had been cut off from the outside world for weeks, and that their only mode of egress and ingress was by tunneling through the snow and getting about on snow shoes. . . . If Mr. Deeble is right and there were quantities of game, no snow, and those idyllic conditions really prevailed, how does it come that Loutsenhizer and his party testified to having discussed the advisability of drawing lots to see who should furnish food for the others? Does he suppose they talked of eating one another while grouse squatted on the ground waiting to be killed?[2]

+ + +

As Pry threw herself into her crusade, her defense of Packer grew increasingly impassioned. Whereas he had initially struck her as "cynical" and "repulsive," she now described him as a dauntless embodiment of American manhood—a soldier, scout, and wilderness guide who "did not know how to fear and had a constitution of iron." His perilous climb on the day before the murders was, in her telling, a feat of selfless and nearly superhuman courage:

> Can you conceive of anything more heartrending than the heroic ascent of that lonely mountain peak by that man of iron?

Can you not see him taking his farewell of that famished band, pulling the belt tighter around his empty stomach, shouldering the rifle and taking his solitary way toward the dread heights above him? For what? To see if he cannot, from that great altitude, locate a place of succor for the little band who are standing at the very threshold of death unless he can find a way to help them! . . . With shoeless feet, bleeding and painful, with ragged clothes through which the icy winds cut and stung, oppressed by the awful danger, famished, cold and half blinded, he struggled up the dizzy heights, animated with the desire to save not himself alone but his comrades.[3]

She freely acknowledged, as Packer had done, that he ate human flesh. "But what of it?" Pry cried. "What would you have done? What did Perry's men do? What have innumerable men done under like conditions?"[4]

"Personally I believe the man is innocent," she declared. "I believe that he has been most unjustly, most terribly punished for a frightful misfortune and not for a crime." Even if he were guilty, however, "his crime did not merit so relentless and barbarous a sentence." Just the previous day, a man, convicted of shooting his wife in a fit of rage, had been sentenced to three years in the penitentiary. "And Packer," Pry exclaimed in an incredulous tone, "after months of starvation, attacked by a madman, to save his own life, shoots him, and they give him forty years! And for twenty years he has walked his narrow cell and cried aloud at the cruelty of man and the injustice of God!"

She urged her readers to join in her crusade. "It is time for the enlightened people of this state to make a demand that justice be done for this, their unfortunate brother," she proclaimed. "Mr. Packer's attorneys are about to petition for a pardon for their client. I want to ask the men and women of this great state, who believe in right, in justice and humanity, to come to the front and help them obtain it. To either make a petition of their own, sign one of those that are going the rounds, send in their signatures to the *Post*, or write directly to his excellency, the governor of the state, urging executive clemency for this man."[5]

+ + +

Not everyone was moved by Pry's appeal. "It strikes me that Polly Pry is 'prying' into something that is none of her business when she monkeys with the Packer case," one reader wrote. Another, deploring "the indiscriminate paroling of murderers, thieves, rapists, and similar characters," opined that "the Man-Eater ought to stay right where he is."[6]

For the most part, however, the Denver public responded with expressions of support. Letters praising Pry's efforts poured into the *Post*. "I beg leave to offer you manifold heartfelt thanks for your valiant and noble defense of Alfred Packer. . . . Oh, keep on fighting for the outraged and downtrodden!" a gentleman named Otto Werner wrote. Another writer, one Harrison Ainsworth, offered his heartiest congratulations "on the brave fight your 'Polly Pry' is making for the liberty of Alfred Packer," while a man who identified himself only as "a Two-Years' Reader of the Post" expressed his desire "to shake Polly Pry's hand for the manner in which she has defended Packer." Even some Coloradans who believed that Packer was guilty as charged sent appreciative words. Alva Adams of Pueblo, for example, while admitting that she "never had any doubt as to the justice of the sentence," wrote to convey her good wishes to Pry. Adams declared, "I shall not be unhappy if you succeed in this work which does so much credit to your woman's heart."[7]

Pry was assisted by the ongoing efforts of the ever-devoted Duane Hatch, who set up a red barrel on the corner of Sixteenth and Larimer Streets where Denverites could deposit their letters endorsing Packer's release. Eventually more than three thousand letters of support were left in the "Packer barrel."

Speaking to a reporter following a three-day visit to Cañon City, Hatch expressed deep concern for his former benefactor. "Packer is in very bad shape," he said. "So many efforts have been made to secure a pardon for him that he has been alternately buoyed up by hope of freedom and then reduced to despair by failure to gain it. The nervous tension has worn him out. I don't expect he will live six months unless he is pardoned."[8]

In the meantime, Pry herself set about circulating a petition among the city's most prominent citizens. "We, the undersigned, believe that

Alfred Packer has been fully punished for whatever crime he may have committed," it read, "and his nineteen years' imprisonment entitle him either to a parole or a full pardon." Within weeks, she had collected the signatures of Mayor Henry V. Johnson, Chief of Police John F. Farley, Fire Chief W. E. Roberts, Postmaster John C. Twombly, former state treasurer H. A. Mulnix, County Commissioner Fred P. Watts, County Coroner R. P. Rollins, City Auditor Edward Keating, District Judge F. T. Johnson, Justice of the Peace A. H. Pickens, plus dozens of distinguished businessmen, bank presidents, attorneys, law enforcement officers, company managers, merchants, and more. "I do not believe that a stronger petition was ever presented to the chief executive of this state," Pry declared with some justification, "nor one which should command more respectful consideration."[9]

+ + +

Immediately following Hatch's visit in early July, Packer, newly energized with hope, sent a letter to the state board of pardons, formally renewing his application "for release from further imprisonment." It was accompanied by a strong letter of endorsement from Warden Hoyt:

> Alfred Packer, Prisoner No. 1389, has been an inmate of this institution for thirteen years, and, previous to coming here, was confined in the county jail at Gunnison for about three years. He was under my charge in 1887 and 1888, and I have known more or less of him ever since. During these years he has been an exemplary prisoner. I shall leave the enormity of his alleged crimes aside. I will not bring up the question whether he is guilty or not, nor shall I argue about the legality of his sentence. Of his sentence, however, I have always thought it was excessive. Public opinion had more or less to do with the trial of a prisoner. This man is now nearly sixty years of age, and sixteen of them have been spent behind prison walls. I believe that justice has been satisfied, and that Packer should be allowed to go out from here without delay.[10]

Serving as the secretary of the Colorado State Board of Charities and Corrections was a gentleman named C. L. Stonaker (who would become the subject of much local newspaper coverage himself when a convict named Sykes publicly accused him of demanding a $500 bribe in exchange for a pardon).[11] After receiving Packer's application, he proceeded to gather testimony from various individuals who might assist the board in making its decision. One of these was Professor Leslie R. Mutch.

A self-described "master in psychology, anthropology, phrenology, physiognomy, physiology and the laws of health," Mutch was a frequent contributor to such journals as the *Dietetic and Hygienic Gazette* and the *Character Builder*, where he promoted his pet theories on the relationship between the climate of a particular geographical region and the mental and moral faculties of its inhabitants.[12] Several years earlier, he had managed to make himself a highly public laughingstock. During a lecture tour that had brought him to Los Angeles, he decided to drum up publicity for himself by staging a dramatic display of his ostensible analytic powers. After badgering the sheriff for several days, he received permission to examine one of the prisoners.

The following afternoon, with various reporters in attendance, he spent several hours in the corridor of the county jail interviewing a young man introduced as James Sharp, recently charged with having sexually assaulted his neighbor's seven-year-old daughter. Afterward, Mutch confidently declared in a written statement that Sharp's "face and eye reveal an emotional type of mental and moral weakness. This points to insanity rather than to either semi-idiocy or criminality. He is not vicious by nature but instead is apparently at the point of nervous degeneracy." His analysis continued in this vein for several pages, concluding with the diagnosis that "James Sharp is undoubtedly of the curable class, owing to the fact that there are few anthropologic signs of inherited mania, his condition arising from the visionary and romantic nature of his mind, together from his weak physical state from excess."

There was only one problem with Mutch's analysis. As it turned out, the man he had interviewed was not the alleged child-rapist, James Sharp, but a local prankster, Bill Nye Jr., who had been enlisted by several deputies eager to expose the blustering "professor" as a charlatan.

"Made Mutch a Monkey," crowed the following day's *Los Angeles Herald*, which devoted much of its front page to describing the hoax. "The officers at the jail are jubilant over their practical joke," the article concluded, "and declare that now they can live in peace for a while as the professor is not likely to bother them again soon. This is certainly a case of too Mutch."[13]

However momentarily chagrined, Mutch continued to promote himself—and was widely accepted—as a scientific expert on the human mind. Residing in Denver at the time of Packer's new pardon application, he was called in to examine the Man-Eater. After spending "two hours carefully observing [Packer's] makeup from the standpoint of anthropology," Mutch delivered an oral report to Stonaker, who transcribed it for the board of pardons.

"With regard to the question of the commission of crime I deem him perfectly capable of committing any crime of which he is accused," said Mutch. "I found him to be in a very bitter state of mind against his fellow men, morbid, vindictive, revengeful in his mental state. Compared with other criminals who have come under my observation during ten years past, I count him to be one whose liberty would be a menace to anyone whose circumstances would make it to his interest to commit crime against him."

"Do you think it would be in the interest of the public to allow this man his liberty?" Stonaker asked.

"Most certainly not."

"Would you class him as a natural born murderer?"

"Yes, sir," said Mutch. "And by years of cultivation of a spirit of intense bitterness and a state of hate against all the world."[14]

+ + +

Former judge Gerry also weighed in with his opinion. Arranging to meet Stonaker in Denver, Gerry expressed his long-held belief that "Packer willfully led the men into the hills solely to murder them and that he secured over $2,000 in currency. He is by nature a murderer and will not be out three months before he will commit another murder or two to satisfy his lust for revenge on those who he thinks have injured him."[15]

+ + +

In August, with the meeting of the board of pardons two months away, Stonaker sent letters to Oliver Loutsenhizer and Preston Nutter, requesting from each a written "statement of your knowledge of Packer, when you first met him and what you know of his character and habits."

Loutsenhizer responded promptly and at considerable length, providing a detailed history of the ill-fated prospecting party, from their departure from Bingham Canyon, Utah, to the discovery of Packer's five murdered companions. The years had done nothing to soften his ill feelings toward Packer. His statement (dictated to a stenographer named Lucy Harrington and typed up on four oversized pages) portrays Packer as a bloodthirsty brute who, after slaughtering his five companions while they slept, "just laid around and gorged off of them" for the next several months.

"I don't think he is fit to be out among men," Loutsenhizer concluded. "He is in the best place right where he is. He is a bad man and a dangerous man."

In contrast to Loutsenhizer, Nutter replied with a brief handwritten note, expressing his long-held view of Packer as a man utterly "without character." Like Loutsenhizer, he was vehemently opposed to a pardon. "If any sane man could have seen the mutilated bodies of those men," he wrote, "and heard the different stories Packer told about the affair and then want to turn that kind of man loose on the community, I would say open all doors and turn all criminals out."

It was a forceful statement. Nutter, however, who had apparently mislaid Stonaker's request and forgotten about it for several months, did not get around to sending it until late December—too late to make a difference.[16]

+ + +

At its meeting on the evening of Saturday, October 14, 1899, the board of pardons considered the applications of a dozen prisoners, among them one Robert "Baldy Bob" Penton, whose conviction for the murder of a saloonkeeper in Goldfield, Colorado, was based entirely on what had since been shown to be the perjured testimony of a prostitute named Nellie Taylor. The board unanimously voted to grant Penton a pardon, deeming his conviction "the grossest miscarriage of justice recorded in Colorado for many years."

A fellow named J. W. Kelly, convicted of stealing a bicycle the previous December, had his two-year sentence commuted. A decision on another case was postponed: that of Alfred Russell, a young man who, lacking money to attend the circus which had just rolled into town, had held up a stranger and ended up shooting him to death.

Nine other prisoners were denied pardons: two other murderers, Louis Buchberger and Harley McCoy; two burglars, Thomas Reynolds and George Bronson; an embezzler named Joe Sampson; a forger, Fred Rice; a rapist, George Gordon; a "tough" named Dick Pickenstell, serving six years for assault to kill; and Alfred G. Packer, sentenced to forty years for manslaughter.[17]

43.

GOVERNOR THOMAS

Occupying the governor's office at this period was the Honorable Charles S. Thomas. Twenty-five years earlier, as a young attorney, Thomas had—indirectly and with no such intent—helped keep Alfred Packer from the gallows. As the defense lawyer for the notorious murderer Filomeno Gallotti in 1875, it was Thomas who—by having his client plead guilty—exposed the flaw in Colorado's murder statute that saved Gallotti's life. The subsequent passage of a revised statute—which, owing to the legislature's oversight, lacked a savings clause—had done the same for Packer.[1]

The board of pardons having refused Packer's petition, any hope for his release now rested with Thomas. "The chief executive of this great state is said to be a man of ice by his detractors," wrote Polly Pry. "If it is not true, here is his opportunity. Let him investigate this case, and if he finds it as I have told it, let him do justice to this man whose sufferings and whose wrongs should touch a heart of stone."[2]

Rallying to Pry's cause, various groups lent their prestige to the fight for Packer's freedom. Members of the Denver Typographical Union; Local Union Number 79 of the Brotherhood of Painters, Decorators and Paperhangers of America; and other labor organizations passed unanimous resolutions, urging Thomas "to mercifully pardon [Packer], that he may know, though friendless, that Coloradans have hearts." Recognizing Packer, a veteran of the Union army, as a comrade, members of the James H. Platt Post, Number 99, Grand Army of the Republic, wrote:

> whereas the keystones of our existence are fraternity, charity & loyalty . . . we petition the governor to show mercy to this comrade by exercising the parole law to him. We plead his services to this country & the testimony of the Warden to his good character as a special reason for this mercy. Charity, which is love, covereth a multitude of sins, and we acknowledge his great crime as defined and punished by law. We claim the higher & noble interpretation of the law, which is mercy and ask that this man be given a parole. If we all had justice "who would 'scape whipping"; but if we all had mercy we should be more patient.[3]

Scores of individuals also wrote to Thomas. While some insisted that "it would be a travesty of justice to set Packer free," the majority called for mercy. Several drew Thomas's attention to an argument that none of Packer's defense lawyers had ever seen fit to raise: the issue of diminished responsibility. Describing the "awful operation of starvation on the human mind," for example, a gentleman named Otto Werner argued that Packer, a "famishing imbecile, frenzied with the thought of food, was an irresponsible madman when he committed the deed. Can such a one commit any act of violence under the irresistible power of this gaunt and ghastly monster that ought not to be excused by an intelligent and advanced public opinion?" The Western Slope pioneer John Lawrence, who had undertaken his own investigation of the case, concluded that, combined with Packer's epileptic "fits," his "suffering in the cold and then starving . . . may have brought on insanity."[4]

+ + +

Taking up Pry's challenge to "investigate this case," Thomas made an overnight visit to Cañon City to interview Packer, who did not make a favorable impression. The governor also corresponded with Sheriff Doc Shores, who sent him copies of the letters Packer had written to his sister, Melissa Fought, while in Shores's custody. Thomas later described them as "the foulest compositions that I ever read, filled with all sorts of threats against [his family] in the event he regained his liberty." So vile were the letters, according to Thomas, that they "were sufficient to justify a refusal of pardon even if he had any claim for consideration."[5]

On October 21—a week after the board of pardons met—Thomas received a visit from Otto Mears. By then, Mears was such a prominent figure in Colorado politics that, a few years later, his stained glass portrait would be permanently installed in the senate chamber of the state capitol building. As the Republican Party's most influential power broker, "he was able to claim that no governor or senator could be elected without his support."[6]

At Thomas's request, Mears provided a lengthy account of his first-hand knowledge of the Packer case. Mears would later insist that, in making this statement, he "never said aught that could in any way bias [the governor's] mind against the man."[7] It was a flagrantly disingenuous claim, since Mears was emphatic that Packer had deliberately led his five companions into the mountains to murder and rob them, that his entire story of having killed Bell in self-defense was "absurd," and that Chief Ouray himself—"whose good repute is proverbial on the Colorado frontier"—had "no doubt of Packer's guilt."[8]

A month and a half later, on Saturday, December 9, Governor Thomas released a statement to the press, announcing his decision in the Packer case:

> I have given it continued and earnest attention and have investigated as far as possible all the facts and circumstances surrounding the offense of which the prisoner claims he is not guilty. The story told by Packer in his statement to the board of pardons is not, in my opinion, the true one. It contained many elements of improbability, some of which are preposterous. It is not consistent with his conduct from the day he reached the agency up to the time it was made. I am firmly convinced that he murdered and robbed his companions and that the penalty he is now suffering is a milder one than the circumstances justify. So believing, I cannot consent to grant this application and thereby relieve the prisoner from the

consequences of the most horrible and atrocious crime ever committed in the state.[9]

With the governor's refusal to grant him executive clemency, Packer, the *Post* reported, had "at last given up all hope."[10]

44.

UNDER FIRE

Thomas's decision may have snuffed out whatever remained of Packer's fighting spirit—"the smoldering fire in his black eyes has at last died out," reported the *Post*[1]—but it had the opposite effect on Polly Pry. Aflame with indignation, she fired off a pair of blistering attacks within a matter of days.

The first was directed at Otto Mears—"The Man Whose Insane Fear Has Kept Alfred Packer behind Bars for Seventeen Years," as the headline read. Deriding Mears as a "little old man with a shrewd face and shifty eye . . . who never gets the worst of a bargain"—language that smacked of anti-Semitic stereotyping—Pry accused him of exerting his political clout to ensure that Packer remained permanently incarcerated. Though seventeen years had passed since Packer's trial—and though Packer himself had repeatedly expressed his regret at his courtroom outbursts—Mears, so Pry claimed, lived in a constant state of terror:

> He remembers the terrible figure that stood in that court and, with blazing eyes and passion-choked voice, flung at him a threat so terrible that it drove the blood to his head and left him trembling with the icy horror of pure physical fear. . . . The days have run to months and the months into years, but the man who was afraid does not forget.

When Mears learned that Governor Thomas was considering a pardon, he caught the next train from Washington, DC—where he was overseeing construction of the Chesapeake Beach Railway—and persuaded his "devoted friend" to refuse Packer's appeal. Pry concluded her tirade with a reference to the stained glass portrait of Mears planned for the state senate chamber: "The governor wants to see Otto's picture hung in the Capitol building. It should be done, and under the picture they should print the word: COWARD!"[2]

Five days later, she took aim directly at Thomas. Proclaiming that, despite the craven manipulations of Otto Mears, the Packer case was not yet closed, Pry published a list of every prisoner who had received a pardon, parole, or commutation of sentence from "tender-hearted Governor Thomas." Among these were no fewer than nine men guilty of the most "hideous, revolting, atrocious" crime imaginable: the sexual violation of "young girls and little children." These wretches included nineteen-year-old John Lippe of Boulder who, along with a friend, "got hold of a little girl of twelve years of age, took her to a secluded place," and, after savagely assaulting her, "left her, half dead, to lie upon the ground." Sentenced to eighteen years in prison in April 1898, Lippe was granted a parole in October 1899. "One year!" cried Pry. "Mothers and fathers, what do you think of this?"

Even more horrifying was the case of William Bloodsworth and his adult son John, who "were arrested for crimes committed upon the person of the little 8-year-old stepdaughter of William." The judge who tried these "inhuman fiends" declared that "in the whole of his career he had never known a more shocking case, nor one where the criminals were entitled to less sympathy." After having served only eight years of their twenty-year sentence, however, both were paroled by Governor Thomas.

In contrast to these creatures there was Alfred Packer, who, in the course of Pry's campaign, had evolved from a victim of injustice into an authentic American hero:

a man who has lived a wonderful life, a life full of danger and hardship and great privation; a man who has feared nothing on earth, whose courage is absolute, unquestioned; a man who has

given seven years of his life to this country, who has been soldier and scout and guide, when to be either meant to take your
life in your hand and bravely face the grim destroyer almost
every hour of your days; a man who earned a pension as a scout
in that wonderful campaign where Custer and his immortal
band met a heroic death and filled a nation's heart with tears.

In words ringing with scorn, Pry concluded with a final blast at
Thomas:

The tender conscience of your great and good chief executive
balks at a case like Packer's—a case where a man in the throes of
starvation kills a maniac in self-defense. Nothing can convince
him that such a crime can be sufficiently punished. Seventeen
years in the penitentiary—it is nothing. For so frightful a crime
he should lie in his narrow cot until he rots. But for two brutes
who ravish a child they are bound in honor and decency to
protect and cherish—for these men the icy heart of your great
governor doth drip tears of pity! Citizens of Colorado, what do
you think of it?[3]

+ + +

Pry herself came under attack for these articles. In a letter to the *Denver
Times*, D. A. Bradley of Lake City, speaking for the entire community,
applauded Governor Thomas's decision, while accusing Pry (with
some justification) of having swallowed Packer's version of events in its
entirety without checking it against the official court records of the case.

"Why is it that the sympathies of such misguided people as Polly
are always extended to the criminals instead of the people who have
suffered at the hands of these murderous villains?" wrote Bradley. "I was
an old time San Juaner, and believe I am in a better position to know
the facts than is your sickly sentimental correspondent who comes here
many years after the crime was committed and presumes to know more
about the case than anybody else. . . . Polly Pry is frantically searching
for justice. Yes, so are those brutally murdered men's lonely skeletons

and grinning skulls calling for justice these many years. Shall the dead be forgotten?"

Bradley's sentiments were echoed by another Hinsdale County resident, Sally B. Cross, who fumed, "What does Polly Pry know about Packer's innocence? She wasn't even in Colorado at the time Packer killed the five men. . . . There is not a man, woman, or child in Hinsdale County who believes Packer innocent."

If Pry was so intent on righting an injustice, Cross continued, she should "take up the defense of one of her own sex," who was sentenced to prison "for a much lesser crime." A worthy candidate, Cross suggested, was Jessie Landers, a young woman from Lake City who, in a fit of insane jealousy, had attempted to shoot her "recreant lover," Frank McDonald, at the Crystal Palace dance hall in June 1897 and killed a bystander named Louis Estep instead.

Cross concluded by quoting one of the surviving jurymen from Packer's first trial, Jack Henderson: "Yes sir, Packer was guilty. And I tell you he should have been hung instead of being sent to the penitentiary."[4]

+ + +

Bradley and Cross lashed out at Pry in the first week of the new century, January 1900. Up until that point, the efforts to free Packer had generated purely verbal attacks: potshots fired back and forth in the form of insults and vituperation.

On January 13, however, in a bizarre turn of events, real bullets began to fly.

45.

PLUG HAT

Sometime in late December, Alfred Packer received a letter from a man who expressed his heartfelt sympathies and assured him that, with the right legal representation, he could still win his freedom. The man's name was Charles M. Fegen-Bush.

There were, of course, things about himself that Fegen-Bush didn't reveal in the letter: namely, that he himself had spent time behind bars in the past several years. In 1897, he had been arrested in Denver for a swindle in which he mailed official-looking letters to several hundred individuals, promising them free expensive pocket watches. All they had to do was send $2.50 for shipping. A sucker who fell for this scam received a neatly wrapped box containing—as the *New York Times* reported—"a toy watch worth a fraction of a cent, nicely packed in salt."[1]

Fegen-Bush was arrested again in October 1900—just a few months before writing to Packer—this time in Chicago for selling $10,000 worth of stock certificates in a nonexistent gold mine. Jumping bail, he headed back to Colorado, where he promptly got in touch with Packer.

Though he intimated that he was motivated purely by a sense of outrage over Governor Thomas's decision, Fegen-Bush had, of course, ulterior motives. As he later explained, he planned to open a cigar store in Denver and believed he could ensure a steady flow of customers by putting the infamous Man-Eater behind the sales counter. If that didn't pan out, he thought he might start a dime museum and make Packer the star attraction.[2]

In his letter to Packer, Fegen-Bush went on to say that among his acquaintances was William W. Anderson, "one of the greatest lawyers in Colorado," who would surely be willing to take on the case.[3] Packer wrote back, expressing his gratitude. He then sent a letter to his unflaggingly loyal friend, Duane Hatch, informing him of this latest development.

No sooner had Hatch received Packer's letter than he called on Anderson, who kept an office in the Cooper Building on Seventeenth and Curtis Streets. Nicknamed "Plug Hat" after the black silk topper he sported, Anderson explained that, because Packer's alleged crime had been committed on an Indian reservation, the territorial court that had tried him had no jurisdiction over the case. It might therefore be possible to secure Packer's release on a writ of habeas corpus.[4]

Hatch, who had been in regular contact with Polly Pry, immediately informed her of his conversation with Anderson. Pry paid her own visit to the lawyer, and—having satisfied herself that "there was something in" his idea—she set up a meeting between him and her bosses.

The following day, Wednesday, January 10, Anderson, wearing his trademark headgear, showed up at the *Post* building, where he was ushered into the Red Room, Bonfils and Tammen's garishly painted private office. After hearing Anderson out, Bonfils, despite some reservations, agreed to support the attempt and offered to cover all legal expenses. First, however, he wanted the paper's attorney, I. N. Stevens, to review the plan. Anderson agreed to return the next morning at ten o'clock to confer with Stevens.

He never showed up. After waiting all Thursday morning with growing impatience, Bonfils telephoned Anderson's office and was told by his secretary that her employer was "out of the city." In answer to Bonfils's further inquiries, she revealed that Anderson had left the previous evening on the 7:15 train to Cañon City.[5]

A phone call to Warden Hoyt confirmed that Anderson had shown up at the penitentiary first thing that morning and asked to see Packer. Knowing that the lawyer associated with the likes of the notorious "bunco artist" Fegen-Bush, Bonfils was immediately suspicious. He shared his concerns with Polly Pry, who agreed to take a trip to Cañon City and investigate the matter.

She left the next day on the afternoon train, arriving at the penitentiary at nine on Friday evening. By then, Packer was asleep. Roused by a guard, he threw on his clothes and was escorted to Hoyt's office, where Pry was waiting.

His story made Pry seethe. "Packer informed me," she later testified, "that Anderson said that he had come on my recommendation, that he was a director of the *Post*, and that the newspaper endorsed him in every way." After years of feeling hoodwinked by lawyers who took his money and failed to deliver on their promises, Packer was leery of the fast-talking Plug Hat. Believing, however, that Anderson had been sent there by Pry and her employers, "he had agreed to everything and signed whatever he was asked to," including a power of attorney that Anderson had prepared in advance. At Anderson's request, Packer also gave him an advance of twenty-five dollars.

Keeping her anger in check, Pry explained to Packer that, far from having the backing of the *Post*, "we did not consider Mr. Anderson competent to manage such a case alone, and that after his misrepresentations, we naturally could have nothing to do with him." She then had Packer sign a letter to Anderson that said, "My employment of you and the authority to represent me in any matter are hereby fully and completely revoked." With the letter tucked away in her handbag, she caught a train at two in the morning and was back in Denver a few minutes past seven thirty on Saturday.[6]

Proceeding directly to the *Post* building, she gave Bonfils a report of her meeting with Packer, showed him the letter, and asked if she "should take it to Anderson or send it by messenger." Bonfils advised her to deliver it by hand. Telephoning Anderson, Pry arranged to see him at his office at ten o'clock that morning.

Arriving at the appointed time, she knocked on his door and was summoned inside. From behind his desk Anderson greeted her pleasantly and invited her to be seated.

"I have a letter for you," said Pry, handing it across the desk.

After reading it over twice, Anderson looked up at her. "In what way," he asked, "have I misrepresented the facts?"

"Are you a director of the *Post*?"

"I never said that I was," he replied.

"Did you go to the penitentiary on the recommendation of the *Post*?"

"I never said that I did."

"But I have just come from the penitentiary," said Pry, "and both Warden Hoyt and Packer said you did."

A flush of anger rising to his cheeks, Anderson explained that, immediately after leaving his meeting with Bonfils and Tammen on Wednesday, he had been called to Cañon City on an urgent business matter and, while there, "thought he might as well see Packer." He had "done nothing underhanded," he insisted, and would like to speak to Bonfils and Tammen in person and straighten things out.

"They are in the office now," said Pry.

Anderson said that he had some pressing business to attend to but would be there at eleven thirty.

Back in the Red Room, Pry told Bonfils that Anderson emphatically denied any wrongdoing. He was eager to clear the air, she said, and intended to come by in an hour.

"I don't see what the point is," said Bonfils. "As far as I'm concerned, the *Post* will have nothing more to do with the man. But all right."

+ + +

Anderson, wearing a light overcoat and his black silk high hat, arrived promptly at eleven thirty and found Bonfils and Polly waiting in the Red Room. Bonfils, who was working on an account book, motioned him to a chair beneath a window. A moment later, Tammen entered and seated himself behind his desk, facing the lawyer.

"Anderson," said Tammen without preliminaries, "I want to have a plain talk with you."

"That's just the kind of talk I like," the lawyer replied.

Tammen leaned forward, elbows on his desktop. "Anderson, you came here the other day and talked a lot about professional honor. You agreed to do certain things with us. You made an agreement to come here Thursday morning. Instead, you left, and in an hour's time you were on your way to Cañon City, where you buncoed a poor old man out of $25. You are a cheapskate and a liar, and I don't want anything more to do with you."

Anderson leapt to his feet. "I don't allow any man to talk to me that way!" he shouted.

What happened next became a matter of heated dispute. Bonfils would later testify that he saw Anderson "move his right hand toward his overcoat pocket," as though reaching for a weapon. Anderson claimed that he was the victim of an unprovoked attack. Whatever the truth of the matter, both agreed that, at that moment, Bonfils jumped up and delivered several blows to the lawyer's face.

"Gentlemen, gentlemen!" cried Pry, rising to her feet. "This won't do! Stop it!"

Snatching up his hat, which had fallen to the floor, Anderson started for the door. "Get out, you damned faker," Tammen shouted after him, "and don't ever come back."

With Bonfils following close behind, Anderson left the Red Room and headed down the hallway for the exit. He later claimed that, just as he reached the outer door, Bonfils kicked him in the seat of his pants. "That was one kick too many," Anderson would testify, "and I let him have it."

Bonfils told a different story. He acknowledged delivering a parting shot to Anderson—not a kick in the pants, however, but a vow to have the lawyer disbarred for cheating Packer out of his money. With that, Anderson "put his right hand down in his overcoat pocket, drew a gun, and fired point blank at me."

The bullet entered the left side of his chest close to the nipple. Bonfils, believing he had been shot through the heart, staggered back into the Red Room and leaned his hands against his desk. An instant later, Anderson appeared in the doorway, took aim with his .38-caliber Smith & Wesson revolver, and shot Bonfils in the back, the bullet passing through his right shoulder blade and lodging in his chest.

As Pry let out a scream, Anderson turned his gun on Tammen, who had rushed to his partner's side. Seeing the pistol aimed at him, Tammen threw up his left arm protectively just as Anderson pulled the trigger. The bullet entered his forearm, smashing the bone. As Tammen went down, Anderson fired again, hitting him in the left shoulder.

Pry, who had been standing by the closed window, desperately trying to pull it open and shout for help, now threw herself between Anderson and Tammen, who lay moaning on the floor. Kneeling beside him and shielding him with her body, she raised her hands and cried, "For God's sake, Anderson, don't shoot again!" Anderson stood above her, aiming his pistol over her shoulder, as if trying to get another shot off at Tammen. Finally, he lowered the gun and stepped over to the telephone on Bonfils's desk.

"I'll call the police," he said.

"Not the police, a doctor," said Pry. "You've done murder enough!"

By then, a crowd of *Post* employees had gathered at the door. Still clutching his smoking revolver, Anderson coolly walked toward them.

"Don't let that man go!" Pry cried. "He's shot Bonfils and Tammen."

No one made a move to stop him. They stepped aside and let him go. He proceeded directly to the office of a doctor named Blair, who tended to the facial injuries inflicted by Bonfils, applying a large piece of adhesive bandage—court plaster, as it was known—to the nasty cut on Anderson's right cheek and three smaller patches to the scratches on the left side of his face.

By then, the police had learned of the shooting. It didn't take them long to locate Anderson, who was still in Blair's office. Taken into custody, Plug Hat was led to the city jail. "He walked jauntily across the street," the *Denver Times* reported, "smiling and evidently rather proud of himself." Word of the shooting had already spread through the city, and as Anderson approached the jail, he was surrounded by a swarm of people: not a lynch mob but a crowd of admirers who were eager to shake his hand.[7]

46.

WITNESS FOR THE PROSECUTION

Tammen, with his arm in a cast, was back at the office within days. Though physicians initially feared for Bonfils's life, he, too, recovered and returned to work three weeks after the shooting. Not everyone celebrated their survival. The editors' two-fisted, no-holds-barred style had earned them a host of enemies. The *Post*, railed one journalistic rival, was a disgrace to the profession—a "blackmailing, blackguarding, nauseous sheet which stinks to high heaven and which is the shame of newspapermen the world over." A prominent Denver attorney, referred to in the local press as a good friend of Bonfils, proclaimed that he would "rather be a friend of the rat that breeds bubonic plague in the foul miasmas of the sewer." It was even reported that, while Anderson was in jail, he received a bouquet from Governor Thomas, accompanied by a letter that read, "I congratulate you upon your intention, but must condemn your poor aim."[1]

Anderson's trial on a charge of assault with intent to commit murder was scheduled to commence on April 23, 1900. A week before opening day, the newspapers broke a story that sent a thrill of excitement through the city. The *Rocky Mountain News* trumpeted in a page-one headline, "Convict Packer Will Come to Denver!"[2]

For the Denver public, Packer's appearance as a witness for the prosecution meant a chance to get a firsthand look not only at the infamous Man-Eater but at a figure who (as one paper put it) "belongs to the pioneer period" of the West, an era already entering into the realm of myth. In stories speculating on how he would experience his first taste of freedom since his arrest in 1883, Packer was portrayed as a kind of Rip Van Winkle, who, after being cut off from the outside world for nearly twenty years, would be overwhelmed by the marvels of the modern world. By his own admission, he had never even spoken on a telephone and had no idea how to use one.

"Think of it!" the *Post* exclaimed. "What child is not now familiar with the telephone and its uses? Why the world, marveling at countless new things, has almost forgotten that it once never had a telephone! What will Packer say in the presence of the X-ray, the wireless telegraph instrument, the linotype, the pneumatic mail tube, the many, many wonders that are familiar to the least of us today?"[3]

Escorted by Deputy Sheriff Perry Clay of Arapahoe County, Packer—dressed in a black frock coat, light-colored trousers, and a black slouch hat, all newly purchased for the occasion—boarded Denver & Rio Grande train number 4 at 7:15 p.m. on Saturday, April 21. Occupying the third seat from the front end of the smoking car, he gazed through the window until darkness hid the passing landscape from view. For the most part, he sat silently, though at one point Deputy Clay, seated directly behind him, heard him remark in a wondering tone: "The world moves, doesn't it?"

Arriving in Denver at 1:10 a.m., he was taken directly to the county jail and placed in the remote second-floor "condemned cell," unused since the abolition of the death penalty in Colorado. He immediately fell asleep. When he awoke early Sunday morning, the jail was already besieged by curiosity seekers, hoping for a glimpse of "Packer the Cannibal." Warden Sidney McDermott, however, refused to allow inside anyone not authorized by Packer, who agreed to see only a handful of visitors, including his faithful friend Duane Hatch and a young man named George Packer, who presented himself—falsely—as a distant relation.

Later that morning, Warden McDermott took Packer on a brief carriage ride through City Park, around Capitol Hill, and down through the business section. In the seventeen years since he'd last been there, Denver had undergone a dizzying transformation—"from a half-grown city with horse cars and miserable streets," as Packer remarked, "to a thriving metropolis." Back in his cell, he declared that "the trip through the city was one of the great events of his life."[4]

Though the Anderson trial featured dramatic testimony by all of the principals, particularly Polly Pry and Frederick Bonfils, Packer was the star attraction. He was the first to take the stand on day two, Tuesday, April 24. A great crowd had assembled in front of the courthouse early that morning. When the courtroom doors were opened at 9:45, they rushed inside, men and women alike, "jamming and pushing like a herd of sheep."[5] Within minutes, every seat in the spectator section was occupied, and the rear of the courtroom was crammed with standees. When Packer was called a few minutes later, "a hushed chorus of happy little 'Ohs!' arose quiveringly from the audience," who strained forward for a good look at the celebrity cannibal.

What they saw was a slender man of medium height, dressed in a black worsted suit with a sack coat, a stiff white collar, and a plain black bow tie. His coal-black hair, worn "tolerably long," was so devoid of gray that he was rumored to have "made liberal use of dye." His long drooping mustache and slightly scraggly goatee were "of the same somber hue."

Still intent on eliciting as much public sympathy for Packer as possible, the *Post* described him as "much faded," with stooped shoulders, a "hollow and sunken" chest, and a ghastly jailhouse pallor. Rival papers, on the other hand, portrayed him as surprisingly fit. At fifty-eight years old, wrote the *Denver Times*, Packer "would not be taken for a man above 40 years of age. His prison life seems to have preserved rather than aged him."[6]

His manner on the stand was "a study in simplicity. He was as ingenuous as a child." Speaking somewhat nervously at first, he gradually became more assured, corroborating in every detail the testimony of Pry and Bonfils. By the time he was finished, he had so impressed the courtroom with his unassuming candor that, in the view of one observer, it was impossible to conceive of him as a criminal, let alone a cold-blooded killer. "That such a man is a murderer at heart is so preposterous a notion that none so poor in perspicacity, none so weak in intuition, and none so hard in sentiment as not to know at the first glance that here is a misjudged and persecuted man."[7]

Before returning to Cañon City, Packer was treated to a day in Denver. Had he been given a guided tour of the Emerald City of Oz, he couldn't have been more dazzled by the sights. Accompanied by Warden McDermott, he rode a trolley and was awestruck by "the invisible power that propels the juggernaut." An ascent in an elevator made him so nervous that he held his breath all the way up to the fourth floor. His first spin in an automobile left him with a strikingly astute idea of a future in which machines traveled through the air. If his prison term lasted another seventeen years, he remarked, he "fully expected to have a drive in the sky" when he got out.[8]

Everywhere he went, people greeted him warmly, shaking his hand and wishing him success in his efforts to win his freedom. Women flocked to him in such numbers that one regional paper, the *Silverton Standard*, joked that the "Man-Eater" would soon be known as the "Lady Killer."[9]

Before boarding the Rio Grande train back to Cañon City on Saturday, April 28, Packer spoke to reporters at the criminal court building. "I feel now that I really have friends," he said. "Before I came I did not think so. But I have received nothing but kindness during my visit to Denver. All the men I have met have been like brothers to me. And the ladies have been so kind to me. I want to thank everyone. I will never forget them and their kindness to a poor old man, who thought he had no friends left."[10]

+ + +

As for Plug Hat Anderson—owing partly to the public's decidedly mixed feelings about his targets, he would get away with near murder. After his trial resulted in a hung jury, he was tried again with the same result. A third trial, in late October 1901, ended with his acquittal.[11]

47.

FREE AT LAST

During his brief stay in Denver, Packer made such a favorable impression on the public that, in the weeks following his return to the penitentiary, Governor Thomas was once again besieged with petitioners, urging that he reconsider his opinion and issue a pardon or parole. Some continued to argue that Packer should never have been convicted in the first place. "I fully believe he should have been cleared at his first trial," wrote a physician named H. K. Braisted. "That he ever misled his party for the purposes of robbery is too preposterous for consideration. He did no more under distressing circumstances than any person would do. In starvation, the animal nature will assert itself, and the strongest and fittest to survive will do so."[1]

Others, while conceding his guilt, urged Packer's release on the basis of Christian charity. Packer "has been sufficiently punished and should be shown mercy in his old age," wrote H. E. Garman, secretary-treasurer of the Allied Printing Trades Council. "He is old and broken down and penniless and cannot live much longer," said R. J. Unger, president of the Press Assistants' Union Number 14. "We therefore appeal to you to grant Alfred Packer a pardon and instill in the hearts of thousands of good men and women the feeling that he is not to be denied mercy by this great state." Speaking for a local ministerial alliance, the Reverend D. N. Beach sent a particularly fervent plea:

In the name of humanity, we ask you to extend the parole system in the case of Alfred Packer. We raise no question as to his crime or conviction, but prayerfully submit to your heart, as a man, that after some nineteen years of servitude, and in consideration of his age and weakening physique, you can conscientiously extend mercy to him in the form of a parole. That he sinned we believe, and that he has suffered for his sin we believe. Therefore meet our plea, which is founded in mercy. . . . Our plea is solely for mercy, and in no sense do we seek to move you on any other ground. Mercy, which in the spiritual life is Christ-like, will be most noble in your human capacity in this case.

Like the Reverend Beach, a number of citizens stressed that freeing Packer would redound to Thomas's credit. "There will never come a time again when you can, by one act, place so many laurels upon your own head and wreathe for yourself a crown that will be immemorial as the present time affords," one Denverite declared. Joseph Pendery, an attorney who had known Thomas for many years, wrote to say that paroling Packer was a "righteous cause" that would "reflect well" upon "my good old friend Charley."[2]

Such was the outpouring of public support that friends of Packer were already anticipating his release. Among them was the proprietor of the Scholtz Drug Store, who began selling souvenir photographs of Packer for twenty-five cents each, the proceeds going into a fund "to aid him in beginning life over again when he has gained his freedom."[3]

On Tuesday, May 8, the *Post* published yet another extensive list of local luminaries, beginning with Mayor Henry V. Johnson, who favored Packer's release. Above it was an engraving of Governor Thomas, seated at his desk, pen poised over a document that awaited his signature. The caption read, "Will He Do It?"[4]

The answer came eight months later. On January 7, 1901—one day before the inauguration of his successor, James B. Orman—Charles S. Thomas, in his last official act as governor, granted Alfred Packer a parole. His decision, he explained in his decree, was based primarily on the prisoner's "advanced age" and "precarious" health, the prison physician having certified that Packer suffered from both Bright's disease (a now-outmoded term for nephritis) and hydrocele (a swelling of the scrotum). There was one condition attached to the parole: that Packer could not leave the state.

For the most part, Coloradans hailed the decision. Even the *Grand Junction Evening Sun*, which had been bitterly opposed to Packer's release, took a lighthearted view of the matter. "Alfred Packer has been given a conditional parole, the condition probably being that he would not eat any more of the sovereign people of Colorado," quipped the editor. "Now that he is approaching his end and has lost most of his teeth, it is probably safe to let him out."[5]

+ + +

Polly Pry was gracious in victory, immediately composing a lengthy editorial, thanking Thomas for doing the "humane thing . . . an act which should win for him the admiration and good will of every man and woman in the state, and one of which he can well feel proud." Her highest praise, however, was reserved for herself and her publishers. "Many efforts were made to get Packer a pardon, but without avail," she reminded her readers. "Then the *Post* took up the case, and for a year and a half has spared neither expense nor effort to secure his release." She applauded the heroic resolve of her bosses, Bonfils and Tammen, who "so nearly lost their lives one year ago, but believing absolutely in the justice of their cause . . . have never faltered in their determination to secure the release of the man they believe to have been more than sufficiently punished. The dawn of the twentieth century has seen their efforts crowned with success."[6]

Below Pry's article, the *Post* ran a mawkish bit of verse titled "Free at Last," ostensibly about Packer, though really a shamelessly self-congratulatory paean to the newspaper itself and the "angel" responsible for his release:

Swing it back! Yes, gently swing it!
    Open wide the iron door!
Let him breathe the air of heaven

Till his soul thrills to the core.

See, he's coming! Yes, he's coming!
    Stand aside and let him by!
Note the heaving of his bosom,
    Note the startled glance of eye!

"Is it true what you are saying?
    Will they let me go away?
Tell me if I am a free man—
    Don't deceive me! Don't, I pray!

"Life to me has been a burden—
    Oh how bitter was the bowl!
And you say that he has signed it?
    That I'm going on parole?

"For a lifetime I have suffered!
    Suffered all the pangs of death!
In the last despairing moments
    Bursts a light upon my path!

"Oh, my friend and benefactor,
    You have raised me to the light.
Led me from the stygian darkness
    Into freedom's glorious light!

Tell the *Post* I'll ever bless it;
    Tell my loyal friends for me
That an angel came and found me,
    Swung the door and set me free!"[7]

It was Pry herself who delivered the news to Packer, taking the
8:00 p.m. train to Cañon City and arriving after midnight on Tuesday,
January 8.

"You're not fooling me? It—it's true?" Packer stammered when she told him of Thomas's act.

"Yes, it's true," she said. "The governor signed the papers today. Tomorrow you will have your parole, and within a day or two you'll be free to come to Denver."

"I had given it up," Packer said in a tremulous voice. "I thought that I would die within these wretched walls." Reaching out to clutch Pry's hands, he began to pour out his thanks to her and the *Post*.

"Not now," she said. "When you are free, you can do that."

Before being led back to his cell, Packer promised to come see her as soon as he arrived in Denver. Then, "big tears in his widely dilated eyes," he bid good night to the woman he would forever after refer to as his "liberator."[8]

48.

THE OLD SCOUT

Dressed in a new suit and hat, purchased only that morning, and clutching a small grip containing his meager possessions, Packer—"the most noted convict in America," as the papers labeled him[1]—arrived at the Union Station in Denver at six in the evening on Thursday, January 10. In his pocket was $400 in cash, the savings he had accumulated over eighteen years from his prison work and the sale of his handicrafts.

His first stop was the *Denver Post* building, where he offered fervent thanks to Frederick Bonfils, Harry Tammen, and especially his great benefactor, Polly Pry. That same evening, the paper would carry Pry's final impassioned plea on his behalf, urging "the good people of Denver to let Packer forget the unholy events of the past which had earned him such epithets as 'man-eater,' 'human hyena,' and 'ghoul.'" In a particularly astute observation, she asserted that the morbid fascination exerted by Packer's case revealed a dark truth about human psychology in general:

It is true—as true as the immutable laws of God—that there is within us all a double nature—that the best as well as the worst of us harbors a 'Hyde' of whom we are afraid and before whom we tremble. And a story like this, a story of a man who after suffering incredible hardships and frightful misery came to that point where the ravenous beast within him could no longer be denied—well, a story like this throws a light on spots in our own nature which we do not care to see.[2]

Taking leave of Pry, Packer checked into the Midlands Hotel, where he would lodge during his extended stay in Denver. The following morning, he was visited by various well-wishers, including the man who had worked so tirelessly for his release, Duane Hatch. Suffering from advanced tuberculosis—or consumption, as it was called at the time—Hatch, his body ravaged by the disease, looked older at forty-two than his sixty-nine-year-old friend. But his face glowed with pleasure as Packer pumped his hand and showered him with thanks.

Several reporters also arrived that morning. "It all seems like a dream," Packer told them. "I can hardly realize that I am at liberty." He had spent so much of his adult life behind bars that he worried about adjusting to the outside world. "When I came out of the penitentiary yesterday morning," he said, "a feeling came over me of such uncertainty that, for a few moments, I was tempted to ask Warden Hoyt to let me back in." Though he had "conquered the feeling and come on to Denver," he "hoped nothing would happen to make me regret leaving prison."

Asked about his plans, he explained that he would remain in Denver until the spring, then "take up the work where I left off. In the old days, I followed mining altogether, and that is the only occupation I am familiar with. When the season opens and the ice clears out of the gulches and the sun melts the snow on the hills, I expect to go prospecting again."[3]

Over the next few days, Packer visited the theater and saw a production whose shocking immodesty left him "thoroughly disgusted" and attended a prizefight between the "California Negro" Rufe Turner and "German pugilist" Otto Sleloff that induced a similar response.

"When two honest men have a dispute and can't settle it without bad blood," he told a reporter after the bout, "let them haul off their coats and go at each other like men. That kind of fighting is manly and inspires respect, but this fighting like two goaded bulls is degrading."

"You're just not used to the modern world," the newspaperman replied. "You haven't seen anything for so long that you really don't know what is going on in the world. People's ideas have changed."

"I suppose they have," said Packer. "But on those questions, I can't change my views. Such things seem to me foolish. Of course I don't know anything about this city life. It is all strange to me, and the sooner I go back into the mountains, the quicker I'll be happy."[4]

+ + +

True to his word, Packer left the city as soon as spring arrived, moving to the ranch of an acquaintance named Ed Connelly in Deer Creek Canyon, about twenty miles west of Littleton.[5] When the weather allowed, he made his way into the mountains and did some prospecting, without any notable results. Once a month, he traveled to Denver to collect his pension and pay a visit to Duane Hatch, whose health was declining rapidly.

On Thursday, February 6, 1902, Hatch—the man who "Aided Packer in His Dark Hour," as the headlines read—died at home at the age of forty-three, with his wife, Millie (née Shipperson), and his two teenaged children, Lola and Duane Jr., at his bedside. Packer, looking less sickly than he had upon his parole a year earlier but clearly stricken with grief, served as a pallbearer when his friend was laid to rest in Riverside Cemetery three days later. Following the funeral, Packer, fighting back tears, spoke to reporters. "It is all over now," he said in a broken voice. "There is very little left for me in this world." Then, as if suddenly abashed at such self-pity, he brightened up a bit and said, "But I have my freedom, thank God—and thank Duane, too, and several other true friends. I cannot complain."[6]

Not long after Hatch's death, Packer moved to the town of Sheridan, where he built a little frame shack and spent his days raising chickens and rabbits and tending to his half-acre vegetable garden. Now in his sixties, the former "fiend" was portrayed in the press as a "kindly old man," well liked by his neighbors, who vouched for his "quiet and steady" character. As one of the last of a rapidly passing breed, he was seen as a living link to Colorado's proud frontier past. On his weekly trips into town to stock up on supplies, children would flock to his side. Packer would pass out handfuls of penny candy and regale them with "brave tales of pioneers, Indian battles, and encounters with grizzly bears." The "gentle old man," one paper reported "was the 'Pied Piper' to the youngsters who followed him in droves each Saturday afternoon to thrill to his stories and munch his candy."[7]

In 1905, Packer moved back to Deer Creek Canyon, close to the ranch of his old friend and prospecting partner Ed Connelly. Early in the summer of 1906, the Connelly family took a long-planned trip to Salt Lake City, leaving Packer as temporary caretaker in their absence.

Early one morning in July, a neighbor of the Connellys, a state game warden named Charles Cash, was riding past the Connellys' place when he spotted a body lying in the front yard. Leaping down from his horse, he ran over and found Alfred Packer lying unconscious in the grass. Wrestling Packer's limp body onto his horse, Cash brought him to the log cabin of his widowed mother-in-law, S. A. Van Alstine. For the next few days, Packer lay unconscious in the cabin's only bed, his body convulsed by such terrible seizures that it seemed impossible that anyone could survive them. Under Van Alstine's ministrations, however, Packer made some improvement. Assisted by her daughter, Mrs. Cash, the good woman would care for Packer at her home for the next ten months.

During that time, he would continue to suffer seizures that "were terrible spectacles to behold. Packer's screams and cries filled the air, accompanied by violent contortions of his body and limbs. When the seizures passed, deep sleep followed only to strengthen Packer for another onslaught. In his delirium he relived many times the days of his black horror." During one twenty-four-hour stretch in the fall of 1906, Packer had fifteen such "fits."[8]

By then, news of Packer's dire condition had spread throughout the state. "Alfred Packer, Old Scout, Is Dying," the *Post* reported in December. On the first of that month, two acquaintances of Packer's, Charles Hanford and G. W. Eller of Englewood, traveled to Deer Creek Canyon to see him. Like other witnesses to his epileptic seizures, they were rattled by both the frequency and howling violence of these episodes.

"In the grasp of these convulsions," Eller reported afterward, "he cries out that wild animals and reptiles are attacking him. His face at these times wears an expression of great fear, and the glassy, staring eyes seem to see again the awful sights they gazed upon thirty-three years ago in the snowbound mountains.

"The old man is sinking rapidly," Eller concluded. "His death may occur at any moment."[9]

+ + +

Despite such predictions, Packer endured for another four months. By early April, however, he knew he was nearing the end. Asking Van Alstine for a pen and paper, he managed to scrawl a final appeal, this one to the current chief executive of the state, Governor Henry A. Buchtel:

> I am dying and I am innocent of the crime. I wish to meet my maker without a shadow hanging over me, and so I ask that I be given an unconditional pardon for the crime of which I am convicted. I have asked nothing in the past, but I want to die clear in the opinion of my fellowmen.

Buchtel never sent a reply, forwarding the letter instead to the state board of pardons. No action was ever taken. By the time the board received the letter, Packer was dead.[10]

He died at ten minutes before seven o'clock on Wednesday evening, April 23, 1907, with Van Alstine, her daughter, and her son-in-law at his bedside. The following day, he was buried on a little knoll in the Littleton Cemetery. Because of his military service, the local post of the Grand Army of the Republic buried him with full GAR rites. Later, a simple stone would mark his grave:

ALFRED PACKER
Co. F
16 U. S. INF.[11]

+ + +

Interviewed about Packer's final moments, Van Alstine told report-ers that he had made no deathbed confession: "He always said that he was innocent. It seemed to trouble him in some sort of a way that men thought him guilty still. That seemed to be a greater hardship to him than his long imprisonment. He thought it hard that after fighting as a Union soldier and being a scout and guide in the army, he should be thought capable of the things they charged against him."

Here, her voice broke slightly and she took a moment to get hold of herself. "He was a very gentle, poor old man," she said at length, "and we got to love him."[12]

49.

LEGEND

In delivering his florid sentence at the climax of Packer's first trial in 1874, Judge Melville B. Gerry had solemnly proclaimed, "While society cannot forgive, it will forget. As the days come and go and the years of our pilgrimage roll by, the memory of you and your crime will fade from the minds of men." Whatever his merits as a jurist, Gerry clearly wasn't much of a prophet.

Within a few years of Packer's death, the Man-Eater had already evolved into a creature of folklore and myth. In its Sunday edition of March 12, 1911, the *Rocky Mountain News* ran a long story headlined "The Beckoning Spirit of Dead Man's Gulch." "Does the Spirit of Packer the Man-Eater Haunt Colorado Mountains?" the story asked.

Accompanied by a spooky illustration of a menacing Packer riding a hollow-eyed steed, the article described a "wraith-like cloud" that had settled over the collective grave of the five butchered prospectors on Cannibal Plateau. Though acknowledging that the "phantom mist" might be a simple meteorological phenomenon, the story—which was syndicated nationwide—suggested a supernatural alternative: that "the spectre-like cloud hovering like a soul in distress above the graves of those five prospectors . . . is the unhappy wraith of Alfred Packer seeking relief as the winds moan through the pine trees and the quaking aspens shake their trembling leaves in the moonlight."[1]

+ + +

Until the mid-1920s, the burial spot atop Cannibal Plateau ostensibly haunted by Packer's restless ghost was marked only with a flimsy wooden fence. In the summer of 1926, deciding that the five murdered prospectors deserved better than an anonymous, unkempt grave, the members of the Ladies' Union Aid Society of Lake City embarked on a mission to improve the site. After replacing the half-fallen wood rails with an enclosure of white-painted stone, they contacted Michael B. Burke, a Denver mining magnate and frequent visitor to Lake City, who agreed to donate a memorial to the five "Packer victims."

"Recognition of their sacrifice should have been accorded many years ago," Burke explained in a press statement. "I honor them as the earliest venturesome prospectors penetrating that wild country which in later years has produced so many millions in Colorado wealth."[2]

On the morning of August 1, 1928, the bronze "Pioneer Memorial Tablet," affixed to a boulder quarried from the hills overlooking the grave, was unveiled in a solemn ceremony. The inscription read:

THIS TABLET ERECTED
IN MEMORY OF

ISRAEL SWAN
GEORGE NOON
FRANK MILLER
JAMES HUMPHREY
WILSON BELL

WHO WERE MURDERED ON THIS SPOT
EARLY IN THE YEAR 1874
WHILE PIONEERING
THE MINERAL RESOURCES
OF THE SAN JUAN COUNTRY

The dedication service, which commenced with the singing of "My Country, 'Tis of Thee" and concluded with "a magnificent fish fry with all the trimmings," was deemed a resounding success.[3]

+ + +

Twelve years later, another, far weirder service took place, this one at Packer's grave in the Littleton Cemetery. The event—an absolution ritual inspired by "the Hebrew Scapegoat ceremony"—was the brain-child of Frank Hamilton Rice, founder and self-anointed bishop of the Liberal Church of America Inc. A former streetcar conductor, parole officer, and door-to-door salesman, Rice was a master of wacky public-ity stunts. At the funerals of his parishioners, he would use an adding machine to "count up their sins." Brides and grooms joined in holy mat-rimony by Rice were never in danger of violating their sacred wedding vows since he did not have them exchange any. In what were described as "the shortest marriage services on record," he simply waved his hands over a couple and declared them married. In 1935, he ran for mayor of Denver on a platform consisting entirely of his objection to a proposed $150 city licensing fee on fortune-tellers.[4]

For all his Barnumesque tendencies, however, Rice was a genuine "champion of the down-trodden . . . one of the greatest social workers Denver ever had," in the estimation of one biographer. "His church was always in the slum area. He was a friend of every down-and-outer. Any bum on Skid Row could be assured of a meal and a bed in his church. A barber chair was part of his church equipment." His "crack-pot publicity stunts" were his way of drawing attention to his work and reminding the public "that he could use money to care for the needy" in the grim days of the Depression.[5]

On Sunday afternoon, September 27, 1940, Rice and six of his fol-lowers filed into the Littleton Cemetery, accompanied by a nanny goat named Angelica, loaned for the occasion by a local sculptor, Arnold Rönnebeck. One of the six participants—meant to represent Packer's sin-shrouded spirit—was garbed in a black robe, reportedly borrowed without permission from a Denver church. The other five, representing the ghosts of his murdered comrades, wore white hoods and sheets, lead-ing onlookers to believe they were witnessing a gathering of Klansmen.

After Packer's black robe was laid on Angelica's back, a bit of goat's milk was placed on his tombstone. Bishop Rice then solemnly intoned his official statement of absolution:

O kind and merciful Father, who looketh down upon this scene knowing full well that we are met here today to transact Holy Business which probably should have been transacted many a year ago, give us thy blessing.

Here in the cemetery of Littleton, Colorado, lies whatever remains of the body of one Alfred Packer. Since no man knows where his soul may be, this spot will do as well as any other for the observance of this Holy and Divine Ritual.

And we beseech thee, O Heavenly Father, to spread the ample mantle of thine incredible goodness over the departed souls of the five men who were eaten by Alfred Packer, so that it might never be said that Your compassion favored those whose major sins brought to them a surpassing amount of attention.

By way of showing that Packer's supposed sin of cannibalism was actually approved by the Bible, Rice concluded by citing "the comforting words spake by Jehovah, who frequently did entreat his chosen people to kill and eat one another":

In Leviticus, 26th chapter, 29th verse, the Bible sayeth, "Ye shall eat the flesh of your sons, and the flesh of your daughters shall ye eat." And again in Deuteronomy, 28th chapter, 53rd to 57th verses, doth it say, "And thou shalt eat the fruit of thine own body, the flesh of thy sons and daughters." Again in Jeremiah and in Ezekiel doth the One God proclaim his espousal of cannibalism. Therefore, Alfred Packer, we won't hold that against you.

The ceremony over, Angelica—seemingly oblivious of the burden of sin she now bore—was returned to her owner. The borrowed black robe was also returned "after Rice reluctantly had it dry-cleaned at the insistence of the church."[6]

+ + +

In the way of all legends, misconceptions about Packer have continued to flourish. Throughout the years, supposedly authentic accounts of his life have perpetuated various myths—that his real name was "Alferd," that he was "the only man ever convicted of cannibalism in the United States," that he decimated the Democratic population of Hinsdale County. By a considerable measure, the most egregious of these biographies is one composed by a former miner named N. E. Gruyot, who claimed to have been personally acquainted with Packer—a highly dubious assertion given the breathtaking inaccuracies in his work, beginning with its title, "The Story of Joseph Packer, The Colorado Cannibal."

In Gruyot's bizarre telling, "Joseph" Packer was "born in the city of Boston in 1840 and at an early age was taken to the Sandwich Islands by his father, a missionary, Cotton Mather Packer. There he remained until the age of twenty, when the missionary died." Gruyot speculates that it was Packer's early experiences in the South Seas that accounted for his singular personality, which "combined the pure, unselfish qualities of the missionary and the savage and predatory rapacity of the Pacific Ocean cannibal."

Following the death of his father, declares Gruyot in the same authoritative tone, Joseph Packer returned to his birthplace, Boston, where "he became a student at Harvard College in Cambridge Massachusetts and graduated about the year 1866" with a law degree. "It is a curious thing," Gruyot marvels, "that Packer selected as the subject of his thesis while at Harvard the French revolutionist and terrorist of 1789, Robespierre, who was also a lawyer and . . . the most sincere and gigantic murderer of modern times." Even stranger, exclaims Gruyot, is the fact that "a scrutiny of Packer's picture shows a startling resemblance between him and Robespierre." For all the similarities between the two men, however, there was a major difference: "It is not recorded of Robespierre that he devoured any of his victims."

Continuing with his lunatic narrative, Gruyot writes that, after briefly practicing law in Boston, Packer was seized with an "irresistible impulse" that caused him to "abandon his profession" and head out to the Colorado Territory, where he soon joined up with "six companions" and embarked on a prospecting trip. "It was the first time in the history of mining," observes Gruyot with his usual crackpot self-assurance, "that any party of miners had ever taken or permitted a lawyer to accompany them on a prospecting expedition."

The party "had six burros and ample supplies of all kinds," writes Gruyot. "For about two months, Packer and his companions prospected and located a number of mining claims." Dispensing with anything resembling a documented fact, Gruyot asserts that, "on the tenth of October, 1872," while the party was "crossing a high mesa at an altitude of 13,432 feet, now known as Cannibal Plateau," they became lost in a blizzard. Soon afterward, while the men huddled in a camp, their burros "wandered off one by one in search of water," taking all the food with them.

One night about five days after the burros disappeared, Packer was roused from his slumbers by a "whispered conversation" among his companions, who were "contemplating, in defiance of all law and dignified modes of procedure, to put him to death and were engaged in a controversy over the mode of his assassination and who should perpetrate the deed." Packer's "blood turned to ice" when he "gathered that they planned to consume his body in lieu of the subsistence lost to the party through the desertion of their burros."

Pretending to sleep, Packer "rose before dawn. First securing the weapons of the conspirators," he "proceeded without unnecessary violence to defend his own life, something which primitive law and statutes have defended as justified." Precisely how Packer managed to slay his six sleeping companions "without unnecessary violence" Gruyot does not bother to explain.

In the spring, Packer emerged from the wilderness, presenting "a well nourished and robust appearance." When questioned about the fate of his six companions, he "said that he had wandered away from the rest of the party and wintered in balmy Gunnison City," a story quickly refuted by a Gunnison resident. An expedition launched to search for the missing men quickly turned up "a frightful bit of evidence"—human bones "in a wood rat's hole." Arrested and tried for the murder of his six companions, Packer was convicted and tried by Judge Gerry, whose sentence Gruyot quotes with his usual blithe indifference to fact:

Joe Packer, stand up and take your medicine. This court has had many noted criminals before the bar, but you are the most monopolistic rascal that it has been my pleasure to sentence. At a time when the San Juan needed additional population and strong men to assist us in subduing the wilderness and develop our great mines of gold, silver, lead, and copper, and we further needed every Democratic voter that we had, you Joseph Packer, had to kill and eat six of our most esteemed citizens. For this offense against the franchise and for further reasons that I cannot sentence you to be hung, I now consign you, Packer, to the State Pen of Colorado for a period of forty years and be damned to you, damn your hide. Sheriff, take the man-eating, monopoly-mawed cannibal with you!

Gruyot ends by explaining that Joseph Packer—"missionary's son, attorney-at-law, and cannibal"—was ultimately pardoned through the crusading efforts of "a newspaper in the city of Colorado Springs." Packer "at once proceeded to Colorado Springs where he inserted an advertisement in a newspaper, soliciting cooperation of men of moderate means to go on a prospecting trip with him." It was during this time that, so Gruyot claims, he "became well acquainted with Packer, who has long since gone over the range to his reward.

"We shall probably never again see his like," Gruyot concludes, finally favoring the reader with a statement of fact.[7]

+ + +

Though Gruyot's biography, which he copyrighted in 1924, was never published, it nevertheless had an impact on the public's perception of Packer. In the fall of 1930, Will Rogers—the humorist, actor, and "cowboy philosopher" beloved by millions for his folksy wit and wisdom—published an article in his nationally syndicated newspaper column in which he referred to the Donner Party as "the only case of cannibalism ever practiced in our abundant country." Soon after that piece appeared, Rogers, as he subsequently wrote, "received a letter from a man named

N. E. Gruyot," informing him "of the case of a man named Packer in Colorado" and supplying him with "the exact details of this case."

Accepting Gruyot's wild inventions as the "gospel truth," Rogers is much amused by Packer's ostensible background as a Harvard-educated lawyer, a "fact" that allows him to poke good-natured fun at both the East Coast intellectual elite and the legal profession:

> What I am getting at is that the only case of a person willfully devouring human flesh was the alumnus of the great Harvard. So Harvard has not only produced the least understandable English in our fair land, but produced the only living cannibal.
>
> Then he was a lawyer. That of course seems natural. Their profession is an offshoot of the cannibal profession, they generally eat you alive. Packer did have the good taste to destroy 'em and put 'em out of their misery. Most lawyers delight in seeing their victims suffer.

Rogers finds the greatest source of humor in the old chestnut (repeated by Gruyot) about Judge Gerry. In delivering his sentence, says Rogers, Gerry—"a fine old high type Democrat from Arkansas"—"admonished [Packer] for eating up all the Democrats in the County. If he had just eat up a Republican, why the Judge would have perhaps given the man a pension instead of a sentence." Famed for his political satire, Rogers ends on a characteristically comical note:

> They give him 40 years in Canon City jail. That was a little over six years for each one he ate. You would have to eat at least 10 or more to get a life sentence according to Colorado justice. He didn't stay in there that long. Along in '99, when civilization and militant editors hit us, certain newspapers started a campaign to release him. There was a tight election coming on, and them being Republicans, they wanted to let him out, hoping he would eat some more Democrats before Nov. 4.
>
> Then they brought up that Judge Gerry had been biased in the trial, that no Democratic Judge should sit in a case where it

was Democrats that had been eat. That it was a blot on the fair name of Colorado that a Harvard man shouldn't be able to eat what he liked. Well anyhow the papers got him out, and the fair name of Colorado was saved, and since then they have never convicted, or even tried a man, for murdering, robbing or otherwise maiming a Democrat. Viva Democracy![8]

+ + +

One reader of Will Rogers's column was the man who had freed Packer nearly three decades earlier, former Colorado governor Charles S. Thomas, who had gone on to serve as the US senator from Colorado before returning to his law practice in Denver. In a letter to an acquaintance written in late November 1930, Thomas chides Rogers for "repeating the shopworn recital of Judge Gerry's reputed sentence of death after Alfred Packer's conviction." Anticipating the famous line from John Ford's classic 1962 western, *The Man Who Shot Liberty Valance*—"When the legend becomes fact, print the legend"—Thomas dryly notes, "This is merely the last illustration of the fact that if a lie is persisted in, it becomes an accepted truth and passes into history as such. Indeed it may be affirmed that a large preponderance of the legends and traditions of the outstanding figures of the past have just such a basis for their acceptance."[9]

In making the latter remark, Thomas was implicitly acknowledging a fact that must have been hard for him to swallow: Alfred Packer, a man he continued to regard as a reprobate, had taken his place in western lore as one of the "outstanding figures of the past," a legendary character whose name would live on forever, even while the name of Charles Spalding Thomas—former Colorado governor and US senator—would soon fade from public memory.

+ + +

Thomas died in 1934 at the age of eighty-four. That same year, the American public—or at any rate that segment of it that delighted in sophisticated mystery novels—would encounter the story of Alfred

Packer in one of the bestselling books of the day, Dashiell Hammett's
The Thin Man.

The acknowledged father of hard-boiled detective fiction, Hammett
had a particular fondness for a volume called *Celebrated Criminal Cases
of America*, a now-classic anthology of criminal case histories compiled
by one-time San Francisco police captain Thomas S. Duke and published
in 1910. Unlike Hammett, Duke was no writer. His prose is pedestrian,
his storytelling strictly workmanlike. In terms of sheer sensationalism,
however, his choice of subject matter cannot be faulted. His collection,
arranged according to geographical area, comprises a veritable Who's
Who of America's most notorious nineteenth-century sociopaths, from
outlaws like Jesse James and the Daltons to such serial murderers as
Dr. H. H. Holmes, "The Chicago Bluebeard," and the "Boy-fiend," Jesse
Pomeroy, a juvenile sadist who terrorized South Boston in the 1870s.
In his section on "Celebrated Cases East of the Pacific Coast," he gives
pride of place to the story of "Alfred Packer, Who Murdered Five Fellow
Prospectors in Colorado, Stole Their Money and Ate Their Flesh."

By all accounts, Hammett's fascination with Duke's book verged
on the obsessive. According to the testimony of his companion Lillian
Hellman, he frequently carried it with him when he traveled. He also
invokes it in his two most famous novels. Describing Sam Spade's home
in the second chapter of *The Maltese Falcon*, Hammett refers to "Duke's
Celebrated Criminal Cases of America, face down on the table" beside
the hero's bed. Later in the novel, while waiting in Spade's apartment,
the "fat man," Casper Gutman, "smoked a cigar and read *Celebrated
Criminal Cases of America*, now and then chuckling over or comment-
ing on the parts of its contents that amused him."

Duke's anthology makes an even more prominent appearance in
The Thin Man. At one point in the novel, young Gilbert Wynant—an
adolescent oddball morbidly fixated on crime and psychopathology—
questions the hero, Nick Charles, about cannibalism. "I don't mean in
places like Africa and New Guinea," Gilbert explains. "In the United
States, say. Is there much of it?"

"Not nowadays," says Nick. "Not that I know of."

"Then there was once?"

"I don't know how much," Nick says, "but it happened now and then before the country was completely settled. Wait a minute: I'll give you a sample." He then steps to a bookcase, removes a "copy of Duke's *Celebrated Criminal Cases of America* that Nora had picked up in a secondhand-book store," opens it to the entry he wants, and gives it to Gilbert to read.

Up to that point, Hammett's story moves at a breathless pace, but it abruptly comes to a four-page halt while he reproduces verbatim Duke's entire two-thousand-word summation of the Packer case. Scholars of Hammett's work have often wondered why a writer famed for his economical style inserted such a lengthy digression into his novel. Hammett himself claimed that he stuck it in simply to fill out what would otherwise have been an overly skimpy manuscript.[10] Whatever the case, there's no doubt that the Packer segment adds a dollop of pulp titillation to *The Thin Man*, particularly since—though infinitely more reliable than N. E. Gruyot—Duke repeats some of the more sensational myths about the Man-Eater, such as Packer's ostensible claim that, by the time he emerged from the wilderness, he "had grown fond of human flesh, especially that portion around the breast."[11]

+ + +

At some point in the evolution of his legend, by a strange alchemy of the popular imagination, Alfred Packer was transmuted into a comical character. As early as the 1930s, a group of Denver Republicans, taking Judge Gerry's apocryphal words as their motto, formed a "Packer Club of Colorado," each member pledging "to eliminate five NuDeal Dimmycrats." Another fan club, "The Friends of Alfred Packer," offered suitable-for-framing membership certificates adorned with a jailhouse portrait of Packer alongside the slogan "Serving Our Fellow Men Since 1874." The certificate also listed the "Great Moments in the Life of the Leader," beginning with Packer's birthday, November 21, 1842, and ending with April 23, 1907, the day "Al [went] to the big Howard Johnson's in the Sky."

In 1968, the cafeteria in the student union of the University of Colorado Boulder, previously known as the Roaring Fork Grill, was renamed the Alferd Packer Restaurant & Grill in recognition of the quality of its fare: "food that was faithful to the high standards exemplified by Mr. Packer," as one speaker put it at the official dedication. At the conclusion of the ceremony, "a raw hamburger was thrown at the wall, where it stuck for some minutes."[12] That same year saw the inauguration of what would become a hallowed tradition at the university: the annual "Alferd Packer Day," celebrated with a raw meat–eating competition, a "belch-off," a Packer look-alike contest, and the consumption of uncountable kegs of beer. Commemorative T-shirts sold at these festivities boasted such slogans as "When you care enough to eat the very best," "If you can't beat 'em, eat 'em," "Nothin' says lovin' like someone in the oven," and "A kinder, tastier nation."[13]

Richard Lamm, three-term governor of Colorado between 1975 and 1987, struck the same flippant tone when, as occasionally happened, he found himself dealing with some bit of Packer-related business. In 1980, a retired municipal court judge from Paterson, New Jersey, named Ervan Kushner, while researching his own book on the case, became persuaded that Packer had been telling the truth. Determined to clear Packer's name (while drumming up a little publicity for his book), he sent a lengthy petition to Governor Lamm, asking that "an unconditional pardon, as an act of mercy and grace, be granted posthumously" to Packer.

Eight months after receiving the petition, Lamm, having studied the matter and consulted with members of his Executive Clemency Advisory Board, sent a very respectful reply to Kushner, denying the application. "Colorado has taken its pardon process very seriously," Lamm explained. "In all our history, only two posthumous pardons have been granted. Further, despite the admirable research you have conducted and my own distaste for circumstantial evidence, I believe the issue of Mr. Packer's guilt or innocence is still far from resolved."

In stark contrast to this sober reply, however, was the official statement that Lamm—struggling to keep a straight face—delivered at a press conference that March:

> I recently received a formal request for a posthumous, unconditional pardon for Alferd Packer. This issue has been gnawing

at me for some time and I now wish to dispose of it properly. I referred this matter to the Executive Clemency Advisory Board which thoroughly digested the file and sunk its teeth into the evidence. The Board then tendered its recommendation to me.

In the final analysis, I have to follow my gut instincts. Although I personally have no beef with Mr. Packer, the people of Colorado would not swallow an unconditional pardon. The application for a pardon asserted that Mr. Packer received a raw deal. 97 years after the trial, I must presume that the process was kosher and that Mr. Packer received his just desserts. Coloradans would eat me alive if I granted a pardon. It goes beyond the boundaries of good taste.

This application has really subjected me to a pressure cooker environment among my friends in the Democratic Party. Most Democrats just can't stomach Mr. Packer's excessively partisan appetite. In his partisan gall, Mr. Packer bit off more than he could chew. If I excused him at this late date, my Democratic friends would have a piece of my hide.

As a result of this action, I will no doubt receive much ribbing and be the butt of a few jokes. This experience has shown me the wisdom of running a bare bones government and avoiding issues like this which only add extra flavor. I intend to go a long time before I become embroiled in another meaty controversy like this. My plate is already quite full and I don't hunger for any more substance.[14]

Despite his closing pledge, Lamm (whose speechwriters, while racking their brains for every conceivable meat-related pun, apparently overlooked the possibilities inherent in the governor's own name) managed to become embroiled in another Packer-related controversy just one year later. In July 1982, prior to being installed at the Alferd Packer Restaurant & Grill at the University of Colorado Boulder, a limestone bust of the Man-Eater created by local sculptor Tom Miller was put on temporary display in the state capitol building, alongside busts of various politicians, including two former governors, two US senators, and George L. Brown, the state's first African-American lieutenant governor. Present at the unveiling ceremony, Lamm delivered another statement full of groan-inducing puns. "I must admit to you that I have little appetite to appear before you today," he began. "As I told my staff, I have better things to do than come over here to chew the fat with a pack of cannibal lovers. But being an election year, they convinced me that every little bit counts, and, in order to protect my flanks, I appear in front of you today." He then went on to defend his refusal to grant a pardon, declaring that, despite arguments that Packer was innocent, "the proof was in the pudding, and Alferd ate that, too."

Televised on the local news that night, Lamm's participation in the ceremony provoked outraged responses from citizens who excoriated him for honoring "a thief, a liar, a fugitive from justice . . . [a man] so illiterate that he signed his name Alferd instead of Alfred . . . and also probably a murderer."[15] Not everyone, however, took the matter quite so seriously. Along with an avalanche of criticism, Lamm heard from a number of people offering moral support. One letter writer reminded him that "serving the public isn't all gravy and doing a job you don't relish requires guts," another assured him that all the criticism was "merely Republican backbiting," while a third wished him good luck in his "continuing efforts to 'Meat the Press.'"[16]

+ + +

As a figure of folklore, Packer has generated not only countless bad puns but everything from ballads and plays to rock albums and cookbooks.[17] Packer is also the protagonist of a pair of movies released by Troma Entertainment, the gleefully tasteless purveyor of such cheesy entertainments as *Chopper Chicks in Zombietown* and *Surf Nazis Must Die*. In *Devoured: The Legend of Alferd Packer*, he is transformed into a slasher-movie boogeyman—a frontier Leatherface who wields a pickax instead of a chainsaw and who, having sold his soul to the devil, lives on to this day, preying on nubile coeds out on college field trips.

Far more fun to watch is *Cannibal! The Musical* ("All Singing! All Dancing! All Flesh Eating!" as the ad slogan proclaims). Written by, directed by, and starring Trey Parker—who, along with his college buddy Matt Stone, would go on to create *South Park* and *The Book of*

Mormon—this crudely hilarious satire, a kind of demented *Oklahoma!*, introduces Packer as a light-hearted innocent, enlisted to lead a group of prospectors from Utah to Colorado after the original guide, Lucky Larry, is incinerated by lightning. After suffering various ordeals, Packer and his companions are welcomed into an Indian camp populated by Asian Americans who speak Japanese, wield samurai swords, and practice kung fu. Setting off again into the mountains, the men resort to cannibalism after one of them, Israel Swan, goes cheerfully berserk and is summarily executed by Shannon Wilson Bell, who can't bear to hear him sing another chorus of "Let's Build a Snowman!" When Packer returns from his reconnoitering trip up the mountain, he finds that Bell has slaughtered the other three men. Packer kills Bell in self-defense (not, however, by shooting him but, true to the Troma aesthetic, by chopping him in the face with a cleaver, shoving a pointed stick in his eye, and impaling him on a pickax).

Arrested and brought to trial, he is depicted by the district attorney as a flesh-eating monster straight out of *Night of the Living Dead*. Only one person believes in his innocence—Polly Pry, portrayed here as a pretty young reporter who gradually succumbs to Packer's not entirely evident charms. It is Pry who, as Packer stands on the scaffold about to be hanged, rides to the rescue with a last-minute reprieve (much to the disappointment of the assembled townspeople, who have delivered a rousing performance of "Hang the Bastard").

The movie provides a mock-Hollywood ending that, of all the screenwriter's wild inventions, might be the most outrageous of them all: Alfred Packer, noose still dangling from his neck, locked in a romantic embrace with his new girlfriend, Polly Pry.[18]

50.

BONES OF CONTENTION

Forensic anthropologists trace the origins of their discipline to one of the most sensational American homicides of the nineteenth century, the murder of Dr. George Parkman by Harvard chemistry professor John White Webster. A member of Boston's social elite and one of the city's wealthiest men, the sixty-year-old Parkman—who had long since abandoned his medical practice to devote himself to his real estate business—left his Beacon Hill home around noon on Friday, November 23, 1849. He was last seen alive at roughly two in the afternoon in the vicinity of the Harvard Medical School.

After a week of frantic citywide searching, suspicion alighted on Professor Webster, a distinguished member of the Harvard faculty who was hopelessly in debt to Parkman. Though initial searches of Webster's lab turned up nothing, the school janitor, an inveterate snoop named Ephraim Littlefield, took it upon himself to burrow through the basement wall at night. Breaking into a vault beneath the professor's privy with a crowbar and chisel, he discovered a human pelvis and a dismembered leg. Other chunks of the butchered Dr. Parkman were stuffed inside a tea chest in Webster's rooms, while fragments of the skull and his charred but unmistakable false teeth were found in the ashes of the lab oven.

Webster's twelve-day trial in March 1850 was a bona fide media circus, covered by journalists from as far away as Paris and Berlin and attended by an estimated sixty thousand spectators. It also proved to be a forensic milestone. Having examined the remains at the request of the police, two of Webster's colleagues—doctors Oliver Wendell Holmes and Jeffries Wyman, both of the Harvard Medical School—testified that the recovered bones were consistent with a man of Parkman's physique. Holmes further asserted that the person who had dismembered the corpse "very evidently showed a knowledge of anatomy . . . there was no botching about the business."

Even more damning were the findings of Dr. Nathan Keep, who positively identified the cremated dentures as Parkman's. Keep's testimony—the first time that dental evidence was allowed in a court-room—was key to securing the conviction of Webster, who, shortly before his execution, confessed that he had bludgeoned Parkman to death during a quarrel that spun out of control.[1]

A half century later, another milestone was reached when George A. Dorsey became the first professional anthropologist to testify at a murder trial. The case was the notorious Luetgert affair, one of the gris-liest crimes of the era.

A German immigrant, fifty-two-year-old Adolph Luetgert had risen from humble beginnings to become the owner of Chicago's largest sau-sage factory. In 1897, however, after falling victim to a swindle, he found himself in dire financial straits. His second marriage, to his wife Louisa (née Bicknese), was also in trouble. Luetgert had taken to sleeping apart from his wife in a little room beside his office, sometimes sharing his bed with his young housemaid, Mary Siemering. He had also begun a surreptitious courtship of a wealthy widow, Christina Feld, sending her amorous letters in which he rhapsodized about their rosy future.

At around ten fifteen on the evening of Saturday, May 1, while Louisa was chatting with her twelve-year-old son, Louis, Luetgert appeared and told the boy to go to bed. Precisely what happened between the two adults after Louis retired to his room is unclear. Only one fact is beyond dispute. After the boy bid good night to his mother at about ten thirty, she was left alone in the company of her husband. Then she vanished.[2]

In the days following his wife's disappearance, Luetgert casually told friends and family members that "he supposed she had run away." His blasé reaction aroused the suspicions of her brother, who alerted the authorities. Searching the basement of the sausage factory, investigators came upon a large steam vat, about half-full of a thick, greasy fluid, reddish-brown in color and giving off a nauseous stink. When the fetid slime was drained from the vat, they discovered tiny pieces of bone along with two gold rings, one of them a wedding band engraved with the initials "L.L." More bone fragments, as well as a false tooth, a hairpin, a charred corset stay, and various scraps of cloth, turned up in a nearby ash heap.

The story of Chicago's "sausage king" who had slain his wife and disposed of her corpse by dissolving it in a solution of caustic potash became a newspaper sensation. Rumors quickly spread that Mrs. Luetgert had ended up as an ingredient in her husband's meat products. Like all urban legends, this cannibalistic fantasy was widely accepted as fact, leading, as one historian puts it, to a drastic reduction in Chicago's "per capita consumption of bratwurst."[3]

Since Luetgert continued to maintain that his wife had run away from home and was, so far as he knew, still alive, prosecutors were faced with the challenge of establishing the corpus delicti. For this, they turned to George Dorsey. The first Harvard student to be awarded a PhD in anthropology, Dorsey had been responsible for organizing a popular archaeological exhibit at the 1893 Chicago World's Fair. At the time of the Luetgert trial, he was assistant curator of anthropology at the Field Museum of Natural History. Brought in as an expert witness for the state, Dorsey identified the minuscule bone fragments found in the ghastly sludge from the steam vat as the skeletal shards of a human female. His sensational testimony helped send Luetgert to prison for life.[4]

Aside from some occasional consulting work with local lawmen and coroners, physical anthropologists devoted little of their energies to forensic activities during the early decades of the twentieth century. A turning point came in 1939 when Wilton M. Krogman—later to gain international renown as "the bone detective"—published his seminal "Guide to the Identification of Human Skeletal Material" in the *FBI Law Enforcement Bulletin*. Almost at once, anthropologists working at the Smithsonian National Museum of Natural History, just across the street from FBI headquarters, found themselves enlisted for help in homicide investigations. Krogman's methods were put to particularly solemn use during World War II, when the US Army shipped the bones of its unknown dead to a special lab in Hawaii, where physical anthropologists labored to identify them.

In 1962, Krogman expanded his pioneering paper into a book, *The Human Skeleton in Forensic Medicine*, which quickly became the bible in the field. Over the next decade, the discipline flourished, turning out a number of high-profile practitioners like Smithsonian curator J. Lawrence Angel. By the time of his death, Angel had helped the FBI and other law enforcement agencies identify the remains of more than five hundred people, many of them murder victims. His ability to study a skeleton and deduce the person's age, sex, stature, cause of death, general health, and even occupation earned him the nickname "Sherlock Bones." At the University of Tennessee Knoxville, Bill Bass not only trained an entire generation of forensic scientists but gained international renown as the creator of the Anthropology Research Facility, better known as the Body Farm, a two-and-a-half-acre field where human cadavers are studied as they undergo gradual open-air decomposition.[5]

Before 1970, only two anthropologists—Wilton Krogman and Ellis Kerley—were fellows of the prestigious American Academy of Forensic Sciences. Founded in 1948, the AAFS (or the American Medico-Legal Congress, as it was first known) originally consisted of seven sections, each devoted to a particular branch of forensic science: Pathology, Psychiatry, Toxicology, Immunology, Jurisprudence, Police Science, and Questioned Documents.[6] In 1972, however, with the approval of the executive committee, the academy added a section on physical anthropology. It was, in the words of an eminent forensic anthropologist, "the year we came of age as a discipline." Since then, specialists in the field have been an integral part of the academy's annual meetings, where they regale each other with lectures on such technical topics as "Patterns of Postmortem Dismemberment," "Unusual Suicides Utilizing Chain Saws," "Morphological Features of Cranial Blunt Force Trauma Fractures," and "Bone Fragmentation Created by Mechanical Wood Chippers."[7]

+ + +

In 1988, the Jurisprudence Section of the AAFS was chaired by James Starrs. A professor of law at George Washington University, Starrs had been on the faculty for only four years when, in 1968, he was approached by the acting director of the FBI Laboratory about setting up a forensic science program at the school. Starrs, already bored with the tedium of teaching traditional law courses, leapt at the chance. Since that time, he had become a recognized expert in the field, coauthoring a standard textbook—*Scientific Evidence in Civil and Criminal Cases*—and founding the *Scientific Sleuthing Review*, a quarterly newsletter for forensic-mystery buffs. An ardent reader of Conan Doyle's Sherlock Holmes stories, he saw himself as an heir to the great detective and had his business card emblazoned with a suitably Sherlockian logo: a microscope topped with a deerstalker hat.

One of the classic cases that Starrs taught in his criminal law course at GW was the 1884 murder trial of Thomas Dudley and Edwin Stephens, the captain and crew member of the doomed yacht *Mignonette*, who, in the throes of starvation, cannibalized the body of seventeen-year-old Richard Parker after cutting the dying boy's throat. The trial, which ended with a guilty verdict, became a legal landmark, establishing the principle that even the most dire necessity could not justify an act of homicide. Because of its precedent-setting significance, *Regina v. Dudley and Stephens* (as it is technically known) has been treated extensively in various texts, among them Allan C. Hutchinson's *Is Eating People Wrong? Great Legal Cases and How They Shaped the World* and A. W. Simpson's *Cannibalism and the Common Law*.[8]

Simpson's book, considered the definitive account, places the *Mignonette* tragedy in a larger context by recounting other notorious episodes of starvation cannibalism. One of his chapters, titled "Man Eaters of the Frontier," deals with Alfred Packer. It was through Simpson's book that Starrs first became aware of the Colorado Cannibal.

In the summer of 1988, Starrs traveled to the AAFS headquarters in Colorado Springs for a meeting of the board of directors. According to his telling, when the proceedings took a disagreeable turn, he decided to bow out and use the opportunity to satisfy his long-standing curiosity about the Packer case.[9]

Making his way to Lake City, he located its major tourist attraction two miles outside of town, where a large roadside sign announced the "Alferd Packer Massacre Site." A short distance away, on the spot known as Cannibal Plateau, stood the small fenced-off boulder bearing the plaque dedicated in 1928 to Packer's five doomed traveling companions.

Standing before the little memorial, Starrs experienced an epiphany. Why not employ the methods of state-of-the-art forensic science to resolve the century-old questions surrounding the case? He would put together a team of experts to exhume the remains of the five men and determine once and for all what really happened to them. The idea was very much in keeping with a common pursuit among physical anthropologists—the application of their professional skills to solve tantalizing historical mysteries. Besides his criminological activities, for example, Wilton Krogman helped establish the age of Pharaoh Ramses III and was called in to study the alleged bones of the young princes supposedly murdered in the Tower of London by their uncle, King Richard III. Through careful analysis of the skeletons retrieved from the wreck, Doug Owsley and his colleagues identified the crew of the sunken Civil War submarine *H. L. Hunley*. A team led by French anthropologist Pierre-François Puech confirmed the authenticity of a skull said to be Mozart's. William Maples identified the remains of conquistador Francisco Pizarro and Czar Nicholas II, examined the exhumed corpse of US president Zachary Taylor for evidence of rumored arsenic poisoning, and inspected the preserved skeleton of Joseph Merrick, the celebrated "Elephant Man," arriving at the surprising conclusion that, to a large extent, "Merrick's deformities belonged to his skin, not to his skeleton."[10]

For Starrs, the Alfred G. Packer Victims Exhumation Project, as it came to be formally called, presented a unique chance to solve one of American criminal history's most enduring puzzles. Not incidentally, it would also allow him to take on a far more glamorous public role, transforming him, in the eyes of the world, from a bookish academic into a high-profile "forensic investigative scientist."[11]

+ + +

The memorial to the five prospectors stood on private property. After securing permission for the dig from the owners, Starrs set about assembling his team, which eventually consisted of thirteen members, including an archaeologist, two pathologists, a geophysicist, experts in antique firearms and fiber analysis, and one of the country's leading forensic anthropologists, Walter Birkby.

A graduate student of the pioneering physical anthropologist Bill Bass, Birkby had spent the bulk of his professional career in Tucson, where he taught at the University of Arizona, served as curator of physical anthropology at the Arizona State Museum, and worked on over 1,500 cases for the Pima County Office of the Medical Examiner (whose lab was eventually named the Walter H. Birkby Forensic Anthropology Laboratory in his honor, though, to his students, it would always be known as "Birkby's Body Shoppe"). In the course of his distinguished career, he had been called upon to analyze everything from a preserved lock of Beethoven's hair to a clump of fur ostensibly belonging to Sasquatch.[12] Two of his doctoral students at UA, Todd Fenton and Bruce Anderson, would assist him in the Packer investigation.

Partly in the hope of drumming up outside funding for his pet project—whose ultimate cost he estimated at between $12,000 and $15,000—Starrs spread the word to the national press. Before long, newspapers from the *Washington Post* to the *Rio Rancho Observer* were running stories on the planned exhumation—an undertaking of "national significance," according to Starrs, with the potential to "enormously enhance the reputation of anthropology as a tool in criminal cases." "Scientists to Dig Up Cannibal Victims," "Forensic Expedition Seeks to Solve Century-Old Cannibal Case," and "GWU Professor Hopes to Prove That Bones Do Tell Tales" ran the headlines. Television shows from NBC's *Unsolved Mysteries* to the syndicated *Buried Secrets* planned to send video crews to cover the unearthing of the remains.[13]

For the four hundred permanent residents of Lake City, all the attention promised a bonanza. Anticipating a flood of tourists in the grip of "Packermania," gift shops began peddling "Have a Friend for Dinner" coffee mugs and "Alferd Packer—Serving His Fellow Man" T-shirts. A local bar band adopted the name the Rolling Bones, while Murphy's restaurant advertised a "Packer Platter" for "man-eating appetites."[14]

Operations commenced on Monday, July 17, 1989. For Starrs, a lifelong mystery fan who liked to think of himself as a swashbuckling "lawyer-sleuth," the date held special meaning, since it was—as he excitedly pointed out—the one hundredth anniversary of the birth of Erle Stanley Gardner, author of the famous stories starring the brilliant legal detective Perry Mason.[15]

A large crowd of locals turned out for the opening day. Picnic coolers at their sides, they lounged on lawn chairs just beyond the cordoned-off dig site ("the bone zone," as the forensic team had dubbed it). Starrs himself was decked out in a T-shirt of his own design, adorned with a human skeleton and the slogan "Gimme Five," a phrase he had learned from his high-fiving grandson and that struck him as particularly apt, since he was hoping to uncover "five skulls and the bodies to go with those skulls."[16]

The first order of business was confirming the location of the remains. Though the consensus among historians was that the five skeletons lay interred beneath the memorial boulder, some locals believed that the bodies were buried elsewhere. Others insisted that the memorial was actually a *secondary* resting place—that the dead prospectors had initially been buried nearby and only later dug up and transferred to the spot beneath the boulder, where their bones lay hopelessly commingled in a mass grave.

Since the opening of a human grave unavoidably smacks of desecration (one critic of the practice, employing the Victorian slang term for a grave robber, dubbed Starrs and his ilk "forensic resurrectionists"),[17] Starrs was eager to avoid as much disturbance of the burial site as possible. For that reason, he secured the services of a company called Geophysical Survey Systems that specialized in the use of ground-penetrating radar for archaeological, geological, environmental, and other purposes. Once the memorial boulder and its surrounding fence posts were removed with the aid of a backhoe, a radar technician scanned the exposed topsoil with a high-frequency transmitter/receiver antenna. Almost at once, the equipment picked up the presence of something anomalous lying less than a foot beneath the surface.

Wielding their shovels, team members quickly uncovered five parallel rows of small stones that had clearly been arranged as some sort of markers and that ran in an east–west direction—the traditional Christian burial orientation, as Starrs immediately noted. A little more digging turned up what—to the trained eye of Walter Birkby—was unmistakably a fragment of human skull bone. By the end of the day, to Starrs's uncontained elation, his team had brought to light the skeletons of all five prospectors. Lying side by side in their common shallow grave, they were in "almost immaculately preserved" condition, though one was missing its skull. Fibers clinging to some of the bones suggested that the corpses had been interred in burlap sacks that had long since decomposed.[18]

With the discovery of the remains, the dig swiftly turned into a bona fide media circus. Satellite trucks crammed the roads leading to the site, while reporters clamored for interviews with Starrs, who—with a white beard and balding dome that endowed him with a vague resemblance to the middle-aged Sean Connery—found himself likened to the father of Indiana Jones. With swarms of curiosity seekers, many of them children, straining for a glimpse of the burial pit, precautions had to be taken to protect the area, particularly after one prankster sprinkled the site with a bunch of chicken bones.[19]

Armed with commonplace tools of the archaeological trade—paintbrushes, masonry trowels, dustpans, and dental picks—Birkby and his assistants devoted the next six days to the painstaking excavation of the bones, pausing periodically to photograph each phase of the process. The skeletons—identified by letters A through E—were then carefully packed into five cardboard boxes, loaded into Starrs's Chevy Blazer, and transported to Birkby's lab in Tucson.

Three weeks of detailed analysis revealed that all four recovered skulls "bore the marks of repeated blunt-force trauma," evidently inflicted by "the blade of a hatchetlike implement" wielded by a single assailant. Deep gashes on the arm bones were classic defensive wounds, incurred when the victims tried to ward off the blows. Scores of other cut marks on the shoulders, spinal columns, ribs, and leg bones left no doubt that the bodies had been "substantially defleshed" with a knife: butchered after death for their meat.[20]

The results sent Starrs into flights of rhetorical extravagance. "There were skeptics to the right of us," he declared. "There were skeptics to the left of us. There were skeptics at every turning. But we prevailed, and we succeeded magniloquently." At a press conference attended by representatives of the national news media in October, he scoffed at Packer's protestations of innocence. "Packer was as guilty as sin and his sins were all mortal ones. . . . It is plain as a pikestaff that Packer was the one on the attack, not Bell."[21]

Not everyone, however, was impressed by Starrs's sweeping claims of triumphant success. Part of the problem was Starrs himself. A self-confessed "impresario" who basked in the limelight, he seemed to some less interested in science than in self-promotion. Despite his high-minded assertion that his Packer project was motivated by a "deeply sensed need" to bring attention to the overlooked victims whose names had been almost entirely eclipsed by their killer's, it appeared to certain critics that it was his own name he was mostly interested in advertising.[22] To a few especially scathing observers, Starrs's investigation was nothing more than "vanity forensics," a "dog-and-pony show" conducted largely for the benefit of the media—"more for headlines than for historical rectitude." One commentator denounced him as a "kind of historical Peeping Tom, foraging in people's graves more to satisfy curiosity than to unearth critical scientific information."[23]

More seriously, questions were raised about the validity of his finds. "By his own admission," wrote one specialist in forensic subjects, Starrs had no idea which body was which, and the paucity of physical descriptions of the victims had left his team groping in the dark. Even if the scientists had been able to determine whether the wounds were inflicted by cutting left- or right-handed, this would have been of little use, since they didn't know who in the ill-fated party was left- or right-handed. Most important of all, Starrs could not say, with any degree of certainty, which set of bones belonged to Shannon Bell.

Nor could the fact that the bones displayed similar nicks from a skinning knife be presented as conclusive evidence of a single killer. Bones recovered from known acts of cannibalism from around the globe, from the American Southwest to France to England, all display broadly similar cut marks. There are only so many ways one can butcher a carcass, and it would be a brave scientist, indeed, who stood up in court and professed to be able to identify whose hand wielded a skinning knife. Either Packer or Bell could have wielded that knife. Or both could have.[24]

Walter Birkby was far more circumspect than Starrs. At the October news conference, he said, "[Starrs's interpretation] could possibly be the right scenario but scientifically we cannot substantiate it." He was even more blunt at another interview. "We found nothing to corroborate or refute anything Packer said," he told one local reporter. "We'll never know who did it based on any solid physical evidence. We're never going to know."[25] Other forensic anthropologists concurred, noting that, while the expedition had established "the cause and manner" of the five prospectors' deaths, "the identity of the perpetrator . . . cannot be directly illuminated by the skeletal evidence."[26]

Starrs, however, remained adamant, dismissing the doubts of his critics and insisting that the "evidence convicts [Packer] beyond a shadow of a doubt. Packer was having his flesh filets morning, noon, and night, even though he could have lived by killing rabbits. Packer was a fiend, base, brutish . . . barbaric."[27]

But if the matter was settled as far as Starrs was concerned, other investigators would eventually arrive at a very different conclusion about Packer's culpability—and they would base it on evidence collected by Starrs's own expedition.

+ + +

In 1994, David P. Bailey, curator of history at the Museum of Western Colorado in Grand Junction, embarked on a project to inventory the items in one of the museum's prized holdings, the Audrey Thrailkill Collection, a unique assemblage of firearms owned by such celebrated westerners as Kit Carson, Buffalo Bill, and Butch Cassidy. Bailey was especially intrigued by one of the weapons—an 1862 Colt five-shot revolver. There was nothing distinctive about the gun itself. On the contrary, it was a rotted, rusted wreck, its grips gone, its main spring broken, its cylinder corroded. What made it so fascinating to Bailey was its accompanying accession card: "This gun was found at the site where Alferd Packer killed and ate five of his traveling companions."

Researching the provenance of the pistol, Bailey confirmed that it had indeed come from the area of the massacre, where a young historian unearthed it in 1950. Determined to see if he could connect the gun directly to the crime, Bailey began researching the Packer case. After five years of poring over every document he could find, he concluded that Alfred Packer was innocent.

Particularly significant to Bailey was the story Packer told to a *Denver Post* reporter who visited him on his deathbed: "When I got back [from the mountain], Bell . . . came running at me with a hatchet. He had the only hatchet in the camp. I could see that he was mad. He made a kind of grating noise. I ran back. I had a revolver. When I got to the snowdrift, I pulled my gun. He came on the run after me, and when I got to the deep snow, I wheeled round as quickly as I could and fired. He was right on top of me with the hatchet. My first shot killed him."[28] Bailey felt sure that the revolver in the museum's collection was the one wielded by Packer—"physical evidence that matched Packer's story" of having killed Bell in self-defense. Still, without a "way to scientifically tie the gun to the murder scene," Bailey knew he couldn't prove his case. In the spring of 1999, his efforts "came to a standstill."[29]

A year and a half later, a chance discovery revived his investigation. During a visit to Lake City in October 2000, Bailey was startled to learn that bits of evidence recovered from the gravesite by Starrs's team—clothing fragments, buttons, soil samples—had been donated to the Hinsdale County Historical Society. Enlisting the aid of Dr. Richard Dujay of Mesa State College in Grand Junction, Bailey had the samples subjected to analysis by electron microscope and spectrograph. To their delight and astonishment, Dujay and his team not only turned up a fifty-micron fragment of man-made lead but matched it to a sample taken from one of the three bullets still chambered in the rusted-out Colt revolver.

Further examination of the forensic samples revealed the presence of gunshot residue on a bit of wool fabric assumed to be a fragment of Shannon Bell's clothing. A close-up photograph of a pelvic bone, taken by Starrs's investigators, also showed a conspicuous puncture hole, indicating—so Bailey believed—that the individual, presumably Bell, had been shot through the hip.

With this evidence in hand, Bailey lost little time announcing, at a national news conference, that he had scientific proof corroborating Packer's story and giving persuasive, if not definitive, proof of his innocence.[30]

Not everyone was convinced. Most obviously, establishing that Packer shot Bell hardly proved that he did not murder the others. Moreover, until his deathbed interview with the *Denver Post* reporter, Packer had never said anything about killing Bell with a revolver. On the contrary, at his first trial, he testified that the weapon was a gun he had carried up the mountain "as a walking stick," clearly indicating that it was a rifle. Twice later—at his second trial and in his 1897 letter to Duane Hatch—he explicitly identified it as a Winchester.[31]

As for the puncture in the pelvic bone that Bailey confidently pronounced a bullet hole, forensic scientists from the Starrs project scoffed at the claim, declaring that "there was no evidence of perimortem gunshot wounds to any of the five individuals." The ostensible "gunshot trauma" described by Bailey "was, in fact, damage from carnivore activity . . . consistent with bear scavenging."[32]

It was also clear that Bailey's belief in Packer's innocence stemmed largely from Packer's deportment in old age—from Bailey's inability "to reconcile the image of Packer the heartless murderer with Packer the avuncular ex-con who carved dollhouses, gave candy to kids, and loved nothing more than to putter in his garden." "He never seemed like a cold-blooded killer to me," Bailey told one reporter. "He sounded like a nice old gent in his later years and not the kind of guy who would do something like that."[33]

What this statement ignores, of course, is the well-documented fact that, when subjected to starvation, even the most highly civilized individuals can be reduced to a near-animalistic state in which the survival instinct supplants every moral standard by which they have formerly conducted their lives.[34] It is also the case that a perfectly law-abiding citizen can, under conditions of extreme emotional stress, commit a singular act of violence and afterward lead a wholly blameless life. Following the Fall River hatchet murders, for example, Lizzie Borden never did anything worse than (reputedly) shoplift a pair of porcelain paintings from a Providence, Rhode Island, art gallery.

Of course, whether Lizzie Borden really gave her father and step-mother their proverbial whacks will forever remain a matter of dispute. So, it seems, will the question of Packer's guilt. An editorial in the *Grand Junction News* following his second trial put the matter well. Despite his conviction, said the paper, "the testimony and the circumstances are such that there will always be a doubt in the minds of many men."[35]

What we do know for certain is that, for roughly two months in the late winter of 1873, the corpses of five men—at least four killed by savage blows to the skull with a hatchet blade—lay in the snow a short distance from where Packer camped in his crude shelter. Throughout that time—in the jargon of the forensic anthropologists who examined the remains—Packer pursued a "butchering strategy focused on fillet-ing muscle tissue for immediate consumption." To translate into less euphemistic terms: whenever Packer grew hungry, he carved a hunk of necrotic flesh from a part of the body particularly rich in muscle tissue—an arm, leg, rib cage, shoulder, or buttock—roasted it on his campfire, and devoured it. In contrast to shipwreck survivors such as the crewmen of the *Essex* and the *Mignonette*—who were driven to devour every edible portion of their dead shipmates, from their brains, hearts, and livers down to the very marrow of their bones—Packer was so abundantly supplied with bodies that there was no need for him to resort to such unappetizing fare as the viscera. Nor did he have to worry about putrefaction, since the frigid weather of the mountains kept his food from spoiling. Dining on nutritious muscle tissue—"high utility meat units," as the forensic anthropologists so euphoniously put it—he hunkered down until the weather changed, when, with a final portion of human flesh to tide him over, he hiked out of the wilderness and made his way into legend.[36]

AFTERWORD

At the end of Charles Portis's beloved novel *True Grit*, Mattie Ross, the crusty one-armed spinster who has been recalling her adolescent adventures in quest of her father's killer, learns that her old friend, the cantankerous lawman Rooster Cogburn, has been spending his declining years performing in the touring Wild West show operated by the former desperados Frank James and Cole Younger. Traveling to Memphis, where the show is scheduled to appear in a local baseball park, she finds the pair of ex-bandits, now in their sixties, relaxing in a Pullman car, drinking Coca-Cola. Though James remains rudely seated at her approach, Younger, "a stout, florid man with a pleasant manner," rises to greet her and, in answer to her question, sadly informs her that Rooster "passed away a few days before." Mattie soon takes her leave after thanking "the courteous old outlaw," whose gracious ways make a lastingly favorable impression upon her.[1]

Though the scene is, of course, fictitious, historical evidence supports this portrayal of Younger. After interviewing the middle-aged outlaw in prison, for example, a writer named J. W. Buel reported that Younger was a model of civility and "bears himself like a perfect gentleman."[2] Certainly, the impression created in Younger's autobiography—published the same year that Mattie Ross would have visited him—is of a gray-haired sage, eager to impart his hard-won wisdom to the young. "The man who chooses the career of outlawry is either a natural fool or an innocent madman," he attests. "My young friend, if you are endowed with physical strength, valor, and a steady hand, let me warn you to use them well, for the God who gave them is the final victor."[3]

I raise the case of Cole Younger—Alfred Packer's exact contemporary—to illustrate a point. Like David Bailey, who finds it difficult to conceive that such "a nice old gent" as the elderly Man-Eater could have "done something like that," Polly Pry undertook her campaign largely because the Packer she encountered when he was a few years shy of sixty struck her as an admirable specimen of fine, old-fashioned, frontier manhood, capable of cannibalism under appalling conditions but not of cold-blooded murder. Yet there is no accurate way to judge the enormities a man might have committed in his unbridled youth by the benign demeanor of his mellowed old age. No one without knowledge of Cole Younger's history would guess, from his upstanding older self, that at nineteen years old, he had participated in the Lawrence Massacre, one of the bloodiest atrocities of the Civil War, when he and the other members of William Quantrill's notorious band of Confederate "bushwhackers" slaughtered as many as two hundred men and boys in the pro-Union town of Lawrence, Kansas.

As anyone who reads the papers knows, there is no shortage of analogous examples—of neighbors shocked to learn that the kindly old man down the block has been identified as a notorious Nazi war criminal, or that, thanks to new DNA evidence, the hardworking family man living next door has been arrested for an unsolved twenty-year-old homicide, or that—in the most extreme cases—the mild-mannered, church-going Cub scout leader beloved by the community has been unmasked as the serial killer who terrorized the city decades before. In the early 1960s, a New Yorker named Irving "Butch" Grossman, working for the US Geological Survey in Puerto Rico, befriended a fellow he knew as "Nate," a brilliant, highly cultivated man who spoke fluent Spanish, taught math at the University of Puerto Rico, worked as a hospital X-ray technician, and spent his leisure time bird-watching. Grossman was stunned when he discovered that "Nate" was the recently paroled Nathan Leopold, half of the infamous pair of young Jazz Age thrill-killers whose kidnapping and murder of a fourteen-year-old acquaintance in 1924 was one of the twentieth century's most sensational crimes.

All this is by way of suggesting that Alfred Packer's mild late-life deportment says nothing about his possible guilt. Nor do his protestations of innocence. Countless cold-blooded killers have gone to the grave insisting that they were the victims of gross injustice. Some seem so sincere that, were it not for overwhelming evidence of their guilt, any reasonable person would be utterly seduced by their claims. Jeffrey MacDonald is a prime contemporary example. Forty-five years after horribly murdering his wife and two young daughters, the former Green Beret physician continues to maintain—with a fervency so convincing that he has won over many supporters—that his family was slain by a band of Manson-like hippies. Indeed, there is reason to think that he himself might genuinely believe he had nothing to do with the massacre. One forensic psychologist brought in to examine MacDonald found that he was "subject to being amnesiac concerning what he wished to blot out from his consciousness and very conscience."[4]

Such self-protective forgetting is common enough that it constitutes its own category in the standard diagnostic manual of the American Psychiatric Association, where it is labeled "dissociative amnesia" and defined as an inability to remember "one or more episodes . . . of a traumatic or stressful nature."[5] This disturbance may well have been operating in Packer's case. There is another possibility, too: not that he retroactively wiped the memory of the murders from his mind but that he was in a sort of trance when he committed them. As one legal historian has proposed, it is conceivable "that Packer himself never actually knew what happened out there in the wilderness, having been reduced by the combined effects of his long-standing epileptic condition (coupled possibly with the effects of lead poisoning) and by privation almost to automatism."[6]

And, of course, there is always the possibility that Packer was simply lying and that he repeated the lie for so long that, over the course of several decades, he came to believe it himself.

As the heated dispute between James Starrs and David Bailey proves, there is no definitive way of determining who slaughtered Alfred Packer's companions. Unfortunately, as both everyday experience and scientific research confirm, the human mind has a very limited tolerance for uncertainty. We crave what social psychologist Arie Kruglanski was the first to define as "cognitive closure," which he defined as the "individual's desire for a firm answer to a question and an aversion toward ambiguity."[7] Empirically, as demonstrated by the painstaking

forensic analysis to which the bones of Packer's companions were subjected, there is no way to provide such closure. Still, an informed opinion is possible.

My considered belief is that Alfred Packer killed all five members of
his party. It simply seems too impausible to me that, on the very brink
of starvation, he conveniently found himself with a two-month supply
of nourishment, thanks to the fortuitous mental breakdown of Shannon
Wilson Bell, who took care of all the dirty work while Packer was away
and even did the cooking for Packer's first meal of human flesh. In the
end, the image of Packer huddling in his shelter for two months, waiting
for spring to arrive while helping himself, whenever hungry, to a chunk
of meat from one of the five exposed corpses, is a vision so brutish that
it negates his claims of innocence.

Should Packer have been found legally guilty of murder, given the
high degree of reasonable doubt in the case? Almost certainly not. *Was*
he guilty of murder? As in the cases of Lizzie Borden and Bruno Richard
Hauptmann—two other notorious figures whose guilt or innocence will
never be conclusively established to everyone's satisfaction—the question will forever remain unsettled. But for me, when I picture the slayer
of Shannon Bell and the others, I see a man reduced by unimaginable
hardship to a state of feral savagery: a crazed, near-skeletal figure with a
wild beard, long matted hair, a hatchet in hand, and the horribly gaunt
but still recognizable face of Alfred Packer.

ACKNOWLEDGMENTS

My sincerest thanks to:

David P. Bailey, Museum of Western Colorado

Beth Benko

Kasey Brooks, Stephen H. Hart Library and Research Center, History Colorado

Lance Christensen, Stephen H. Hart Library and Research Center, History Colorado

Sarah Gilmor, Stephen H. Hart Library and Research Center, History Colorado

Grant Houston, *Lake City Silver World*

Bruce Kawin

Jessy Randall, Colorado College Special Collections

Katie Salisbury

Laura Ruttum Senturia, Stephen H. Hart Library and Research Center, History Colorado

Tracy Seurer, Colorado State Archives

NOTES

PROLOGUE

1. William Bradford, *Of Plymouth Plantation* (New York: The Modern Library, 1981), 27.
2. Lewis Petrinovich, *The Cannibal Within* (New York: Aldine de Gruyter, 2000), 4–5.
3. In the 1970s, anthropologist W. Arens caused a stir by arguing that European reports of aboriginal cannibalism were purely a product of colonialist propaganda—a view now largely discredited. See W. Arens, *The Man-Eating Myth: Anthropology & Anthrophagy* (New York: Oxford University Press, 1979). The description of Iroquois torture is from Bernard Bailyn, *The Barbarous Years: The Peopling of British North America; The Conflict of Civilizations, 1600–1675* (New York: Alfred A. Knopf, 2012), 12.
4. Christy G. Turner II and Jacqueline A. Turner, *Man Corn: Cannibalism and Violence in the Prehistoric American Southwest* (Salt Lake City: University of Utah Press, 1999).
5. Bradford, 70; Nathaniel Philbrick, *Mayflower: A Story of Courage, Community, and War* (New York: Viking, 2006), 117–18.
6. Bailyn, 58. I have modernized Percy's spelling here and below.
7. Ibid., 60–61.
8. The findings were first reported on the *Smithsonian* magazine website. See Joseph Stromberg, "Starving Settlers in Jamestown Colony

Resorted to Cannibalism," *Smithsonian*, May 1, 2013, http://www.smithsonianmag.com/history/starving-settlers-in-jamestown-colony-resorted-to-cannibalism-46000815/. Also see Nicholas Wade, "Girl's Bones Bear Signs of Cannibalism by Starving Virginia Colonists," *New York Times*, May 1, 2013, sec. C, 1, and Richard Sugg, "The Jamestown Cannibalism Is No Surprise—It's Part of Human History," *Guardian*, May 5, 2013, http://www.theguardian.com/commentisfree/2013/may/05/cannibalism-history-europe-famine-shipwreck.

CHAPTER ONE

1. David Roberts, *A Newer World: Kit Carson, John C. Frémont, and the Claiming of the American West* (New York: Simon & Schuster, 2000), 292.
2. Ibid., 17.
3. Ibid., 288–89; Gail Collins, *Scorpion Tongues: Gossip, Celebrity, and American Politics* (New York: HarperCollins, 2007), 46 and 48.
4. For a particularly vivid re-creation of the fourth expedition, see Roberts, 183–244.

CHAPTER TWO

1. Theressa Gay, *James W. Marshall, the Discoverer of California Gold: A Biography* (Georgetown, CA: Talisman Press, 1967), 521.
2. Phyllis Flanders Dorset, *The New Eldorado: The Story of Colorado's Gold and Silver Rushes* (New York: Macmillan, 1970), 26 and 68.
3. Ibid., 193–94.
4. Robert L. Brown, *An Empire of Silver: A History of the San Juan Silver Rush* (Caldwell, ID: Caxton Printers, 1968), 28, 29, and 57.
5. Dorset, 210.
6. Mark Twain, *Roughing It* (Hartford, CT: American, 1901), 211–12.

CHAPTER THREE

1. *San Francisco Daily Alta*, October 10, 1873, 1 (reprinted from the *Denver Tribune*).

2. In census and other records, Packer's mother's maiden name is variously spelled "Griner," "Criner," and "Crider." Since Packer used the middle initial "G," it seems likely that the name was spelled "Griner." As one amateur genealogist points out, in the past "it was common practice to give children their mother's maiden name to help preserve their genealogy." Hence: Alfred Griner Packer. See www.genforum.genealogy.com/packer/messages/926.html.

   Besides Alfred, the Packers had six daughters—Alvinah, Mary Jane, Adaline, Marion, Melissa, and Eleanor—and another son, Marshall. Two of the children, Marion and Eleanor, died in infancy. See Ann Oldham, *Alfred G. Packer: Soldier, Prospector, Cannibal* (Davenport, IA: printed by author, 2005), 1–2.

3. Often Packer claimed to be Asa's nephew, though at other times he acknowledged a more distant kinship. In an interview following his capture in 1883, he described himself as "somewhere near a cousin to Asa Packer" (*Cheyenne Leader*, March 16, 1883, 3). There does seem to have been a very tenuous family connection between the two men, though genealogists differ on its precise nature, one identifying Alfred and Asa as fifth cousins three times removed, another as eighth cousins twice removed.

   For James Packer's obituary, see *LaGrange Standard*, February 27, 1902, 6.

4. Oldham, 2.

5. *Rocky Mountain News*, August 6, 1886, 2. Also see "Polly Pry Serves a Brief Time at Cañon City," *Denver Post*, May 5, 1899, 9.

6. Copies of two of Melissa Fought's letters are in the files of David Bailey at the Museum of Western Colorado in Grand Junction.

7. Ervan F. Kushner, *Alferd Packer: Cannibal! Victim?* (Frederick, CO: Platte 'N Press, 1980), 223.

8. "Army of the United States Certificate of Disability for Discharge," December 29, 1862, Alfred G. Packer Collection, Stephen H. Hart Library and Research Center, History Colorado, box 1040, file

folder no. 15.

9. "8 Cav Iowa Company Muster Roll," November–December 1863, Alfred G. Packer Collection, Stephen H. Hart Library and Research Center, History Colorado, box 1040, file folder no. 4.

10. "Army of the United States Certificate of Disability for Discharge," April 25, 1864, Alfred G. Packer Collection, Stephen H. Hart Library and Research Center, History Colorado, box 1040, file folder no. 15.

11. Kushner, *Alferd Packer*, 16.

12. Oldham, 8.

13. *The People of the State of Colorado v. Alfred Packer*, 91–92.

14. "Statement of Robert McGrue" as transcribed by John Lawrence, Alfred G. Packer Collection, Stephen H. Hart Library and Research Center, History Colorado, box 1040, file folder no. 5.

15. Blue wrote a memoir of his ordeal, originally published in 1860 and later reprinted in facsimile. See Daniel Blue, *Thrilling Narrative of the Adventures, Sufferings and Starvation of Pike's Peak Gold Seekers on the Plains of the West in the Winter and Spring of 1859* (Fairfield, WA: Ye Galleon Press, 1968).

16. Dorset, 36.

17. According to the recollections of McGrue. See "Statement of Robert McGrue."

18. *The People of the State of Colorado v. Alfred Packer*, 46; *Montrose Messenger*, March 22, 1883, 1; "Statement of O. D. Loutsenhizer" as transcribed by John Lawrence, Alfred G. Packer Collection, Stephen H. Hart Library and Research Center, History Colorado, box 1040, file folder no. 5.

CHAPTER FOUR

1. "Statement of O. D. Loutsenhizer."

2. Ibid. Other, unsubstantiated accounts claim that Packer was in jail for either counterfeiting money or "holding up a Mormon" for twenty-three dollars. See Wilson Rockwell, *Sunset Slope* (Ouray, CO: Western Reflections, 1999), 105, and *Montrose Messenger*, March 22, 1883, quoted in Paul H. Gantt, *The Case of Alfred Packer the Man-Eater* (Denver: University of Denver Press, 1952), 132,

no. 29.

3. Preston Nutter, "Letter to C. L. Stonaker, Secretary of Board of Parole, December 25, 1899," Alfred G. Packer Collection, Stephen H. Hart Library and Research Center, History Colorado Center, box 1040, file folder no. 4.

4. Dorset, 213. There is reason to believe that this peculiarity was a symptom of his epilepsy, the so-called "epileptic voice sign" characterized by one physician as "an expressionless quality of voice rendering speech monotonous." See E. W. Scripture, "The Epileptic Voice," *Medical Record* 75, no. 20 (May 15, 1909), 857.

5. "Statement of O. D. Loutsenhizer."

6. "Statement of Robert McGrue."

7. Kushner, *Alferd Packer*, 18–19; "Statement of Robert McGrue."

8. *The People of the State of Colorado v. Alfred Packer*, 93.

9. *The People of the State of Colorado v. Alfred Packer*, 94; "Statement of Robert McGrue."

CHAPTER FIVE

1. Marshall Sprague, *Massacre: The Tragedy at White River* (Lincoln: University of Nebraska Press, 1957), 61–67; Wilson Rockwell, *The Utes: A Forgotten People* (Ouray, CO: Western Reflections, 1956), 14–18.

2. P. David Smith, *Ouray: Chief of the Utes* (Ridgway, CO: Wayfinder Press, 1990), 38–39.

3. Virginia McConnell Simmons, *The Ute Indians of Utah, Colorado and New Mexico* (Boulder: University Press of Colorado, 2000), 59.

4. P. David Smith, 35; Robert B. Houston Jr., *Two Colorado Odysseys: Chief Ouray and Porter Nelson* (Lincoln, NE: 2005), 22.

5. Marshall Sprague, *Massacre*, 91.

6. P. David Smith, 73–74.

7. Cynthia S. Becker and P. David Smith, *Chipeta: Queen of the Utes* (Lake City, CO: Western Reflections, 2006), 60.

8. Wilson Rockwell, *The Utes: A Forgotten People* (Ouray, CO: Western Reflections, 1956), 99.

9. Peter R. Decker, *"The Utes Must Go!": American Expansion and the*

Removal of a People (Golden, CO: Fulcrum, 2004), 58; Becker and Smith, 62; P. David Smith, 184–85.

10. Kushner, *Alferd Packer*, 19. As with so many details of the Packer saga, there are contradictory accounts of the party's initial encounter with Ouray. In their biography of Ouray's wife, *Chipeta: Queens of the Utes*, Becker and Smith write that the party of twenty-one prospectors "happened into" Ouray's camp (74). In another of his books, however—*Ouray: Chief of the Utes* (Ridgway, CO: Wayfinder Press, 1990)—Smith asserts that, around January 25, while the group was camped on the south side of the Grand River, "three Utes stumbled upon the party and, when asked, told the prospectors of Chief Ouray's whereabouts, a three days' journey away" (118). Packer himself testified, "We was traveling on the south side of the Green River when a band of Indians come whooping and yelling up" (*The People of the State of Colorado v. Alfred Packer*, 94). According to Bob McGrue's account of the initial encounter, "Ouray had a lot of Indians with him in war array" ("Statement of Robert McGrue").

11. "Statement of Robert McGrue"; *The People of the State of Colorado v. Alfred Packer*, 96; "Statement of O. D. Loutsenhizer."

12. "Statement of O. D. Loutsenhizer"; "Story of Packer as Told by Alonzo Hartman," Stephen H. Hart Library and Research Center, History Colorado, box 1040, file folder no. 15.

13. Sidney Jocknick, *Early Days on the Western Slope of Colorado, and Campfire Chats with Otto Mears, the Pathfinder* (Glorietta, NM: Rio Grande Press, 1968), 55–59; "Story of Packer as Told by Alonzo Hartman."

14. "Statement of O. D. Loutsenhizer." Also see Diana Di Stefano, "Alfred Packer's World: Risk, Responsibility, and the Place of Experience in Mountain Culture, 1873–1907," *Journal of Social History* 40, no. 1 (Fall 2006), 185.

15. "Story of Packer as Told by Alonzo Hartman"; "Statement of O. D. Loutsenhizer"; *The People of the State of Colorado v. Alfred Packer*, 87–90.

CHAPTER SIX

1. "Statement of Robert McGrue."
2. "Statement of O. D. Loutsenhizer."

CHAPTER SEVEN

1. Becker and Smith, 58; Rockwell, *The Utes*, 84; P. David Smith, 84.
2. "Story of Packer as Told by Alonzo Hartman."
3. Johnny D. Boggs, *Great Murder Trials of the Old West* (Plano, TX: Republic of Texas Press, 2003), 160.
4. *The People of the State of Colorado v. Alfred Packer*, 55.
5. Ibid., 8.
6. Jocknick, 71.
7. *The People of the State of Colorado v. Alfred Packer*, 9.

CHAPTER EIGHT

1. Sarah Platt Decker Chapter, DAR, *Pioneers of the San Juan County*, vol. 1 (Colorado Springs, CO: The Out West Printing and Stationery Company, 1942), 19; Ervan F. Kushner, *Otto Mears: His Life & Times, with Notes on the Alferd Packer Case* (Frederick, CO: Platte 'N Press, 1979), 12.
2. Kushner, *Otto Mears*, 3–7; E. F. Tucker, *Otto Mears and the San Juans* (Montrose, CO: Western Reflections, 2003), 7.
3. David Lavender, *The Big Divide: The Lively Story of the People of the Southern Rocky Mountains from Yellowstone to Santa Fe* (Edison, NJ: Castle Books, 2001), 93–95; Tucker, 10–16; Michael Kaplan, *Otto Mears: Paradoxical Pathfinder* (Silverton, CO: San Juan Book Company, 1982), 6–16.
4. Federal Writers' Project, *Colorado: A Guide to the Highest State* (New York: Hastings House, 1941), 397.
5. Gantt, 31.
6. *The People of the State of Colorado v. Alfred Packer*, 67.
7. Ibid.

8. Ibid., 118–19.
9. Ibid., 36–37.

CHAPTER NINE

1. James Terry White, ed., *The National Cyclopaedia of American Biography: Being the History of the United States as Illustrated in the Lives of the Founders, Builders, and Defenders of the Republic, and the Men and Women Who Are Doing the Work and Moulding the Thought of the Present Era*, vol. 8 (New York: James T. White, 1906), 248.
2. *The People of the State of Colorado v. Alfred Packer*, 21.
3. Charles Adams, "Letter to the State Board of Pardons," May 31, 1894, Stephen H. Hart Library and Research Center, History Colorado, box 1040, file folder no. 2.
4. *The People of the State of Colorado v. Alfred Packer*, 49.
5. Ibid., 22; Gantt, 34.
6. *The People of the State of Colorado v. Alfred Packer*, 31; Jocknick, 74.
7. *The People of the State of Colorado v. Alfred Packer*, 24; Adams, "Letter to the State Board of Pardons." One colorful, if highly questionable, account claims that Packer finally broke down and confessed "after two Indians arrived at the agency from a hunting trip. They carried strips of flesh in their hands. 'White man's meat,' they called it. . . . When Packer caught sight of the flesh, his face became livid, his breath came short, and suddenly all strength left him, and with a low moan he sank to the floor." See Boggs, 162, and Jocknick, 71–72.

CHAPTER TEN

1. The details of the first confession, as here given, are assembled from accounts given by Alonzo Hartman, Charles Adams, Preston Nutter, and Herman Lauter.
2. Kushner, *Alferd Packer*, 23. Some controversy exists over the authenticity of this document. David Bailey, for example—curator of history at the Museum of Western Colorado—believes that it is ersatz, stitched together at a later date from a blank sheet of official

letterhead and a précis of Packer's statement written on plain paper. Significantly, it was never produced at Packer's 1883 trial.

3. "Letter to Hon. E. P. Smith, Commissioner of Indian Affairs, May 9th, 1874," Alfred G. Packer Collection, Stephen H. Hart Library and Research Center, History Colorado, box 1040, file folder no. 2.

4. Adams, "Letter to the State Board of Pardons"; *The People of the State of Colorado v. Alfred Packer*, 39.

5. *The People of the State of Colorado v. Alfred Packer*, 26.

6. Ibid., 13; Gantt, 39.

7. *The People of the State of Colorado v. Alfred Packer*, 57.

8. Ibid., 15; "Statement of James Fullerton" as transcribed by John Lawrence, Alfred G. Packer Collection, Stephen H. Hart Library and Research Center, History Colorado, box 1040, file folder no. 5.

9. *The People of the State of Colorado v. Alfred Packer*, 57; Gantt, 40.

CHAPTER ELEVEN

1. *Rocky Mountain News*, July 11, 1874, 4.

2. Alice Polk Hill, *Tales of the Colorado Pioneers* (Denver: Pierson & Gardner, 1884), 303.

CHAPTER TWELVE

1. *Rocky Mountain News*, August 28, 1874, 4.

2. "Packer, the Man-Eater: Interview with James D. Martin and Nathaniel Hunter," Alfred G. Packer Collection, Stephen H. Hart Library and Research Center, History Colorado, box 1040, file folder no. 4.

3. Peter Hutchinson, "A Publisher's History of American Magazines," http://themagazinist.com/Magazine_History.html.

4. *The People of the State of Colorado v. Alfred Packer*, 51.

5. "Statement of John R. Pond to John Lawrence," Alfred G. Packer Collection, Stephen H. Hart Library and Research Center, History Colorado, box 1040, file folder no. 5.

6. "Statement of Robert McGrue."

7. Kushner, *Alferd Packer*, 30–31; Gantt, 50–51.

CHAPTER THIRTEEN

1. *Wilmington (NC) Morning Star*, September 13, 1874, 1; *Louisville (KY) Courier Journal*, September 9, 1874, 1; *Reading (PA) Times*, September 12, 1874, 1.
2. *New York Times*, September 9, 1874, 1.
3. Kushner, *Alferd Packer*, 31; Gantt, 51; *Gunnison Daily Review*, March 19, 1883, 1.
4. Bernice Martin, ed., *Frontier Eyewitness: Diary of John Lawrence, 1867–1908* (Saguache, CO: The Saguache County Museum, n.d.), 1–6.
5. "Statement of John Lawrence," Alfred G. Packer Collection, Stephen H. Hart Library and Research Center, History Colorado, box 1040, file folder no. 5.
6. Ibid. Also see the *Denver Sunday Times*, February 18, 1900, 21.
7. The original warrant is reproduced in Gantt, 41, and Kushner, *Alferd Packer*, 30.
8. *Rocky Mountain News*, August 28, 1874, 4; "Packer, the Man-Eater: Interview with James D. Martin and Nathaniel Hunter," 4.
9. *Lake City Silver World*, July 31, 1875, 3.

CHAPTER FOURTEEN

1. Philip Jenkins, *Laying Down the Sword: Why We Can't Ignore the Bible's Violent Verses* (New York: HarperCollins, 2011), 6 and 30; A. W. Brian Simpson, *Cannibalism and the Common Law: A Victorian Yachting Tragedy* (London: Hambledon Press, 1994), 110 and 141.
2. The definitive work on this famous maritime disaster is Nathaniel Philbrick, *In the Heart of the Sea: The Tragedy of the Whaleship Essex* (New York: Penguin Books, 2000).
3. Simpson, 126–127.
4. Ethan Rarick, *Desperate Passage: The Donner Party's Perilous Journey West* (New York: Oxford University Press, 2008), 132.
5. Simpson, 6, 8, 66–68, and 308; Rarick, 132–33. Also see Allan C. Hutchinson, *Is Eating People Wrong? Great Legal Cases and How They Shaped the World* (Cambridge: Cambridge University Press,

2011).

6. Rarick, 240.

7. George R. Stewart, *Ordeal by Hunger: The Story of the Donner Party* (Boston: Houghton Mifflin, 1988), p. 296.

8. Rarick, 223–25; George R. Stewart, 288.

9. Robert L. Brown, *The Great Pikes Peak Gold Rush* (Caldwell, ID: Caxton Printers, 1985), 108.

10. LeRoy Hafen, "Mountain Men—'Big Phil, the Cannibal,'" *Colorado Magazine* 8, no. 2 (March 1936), 57.

11. Robert L. Brown, *The Great Pikes Peak Gold Rush*, 107.

12. E. Hough, "Portraits of Three Westerners," *Field and Stream*, no. 9 (January 1904), 854; Nathan E. Bender, "The Abandoned Scout's Revenge: Origins of the Crow Killer," *Annals of Wyoming: The Wyoming History Journal* 78, no. 4 (Autumn 2006), 2–17.

13. Jay Robert Nash, *The Great Pictorial History of World Crime*, vol. 1 (Blue Ridge Summit, PA: Scarecrow Press, 2004), 296–97.

CHAPTER FIFTEEN

1. Tom Lindmier, *Drybone: A History of Fort Fetterman, Wyoming* (Glendo, WY: High Plains Press, 2002), 15–21.

2. Donald McCaig, "The Bozeman Trail," *Smithsonian* 31, no. 7 (October 2000), 88.

3. R. Kent Morgan, *Guide to the Indian War Battlefields in Eastern Wyoming, Nebraska and South Dakota* (Bloomington, IN: printed by author, 2006), 52; Charles Ritter, "The Early History of Fort Fetterman," *Annals of Wyoming* 32, no. 2 (October 1960), 220–24.

4. Lindmier, 146–48; Charles Ritter, p. 223.

5. Robert B. David, *Malcolm Campbell, Sheriff: The Reminiscences of the Greatest Frontier Sheriff in the History of the Platte Valley, and of the Famous Johnson County Invasion of 1892* (Casper, WY: Wyomingana, 1932), 92–93; James R. Dow, Roger L. Welsch, and Susan D. Dow, eds., *Wyoming Folklore: Reminiscences, Folktales, Beliefs, Customs, and Folk Speech* (Lincoln: University of Nebraska Press, 2010), 43.

CHAPTER SIXTEEN

1. David, 93; Dow, Welsch, and Dow, 43–44; Kushner, *Alferd Packer*, 36.
2. *Rocky Mountain News*, March 13, 1883, 8.
3. David, 94.
4. *Lake City Silver World*, March 24, 1883, 1. All observers agree that Packer was missing the first joint of his left index finger, but there is contradictory testimony about the other mutilated digit, with some observers describing it as his ring finger, others as his pinky.
5. Dow, Welsch, and Dow, 48.
6. *Cheyenne Leader*, March 16, 1883, 3; *Denver Republican*, March 17, 1883, 1; *Gunnison Daily Review Press*, March 19, 1883, 1.
7. *Cheyenne Leader*, March 16, 1883, 3.
8. *Cheyenne Leader*, March 17, 1883, 3.
9. Ibid.; Dow, Welsch, and Dow, 46–48; David, 94–96; Kushner, *Alferd Packer*, 37–38.

CHAPTER SEVENTEEN

1. Decker, 89, 115–16.
2. Sprague, *Massacre*, 248–49; Rockwell, *Sunset Slope*, 176.
3. *Cheyenne Leader*, March 17, 1883, 3; Adams, "Letter to the State Board of Pardons"; *The People of the State of Colorado v. Alfred Packer*, 28.
4. Gantt, 55.
5. *Rocky Mountain News*, March 17, 1883, 8.
6. *Cheyenne Leader*, March 18, 1883, 3.

CHAPTER EIGHTEEN

1. The confession was reprinted verbatim in papers throughout the state and entered into evidence at Packer's 1883 trial. See *The People of Colorado v. Alfred Packer*, 34–35.
2. *Lake City Silver World*, March 31, 1883, 3.

CHAPTER NINETEEN

1. *New York Times*, March 24, 1883, 5; *Alton (IL) Evening Telegraph*, March 25, 1883, 1; *Decatur (GA) Herald*, March 24, 1883, 8; *Harrisburg (PA) Telegraph*, March 30, 1883, 1; *Chicago Daily Tribune*, March 31, 1883, 10.
2. *Jackson (IA) Sentinel*, March 19, 1883, 6.
3. Kushner, *Alferd Packer*, 38.
4. *Gunnison Daily Review*, March 17, 1883, 1; *Gunnison Daily Review*, March 19, 1883, 1; *Rocky Mountain News*, March 13, 1883, 8.
5. *Denver Republican*, March 17, 1883, 8.
6. *Cheyenne Leader*, March 18, 1883, 3; *Rocky Mountain News*, March 17, 1883, 8.
7. *Logansport Daily Pharos*, March 20, 1883, 3; *Montrose Messenger*, March 22, 1883, quoted in Gantt, 132, no. 29; *Jocknick*, 75; Kushner, 38; *Denver Republican*, March 17, 1883, 8.
8. *Gunnison Daily Review*, March 19, 1883, 2.
9. Kushner, *Alferd Packer*, 40.

CHAPTER TWENTY

1. Grant Houston, *Lake City Reflections* (Gunnison, CO: B & B Printers), 1976, 24.
2. *New York Times*, November 3, 1876, 7.
3. Grant Houston, 30.
4. Ibid., 69–70.
5. Margaret Bates, *A Quick History of Lake City, Colorado* (Colorado Springs, CO: Little London Press, 1973), 18; Oldham, 36–37.
6. George A. Root, "Gunnison in the Early 'Eighties," *Colorado Magazine* 9, no. 6 (November 1932), 204–5; Stephen J. Leonard, *Lynching in Colorado, 1859–1919* (Boulder: University Press of Colorado, 2002), 140.
7. Root, 202; Gantt, 78.
8. Root, 207.
9. *The People of the State of Colorado v. Alfred Packer*, 91–92.
10. Kushner, *Alferd Packer*, 42; *Lake City Silver World*, March 24, 1883,

3; Betty Wallace, *Gunnison: A Short, Illustrated History* (Denver: Sage Books, 1964), 53.

11. "Packer, the Man-Eater: Interview with James D. Martin and Nathaniel Hunter."

12. *Lake City Silver World*, March 31, 1883, 3.

CHAPTER TWENTY-ONE

1. Frank Hall, *History of the State of Colorado: Embracing Accounts of the Pre-Historic Races and Their Remains; the Earliest Spanish, French and American Explorations; the Lives of the Primitive Hunters, Trappers and Traders; the Commerce of the Prairies; the First American Settlements Founded; the Original Discoveries of Gold in the Rocky Mountains; the Development of Cities and Towns, with the Various Phases of the Industrial and Political Transition from 1858 to 1890*, Vol. 3 (Chicago: The Blakely Printing Company, 1891), 234.

2. Ibid., 239.

3. Ibid., 239–40.

4. Ibid., 244.

5. Ibid., 243; Gantt, 81.

6. Gantt, 81; Kushner, *Alferd Packer*, 48–49.

7. Hall, 242.

8. Kushner, *Alferd Packer*, 49–50.

CHAPTER TWENTY-TWO

1. Gantt, 145, no. 187; Kushner, *Alferd Packer*, 42.

2. Kushner, *Alferd Packer*, 47–48. According to the April 7, 1883, issue of the *Lake City Silver World*, the grand jury "found a true bill against Packer for the murder of Israel Swan, one of the five victims." In reviewing the history of the case in 1886, however, the *Gunnison Review* noted that "five indictments for murder, one for each man killed, were found by the Grand Jury" (August 2, 1886, 1). Kushner, too, writes that the grand jury "presented five indictments charging Packer with murder" (47). In any case, Packer's first trial was solely for the murder of Swan.

3. *Lake City Silver World*, April 7, 1883, 3.

4. Kushner, *Alferd Packer*, 49.

5. Ibid., 52–53.

6. Adams, "Letter to the State Board of Pardons."

7. *Lake City Silver World*, April 7, 1883, 3.

CHAPTER TWENTY-THREE

1. Kushner, *Alferd Packer*, 58.

2. Ibid., 62.

3. Virginia Price and John T. Darby, "Preston Nutter: Utah Cattleman, 1886–1936," *Utah Historical Quarterly* 32, no. 3 (Summer 1946), 233–36 and 251.

4. *The People of the State of Colorado v. Alfred Packer*, 1–19.

CHAPTER TWENTY-FOUR

1. *The People of the State of Colorado v. Alfred Packer*, 19–33.

2. "Letter to Hon. E. P. Smith, Commissioner of Indian Affairs, May 9th, 1874."

3. *The People of the State of Colorado v. Alfred Packer*, 36–38. In Mears's testimony, the wallets are described as "pocket books" and the money order as a "Wells Fargo draft."

4. Di Stefano, 191–92.

5. *The People of the State of Colorado v. Alfred Packer*, 48.

6. Ibid., 65–76.

7. Ibid., 50–54.

8. Ibid., 57–58.

9. Ibid., 62 and 79.

CHAPTER TWENTY-FIVE

1. *The People of the State of Colorado v. Alfred Packer*, 82–90.

2. Kushner, *Alferd Packer*, 131; Boggs, 180.

3. *The People of the State of Colorado v. Alfred Packer*, 96–115.

CHAPTER TWENTY-SIX

1. *The People of the State of Colorado v. Alfred Packer*, 120–33.
2. *Lake City Silver World*, April 14, 1883, 3. By Kushner's count, Bell asked 318 questions during his cross-examination (*Alferd Packer*, 146).
3. *The People of the State of Colorado v. Alfred Packer*, 154–56.
4. Ibid., 154.
5. Boggs, 180.
6. *Rocky Mountain News*, April 14, 1883, 8.

CHAPTER TWENTY-SEVEN

1. Kushner, *Alferd Packer*, 156; *Lake City Silver World*, April 12, 1883, 2.
2. *Lake City Silver World*, April 21, 1883, 2.
3. *Rocky Mountain News*, April 14, 1883, 1.
4. *Lake City Silver World*, April 14, 1883, 3; Kushner, 157.
5. *Cheyenne Leader*, April 15, 1883, 3.
6. *Rocky Mountain News*, April 14, 1883, 1.
7. The supposed source of this legend was none other than Larry Dolan. According to a piece in the *Rocky Mountain Herald* of June 13, 1942—which is where this undoubtedly apocryphal story originated—Dolan headed straight from the courthouse to the nearest saloon after sentence was pronounced and gave this colorfully mangled version.
8. *Lake City Silver World*, April 14, 1883, 3.
9. *Rocky Mountain News*, April 14, 1883, 1.
10. Albert L. Moses, "Judge Gerry's Sentence of Alfred Packer," *Dicta* 19 (July 1942), 169–71.
11. *Lake City Silver World*, April 14, 1883, 1; Kushner, *Alferd Packer*, 161.

CHAPTER TWENTY-EIGHT

1. *Lake City Silver World*, April 14, 1883, 2.

2. *Breckenridge Daily Journal*, April 16, 1883, 2, and April 21, 1883, 2.
3. *Grand Junction News*, April 21, 1883, 2.
4. *Pueblo Chieftain*, April 17, 1883, 2
5. *Lake City Silver World*, April 28, 1883, 2.
6. *Lake City Silver World*, April 14, 1883, 2.

CHAPTER TWENTY-NINE

1. Kushner, *Alferd Packer*, 162 and 166.
2. Ibid., 167.
3. *Lake City Silver World*, May 5, 1883, 3, and May 12, 1883, 2.
4. *Louisville (KY) Courier-Journal*, October 10, 1884, 4.
5. L. B. France, *Reports of Cases Determined in the Supreme Court of the State of Colorado, Containing All Cases Decided at the December Term, 1883, the April Term, 1884, and the Special October Term, 1884*, vol. 7 (Chicago: Callaghan & Company, 1884), 384–96; Kushner, *Alferd Packer*, 167. Following Judge Beck's ruling, Garvey was transferred from the state penitentiary to the Denver city jail to await retrial. Since the principle of double jeopardy precluded a second trial for murder, it was decided to charge Garvey with manslaughter. Garvey being so obviously guilty, the presiding judge "dispensed with this tedious formality and simply sentenced" him to ten years in the penitentiary, the maximum term for that crime. Garvey was locked up for another year, while his lawyers argued that he should, in fact, have been given a trial. The supreme court agreed, but in October 1884, "it set him free under the Colorado Habeas Corpus Act, which imposed a time limit on criminal proceedings that had clearly been exceeded." See Simpson, 272.
6. Kushner, *Alferd Packer*, 168.
7. Kushner, *Alferd Packer*, 169; *Lake City Silver World*, May 19, 1883, 2, and May 26, 1883, 2.
8. *Lake City Silver World*, May 26, 1883, 2.

CHAPTER THIRTY

1. Gene Smith and Jayne Barry Smith, eds., *The Police Gazette* (New York: Simon & Schuster, 1972), 15.
2. *National Police Gazette*, March 31, 1883, 3.
3. *Albion (IN) New Era*, May 10, 1883, 5.
4. *Lake City Silver World*, May 5, 1883, 3.
5. Doc Shores, *Memoirs of a Lawman* (Denver: Sage Books, 1962); Beau Riffenburgh, *Pinkerton's Great Detective: The Amazing Life and Times of James McParland* (New York: Viking, 2013); *Grand Junction (CO) Daily Sentinel*, May 22, 1938, 4.
6. Shores, 342.
7. The extant letters are on file at the Museum of Western Colorado in Grand Junction.
8. Charles Adams, "Letter to the State Board of Pardons, May 31, 1894," Alfred G. Packer Collection, Stephen H. Hart Library and Research Center, History Colorado, box 1040, file folder no. 2.
9. Shores, 343.
10. Gantt, 79.
11. Wilson Rockwell, "The West End Story," *San Miguel Forum*, January 21, 1965, 10; Shores, 346.
12. Kushner, *Alferd Packer*, 176; Gantt, 79–80.
13. *Louisville (KY) Courier-Journal*, June 2, 1892, 16. Hill's best-known poem is "The Message of the Tree," a work so sappy that it makes Joyce Kilmer's famous poem seem tough-minded by comparison.
14. Alice Polk Hill, *Tales of the Colorado Pioneers* (Denver: Pierson & Gardner, 1884), 301.
15. Ibid., 305.
16. *Golden (CO) Transcript*, September 5, 1884, 2.
17. Kelly Segrave, *Lynchings of Women in the United States: The Recorded Cases, 1851–1946* (Jefferson, NC: McFarland, 2010), 35–39; Leonard, 81.
18. Kushner, *Alferd Packer*, 175.

CHAPTER THIRTY-ONE

1. For a gripping, meticulously researched account of the Greely expedition, see Leonard F. Guttridge, *Ghosts of Cape Sabine: The Harrowing True Story of the Greely Expedition* (New York: G. P. Putnam's Sons, 2000).
2. *New York Times*, August 12, 1884, 1.
3. Michael F. Robinson, *The Coldest Crucible: Arctic Exploration and American Culture* (Chicago: University of Chicago Press, 2006), 82.
4. *New York Times*, August 15, 1884, 1.
5. *New York Times*, August 20, 1884, 1.
6. Reprinted in the *Williamsport (PA) Daily Gazette and Bulletin*, August 9, 1886, 2.

CHAPTER THIRTY-TWO

1. *Lake City Silver World*, June 2, 1883, 3.
2. The ruling is reproduced in an appendix to Gantt's book, 115–19.
3. Ibid., 118.
4. "Petition for a Change of Venue," Alfred G. Packer Collection, Stephen H. Hart Library and Research Center, History Colorado, box 1040, file folder no. 10.
5. Oldham, 96–97.
6. Kushner, *Alferd Packer*, 183; Gantt, 83.

CHAPTER THIRTY-THREE

1. *Gunnison Review-Press*, August 2, 1886, 1. It is possible, of course, that this horror story was a mere urban legend.
2. *Gunnison Review-Press*, August 4, 1886, 1.
3. Kushner, *Alferd Packer*, 187.
4. *Gunnison Review-Press*, August 4, 1886, 1.
5. *New York Times*, August 7, 1886, 3; *Rocky Mountain News*, August 5, 1886, 6.
6. *New York Times*, August 7, 1886, 3.
7. Ibid.; *Gunnison Review-Press*, August 4, 1886, 1; *Rocky Mountain*

News, August 5, 1886, 6. Unfortunately there is no record of Packer's cross-examination or the exact curses he leveled at his enemies, since—for unknown reasons—no transcript of the second trial exists.

8. *New York Times*, August 7, 1886, 3.

CHAPTER THIRTY-FOUR

1. *Gunnison Review-Press*, August 6, 1886, 3.
2. Kushner, *Alferd Packer*, 191.
3. Riffenburgh, 77–78, 92–93, and 144–45.
4. Shores, 346–47. The precise date of Curran's murder is unclear, though evidence suggests it occurred on August 2.
5. Shores, 348; Gantt, 88.
6. Shores, 349.
7. Gantt, 63–64.
8. Shores, 349–50.
9. Kushner, *Alferd Packer*, 191; Gantt, 85; Oldham, 110.
10. *Gunnison Review-Press*, August 5, 1886, 1.
11. *Rocky Mountain News*, August 6, 1886, 1.
12. Simpson, 273.
13. *Rocky Mountain News*, August 6, 1886, 1.
14. Simpson, 273.
15. *Rocky Mountain News*, August 6, 1886, 1.

CHAPTER THIRTY-FIVE

1. Fred Harrison, *Hell Holes and Hangings* (Clarendon, TX: Clarendon Press, 1968), 136. Much of the information in this section comes from a fifty-cent souvenir booklet, *This Is the Prison: Colorado Penitentiary, Cañon City*, printed (as best I can tell) in 1955 and offered for sale to visitors to the prison. I found it on eBay. See also Gerald E. Sherard, "A Short History of the Colorado State Penitentiary," Colorado State Archives, State Penitentiary Records, https://www.colorado.gov/archives.
2. A popular—and probably apocryphal—story has it that, as a reward

for supporting Denver in its bid for the state capital, Cañon City "was offered its choice of payoff: the state university or the state prison." It chose the prison, thus becoming "the first community in America to recognize incarceration as a growth industry." See Jonathan Franzen, *How to Be Alone: Essays* (New York: Farrar, Straus and Giroux, 2003), 218.

3. Victoria R. Newman and the Museum of Colorado Prisons, *Images of America: Prisons of Cañon City* (Charleston, SC: Arcadia, 2008), 9.

4. Harrison, 155–58. After serving sixteen years in the Cañon City penitentiary, Witherell was paroled in 1887, whereupon he promptly committed another murder. On December 4, 1886, he was seized from the jail by a mob and strung up from the nearest telegraph pole.

5. C. W. "Doc" Shores, alias "Doc" Shores, "The Story of Alfred Packer The Colorado Cannibal, Denver, Colorado, April 3, 1927," typescript, Alfred G. Packer Collection, History Colorado, box 1040, file folder no. 5.

CHAPTER THIRTY-SIX

1. Kushner, *Alferd Packer*, 197–98; Gantt, 89.
2. Gantt, 89; Oldham, 116.
3. Oldham, 116–20; Kushner, *Alferd Packer*, 199.
4. Kushner, *Alferd Packer*, 197–98.
5. See, for example, the *Goshen Daily News*, December 23, 1892, 4.
6. *Salt Lake City Tribune*, December 18, 1892, 1.
7. Kushner, *Alferd Packer*, 199–200; Gantt, 91.
8. Kushner, *Alferd Packer*, 199.
9. "Petition of Alfred Packer for a Writ of Habeas Corpus, John R. Smith, Alex Stewart, Attorneys for Petitioner," Alfred G. Packer Collection, Stephen H. Hart Library and Research Center, History Colorado, box 1040, file folder no. 10.
10. *Boulder County Herald*, January 11, 1893, 6.
11. *Rocky Mountain News*, January 4, 1893, 8.
12. Gantt, 122. Packer's case would come before the Colorado Supreme

Court "not less than five times." All of these appeals would be denied. See also Joseph G. Hodges, "The Legal Experiences of Mr. Alfred Packer," *Dicta* 19 (June 1942), 149–52.

CHAPTER THIRTY-SEVEN

1. *Denver Times*, August 9, 1893, 3; *Denver Republican*, August 20, 1893, 3.
2. David Silkenat, *Moments of Despair: Suicide, Divorce, and Debt in Civil War Era North Carolina* (Chapel Hill: University of North Carolina Press, 2011), 63–67.
3. *Denver Republican*, August 20, 1893, 3. The description of Packer's left hand in this article contradicts the testimony of other witnesses, who identified his missing digits as the index and ring fingers.
4. Like all such snake oil, this nostrum contained a number of decidedly insalubrious ingredients, including a heavy dose of ammonia.
5. *Denver Republican*, August 20, 1893, 3.
6. "Letter to Governor Waite," August 16, 1893, Alfred G. Packer Collection, Stephen H. Hart Library and Research Center, History Colorado, box 1040, file folder no. 2.
7. Silkenat, 67.

CHAPTER THIRTY-EIGHT

1. "Letter from Frank P. Blake to John R. Smith," August 24, 1893, Alfred G. Packer Collection, Stephen H. Hart Library and Research Center, History Colorado, box 1040, file folder no. 5.
2. Charles Adams, "Letter to the State Board of Pardons, May 31, 1894," Alfred G. Packer Collection, Stephen H. Hart Library and Research Center, History Colorado, box 1040, file folder no. 5.
3. Kushner, *Alferd Packer*, 209–10.
4. *San Francisco Chronicle*, August 20, 1895, 1; Dick Kreck, *Denver in Flames: Forging a New Mile High City* (Golden, CO: Fulcrum, 2000), 76–77.
5. *Denver Evening Post*, August 22, 1895, 1.
6. Kreck, 86.

7. *Oakland Tribune*, August 19, 1895, 1.
8. *San Francisco Chronicle*, August 20, 1895, 1.

CHAPTER THIRTY-NINE

1. *Wichita Daily Eagle*, September 12, 1895, 1.
2. *Rocky Mountain News*, August 7, 1897, 2.
3. "Letter to Mr. D. C. Hatch," June 27, 1897, Alfred G. Packer Collection, Stephen H. Hart Library and Research Center, History Colorado, box 1040, file folder no. 2.
4. Alfred G. Packer Collection, Stephen H. Hart Library and Research Center, History Colorado, box 1040, file folder no. 2.
5. Alfred G. Packer Collection, Stephen H. Hart Library and Research Center, History Colorado, box 1040, file folder no. 2.
6. Di Stefano, 196.
7. *Denver Times*, August 10, 1897, 3.
8. Kushner, *Alferd Packer*, 220.
9. Alfred G. Packer Collection, Stephen H. Hart Library and Research Center, History Colorado, box 1040, file folder no. 2; *Rocky Mountain News*, August 11, 1897, 8.
10. Kushner, *Alferd Packer*, 220.
11. *Denver Times*, January 2, 1898, 1.

CHAPTER FORTY

1. See, for example, Gayle C. Shirley, *More Than Petticoats: Remarkable Colorado Women* (Guilford, CT: Twodot Books, 2002), 97; Peter V. Hayden, "The Incredible Polly Pry," *Frontier Times* 51, no. 1 (December–January 1977), 16; Sue Hubbell, "Polly Pry Did Not Just Report the News; She Made It," *Smithsonian Magazine* 21, no. 10 (January 1991), 48.
2. Though some writers claim that she did not start using this pseudonym until she went to work for the *Denver Post*, her articles for the *World* appear under the byline Polly Pry.
3. Shirley, 98; Ishbel Ross, *Ladies of the Press: The Story of Women in Journalism by an Insider* (New York: Harper & Brothers, 1936), 563.

4. "Tammen of Denver Tells His Story," *Printers' Ink Magazine* 47, no. 7 (May 18, 1904), 12–14.

5. Gene Fowler, *Timber Line: A Story of Bonfils and Tammen* (Garden City, NY: Garden City, 1933), 44 and 51.

6. *Collier's*, April 1, 1911, 18; Bill Hosokawa, *Thunder in the Rockies: The Incredible "Denver Post"* (New York: William Morrow, 1976), 32–33. Interested readers will find Tammen's complete 1881 *Relics from the Rockies* catalogue reproduced at archive.org/details/relicsfromrockie00hhta.

7. Fowler, 87; John A. Garraty and Mark C. Carnes, eds., *American National Biography* 3 (New York: Oxford University Press, 1999), 171.

8. Hosokawa, 18.

9. Charles Austin Bates, *American Journalism from the Practical Side: What Leading Newspaper Publishers Say Concerning the Relations of Advertisers and Publishers and about the Way a Great Paper Should Be Made* (New York: Holmes, 1897), 279.

10. Fowler, 139; Hosokawa, 23.

11. Fowler, 101; Garraty and Carnes, 172.

12. Garraty and Carnes, 172. Also see Hosokawa, 73–74.

13. Fowler, 101.

14. *Denver Post*, February 14, 1901, 3; August 1, 1901, 8; and April 23, 1899, 20.

15. *Denver Post*, June 16, 1899, 8; February 21, 1900, 3; and March 23, 1902, 6.

CHAPTER FORTY-ONE

1. All quotes in this chapter are from the article "Polly Pry Serves a Brief Term at Cañon City," *Denver Post*, May 21, 1899, 15 and 20.

2. Pry makes a number of significant factual errors in this account, among them that the doomed party consisted of Packer and four other men.

3. It was reinstated in 1901.

CHAPTER FORTY-TWO

1. *Denver Post,* May 26, 1899, 4.

2. Ibid., May 27, 1899, 4.

3. Ibid., May 26, 1899, 10.

4. Pry, who could have used a fact-checker, was guilty of making frequent glaring mistakes. She was evidently referring not to Commodore Perry but to the polar explorer Robert Peary. Since cannibalism has never been connected to any of Peary's expeditions, however, one assumes she meant Greely.

5. *Denver Post,* July 23, 1899, 15. By the time Pry wrote these words, Packer's only hope lay with the governor and board of pardons, the state supreme court having denied his fifth and final appeal. See "Polly Pry Says the Merits of Packer Case Are Unaffected by the Supreme Court Decision," *Denver Post,* June 20, 1899, 7.

6. *Denver Times,* August 4, 1899, 4; *San Juan Prospector,* January 20, 1900, 3, quoted by Oldham, 127.

7. *Denver Post,* July 23, 1899, 15 and 20.

8. *Denver Times,* July 9, 1899, 6.

9. *Denver Post,* August 6, 1899, 10.

10. *Rocky Mountain News,* July 22, 1899, 5.

11. *Colorado Springs Weekly Gazette,* April 17, 1902, 1. Stonaker would be fully exonerated.

12. See, for example, "The Effect of the Climate on Mind," *Dietetic and Hygienic Gazette: A Monthly Journal of Physiological Medicine* 14, no. 7 (July 1898), 591–92, and "Sketch of Prof. Leslie R. Mutch," *Character Builder* 31, no. 10 (October 1918), 34–35. Also see "Rainfall and Intellect," *Western Medical and Surgical Gazette* 1, no. 5 (August 1910), 307–8.

13. *Los Angeles Herald,* September 15, 1895, 1. The fellow analyzed by Mutch was not Bill Nye, an internationally famous humorist of the time, but a local prankster who adopted the name Bill Nye Jr., presumably because of his striking resemblance to the celebrated writer.

14. Kushner, *Alferd Packer,* 220–21.

15. Stonaker transcribed his conversation with Gerry on a sheet of

letterhead stationery from the Hotel Metropole in Denver, which is filed in the Alfred G. Packer Collection, Stephen H. Hart Library and Research Center, History Colorado, box 1040, file folder no. 15.

16. Alfred G. Packer Collection, Stephen H. Hart Library and Research Center, History Colorado, box 1040, file folder no. 15; Kushner, 225–29.

17. *Denver Post*, October 5, 1899, 2, and October 15, 1899, 6.

CHAPTER FORTY-THREE

1. See above, pp. 88–91.
2. *Denver Post*, October 16, 1899, 10.
3. Alfred G. Packer Collection, Stephen H. Hart Library and Research Center, History Colorado, box 1040, file folder no. 2.
4. Alfred G. Packer Collection, Stephen H. Hart Library and Research Center, History Colorado, box 1040, file folder no. 5.
5. Letter "To Hon. Williams C. Blair c/o Silver World, Lake City, Colorado, December 4, 1930," Alfred G. Packer Collection, Stephen H. Hart Library and Research Center, History Colorado, box 1040, file folder no. 5.
6. Tucker, 73; Kaplan, *Otto Mears*, 51.
7. *Denver Times*, January 21, 1900, 8.
8. "Memorandum of Statement Just Made by Otto Mears in the Presence of Herman Lueders to Charles S. Thompson of and Concerning the Circumstances Leading to the Conviction of Alfred Packer, Now Serving a Cumulative Sentence of Forty Years for Murder," October 21, 1899, Alfred G. Packer Collection, Stephen H. Hart Library and Research Center, History Colorado, box 1040, file folder no. 5.
9. *Rocky Mountain News*, December 9, 1899, 1.
10. *Denver Post*, December 10, 1899, 1.

CHAPTER FORTY-FOUR

1. *Denver Post*, December 10, 1899, 1.
2. *Denver Post*, January 3, 1900, 7.

3. *Denver Post*, January 8, 1900, 12. In her depiction of Packer, Pry, as was so often the case, played fast and loose with the facts. Packer received his pension not "as a scout for Custer" but because of the disability he supposedly suffered while a soldier in the Civil War. In truth, there is no hard evidence that he ever served under Custer.

4. *Denver Times*, January 5, 1900, 7, and January 7, 1900, 21.

CHAPTER FORTY-FIVE

1. *New York Times*, June 24, 1897, 3.
2. *Denver Post*, April 23, 1900, 3.
3. *Denver Post*, April 24, 1900, 8.
4. *Denver Post*, January 14, 1900, 1.
5. *Denver Post*, January 14, 1900, 1, and April 23, 1900, 1.
6. Ibid.
7. *Denver Post*, January 14, 1900, 1, April 23, 1900, 1, and April 24, 1900, 1; Hosokawa, 97–99; *Denver Times*, January 13, 1900, 1.

CHAPTER FORTY-SIX

1. Marilyn Griggs Riley, *High Altitude Attitudes: Six Savvy Colorado Women* (Boulder, CO: Johnson Books, 2006), 48; Hosokawa, 15; Fowler, 158.
2. *Rocky Mountain News*, April 15, 1900, 1.
3. *Denver Post*, April 24, 1900, 1.
4. *Rocky Mountain News*, April 23, 1900, 1; *Denver Post*, April 29, 1900, 1.
5. *Denver Times*, April 24, 1900, 1.
6. Ibid.; *Denver Post*, April 24, 1900, 1.
7. Kushner, *Alferd Packer*, 278.
8. *Denver Post*, April 24, 1900, 10; Kushner, *Alferd Packer*, 278–79.
9. Oldham, 128.
10. *Rocky Mountain News*, April 29, 1900, 1.
11. For a good summation of the various legal proceedings against Anderson, see Hosokawa, 104–7.

CHAPTER FORTY-SEVEN

1. *Denver Post*, May 24, 1900, 7.
2. Alfred Packer Collection, Colorado State Archives.
3. *Denver Post*, May 9, 1900, 3.
4. *Denver Post*, May 8, 1900, 10.
5. *Grand Junction Evening Sun*, January 9, 1901, 1.
6. *Denver Post*, January 9, 1900, 8.
7. The poem is attributed to "an Old Soldier," W. A. Simmons. *Denver Post*, January 9, 1901, 8.
8. *Denver Post*, January 8, 1901, 1.

CHAPTER FORTY-EIGHT

1. *Rocky Mountain News*, January 11, 1901, 1.
2. Gantt, 97; *Denver Post*, January 10, 1901, 5.
3. *Rocky Mountain News*, January 11, 1901, 1; *Denver Post*, January 11, 1901, 1.
4. Gantt, 98; *Rocky Mountain News*, January 14, 1901, 7, and January 20, 1901, 28.
5. Connelly's first name is variously given as Ed, Dave, and Dan in different Denver newspapers.
6. *Denver Times*, February 10, 1902, 7.
7. Robert W. Fenwick, *Alfred Packer: The True Story of Colorado's Man-Eater* (Denver: *Empire Magazine* of the *Denver Post*, 1963), 40.
8. Kushner, *Alferd Packer*, 288; *Denver Post*, January 13, 1907, 15.
9. *Denver Post*, December 2, 1906, 15.
10. *Rocky Mountain News*, April 27, 1907, 1 and 4.
11. *Denver Post*, April 27, 1907, 1, and April 26, 1907, 1; Gantt, 110.
12. *Denver Post*, April 27, 1907, 1.

CHAPTER FORTY-NINE

1. *Rocky Mountain News*, March 12, 1911, 8.
2. *Rocky Mountain News Sunday Magazine*, February 13, 1927, 1 and 7.

3. Simpson, 280; Gantt, 142.

4. Gantt, 111–12.

5. Inez Hunt, "The Marryin' and the Buryin,'" *Denver Westerners Roundup* 39, no. 2 (January–February 1971), 39. Also see Inez Hunt and Wanetta W. Draper, *Horsefeathers and Applesauce: The Story of Bishop Frank Hamilton Rice* (Denver: Sage Publications, 1959).

6. Inez Hunt, "The Marryin' and the Buryin'"; Edward V. Dunklee, "Colorado Cannibalism," in *1946 Brand Book: Twelve Original Papers Pertaining to the History of the West*, ed. Virgil V. Thompson (Denver: Westerners, 1947), 112–14.

7. A typed copy of Gruyot's jaw-dropping eight-page document is on file in the Alfred Packer Collection, Colorado State Archives.

8. *Rocky Mountain News*, November 2, 1930, 18.

9. Letter "To Hon. Williams C. Blair."

10. Don Herron, *The Dashiell Hammett Tour* (San Francisco: City Lights Books, 1991), 86–87.

11. Dashiell Hammett, *The Thin Man* (New York: Alfred A. Knopf, 1933), 70–75, and Thomas S. Duke, *Celebrated Criminal Cases of America* (San Francisco: James H. Barry Company, 1910), 307–311.

12. Simpson, 282.

13. Mike Harden, *Among Friends: The Best of Mike Harden* (N.p.: Wing and Prayer Publications, 1993), 9–10.

14. The statement was drafted by Lamm's aide, Eric Sondermann. Kushner's petition and accompanying documents are reproduced as an appendix to a limited edition of his book, *Alferd Packer: Cannibal! Victim?* A typescript of Lamm's statement, along with other documents relating to his ultimate decision, can be found in the Alfred G. Packer Collection, Stephen H. Hart Library and Research Center, History Colorado, box 1040, file folder no. 12.

15. *Denver Post*, July 15, 1982, 23.

16. "Letter to Maurice H. Lannan, Jr.," July 23, 1982, Alfred G. Packer Collection, Stephen H. Hart Library and Research Center, History Colorado, box 1040, file folder no. 12.

17. For example, Phil Ochs's "The Ballad of Alferd Packer" (featuring the refrain "They called him a murderer, a cannibal, a thief / It just doesn't pay to eat anything but government-inspected beef"), a

melodrama titled *They Wuz Et*, the 1990 album *Eaten Back to Life* by death metal band Cannibal Corpse, and James E. Banks's *Alferd Packer's Wilderness Cookbook* (Palmer Lake, CO: Filter Press, 1969).

18. Two other movies have been based on the Packer case: the no-budget horror-western *The Legend of Alfred Packer*, distinguished largely by its (unintentionally) hilarious acting, and *Ravenous*, a darkly comic Hollywood horror film with actual production value, first-rate actors, and genuine shocks that was inspired by screenwriter Ted Griffin's discovery of the Packer story in *The Thin Man*.

CHAPTER FIFTY

1. James W. Stone, *Report of the Trial of Prof. John W. Webster, Indicted for the Murder of Dr. George Parkman, before the Supreme Judicial Court of Massachusetts, Holden at Boston, on Tuesday, March 19, 1850* (Boston: Phillips, Sampson and Company, 1850), 50–59. There have been many accounts of the Parkman–Webster case. One of the best constitutes the second half of Simon Schama's *Dead Certainties: Unwarranted Speculations* (New York: Vintage Books, 1992).

2. John H. Wigmore, "The Luetgert Case," *American Law Review* 32 (March–April 1898), 188. The most complete account of the case is Robert Loerzel, *Alchemy of Bones: Chicago's Luetgert Murder Case of 1897* (Urbana, IL: University of Illinois Press, 2003).

3. Clyde Collins Snow, "Forensic Anthropology," *Annual Review of Anthropology* 11 (1982), 100.

4. T. D. Stewart, "George A. Dorsey's Role in the Luetgert Case: A Significant Episode in the History of Forensic Science," *Journal of Forensic Science* 23, no. 4 (October 1978), 786–91.

5. Jessica Snyder Sachs, *Corpse: Nature, Forensics, and the Struggle to Pinpoint Time of Death* (New York: Basic Books, 2001), 55; William Bass and Jon Jefferson, *Death's Acre: Inside the Legendary Forensic Lab the Body Farm Where the Dead Do Tell Tales* (New York: G. P. Putnam's Sons, 2003).

6. Ralph F. Turner, "American Academy of Forensic Sciences Is Now Firmly Established," *Journal of Criminal Law and Criminology*

(1931–1951) 41, no. 4 (November–December 1950), 477–78; Kenneth S. Field, *History of American Academy of Forensic Sciences, 1948–1998* (West Conshohocken, PA, 1998), 22. By the 1960s, the makeup had altered somewhat. The Police Science section had evolved into Criminalistics, Immunology was folded into Pathology/Biology, and new sections on Odontology and Engineering Sciences were added. See Snow, 107.

7. William R. Maples and Michael Browning, *Dead Men Do Tell Tales: The Strange and Fascinating Cases of a Forensic Anthropologist* (New York: Doubleday, 1994), 103; Snow, 107–8. Programs from AAFS annual meetings from 2002 to the present can be found on the academy's website, http://www.aafs.org.

8. Also recommended: Neil Hanson, *The Custom of the Sea* (New York: John Wiley & Sons, 1999).

9. James E. Starrs and Katherine Ramsland, *A Voice for the Dead: A Forensic Investigator's Pursuit of the Truth in the Grave* (New York: G. P. Putnam's Sons, 2005), 24–25.

10. Maples and Browning, 112; Jeff Benedict, *No Bone Unturned: The Adventures of a Top Smithsonian Forensic Scientist and the Legal Battle for America's Oldest Skeletons* (New York: Harper, 2003).

11. Starrs and Ramsland, *A Voice for the Dead*, 25.

12. Russell Martin and Lydia Nibley, *The Mysteries of Beethoven's Hair* (Watertown, MA: Charlesbridge, 2009), 17–18; Stanley Rhine, *Bone Voyage: A Journey in Forensic Anthropology* (Albuquerque: University of New Mexico Press, 1998), 141–42.

13. *Washington Times*, May 8, 1989, A12.

14. *Rocky Mountain News*, March 16, 1989, 12; *Colorado Daily Record*, July 20, 1989, 9; *Pueblo (CO) Chieftain*, July 19, 1989, 7.

15. James E. Starrs, "Words as True as Bone: A Report on the Packer Victims' Exhumation Project," *Scientific Sleuthing Review* 13, no. 3 (Summer 1989), 6.

16. Starrs and Ramsland, *A Voice for the Dead*, 32.

17. Colin Evans, *A Question of Evidence: The Casebook of Great Forensic Controversies from Napoleon to O.J.* (Hoboken, NJ: John Wiley & Sons, 2003), 30.

18. Starrs and Ramsland, *A Voice for the Dead*, 42, and Starrs, "Words

as True as Bone," 6.

19. Starrs and Ramsland, *A Voice for the Dead*, 44–45.

20. Ibid., 47–49; Evans, 37–38.

21. Starrs, "Words as True as Bone," 1; Evans, 37.

22. Evans, 37.

23. Evans, 30; Amanda Ripley, "Bone Hunter," *Washington City Paper*, March 13, 1998, www.washingtoncitypaper.com/articles/14597/bone-hunter; Geoff Williams, "Death Sleuth," *Biography* 2, no. 7 (July 2998), 50.

24. Evans, 38.

25. *Pueblo (CO) Chieftain*, August 16, 1989, 8A.

26. Rhine, 150.

27. *Gainesville Sun*, October 14, 1989, 3.

28. *Denver Post*, April 26, 1907, 2.

29. David Bailey, "Solving the West's Greatest Mystery: Was Alferd Packer Innocent of Murder?" *Pathways*, no. 1 (2003), 14–19.

30. Ibid.; Evans, 39–41.

31. See above, pp. 164 and 195.

32. Alison E. Rautman and Todd W. Fenton, "A Case of Historic Cannibalism in the American West: Implications for Southwestern Archaeology," *American Antiquity* 70, no. 2 (April 2005), 325.

33. Evans, 39; *Denver Post*, April 26, 1997, 18.

34. See Philbrick, *In the Heart of the Sea*, 172.

35. *Grand Junction News*, April 21, 1883, 2.

36. Rautman and Fenton, 324–37.

AFTERWORD

1. Charles Portis, *True Grit* (New York: Simon & Schuster, 1968), 221–22.

2. J. W. Buel, *The Border Bandits: An Authentic and Thrilling History of the Noted Outlaws, Jesse and Frank James, and Their Bands of Highwaymen. Compiled from Reliable Sources Only and Containing the Latest Facts in Regard to These Freebooters* (Saint Louis: Historical, 1881), 132.

3. Cole Younger, *The Story of Cole Younger, by Himself: Being an*

Autobiography of the Missouri Guerilla Captain and Outlaw, His Capture and Prison Life, and the Only Authentic Account of the Northfield Raid Ever Published (Chicago: Henneberry, 1903), 117–18.

4. Joe McGinniss, *Fatal Vision* (New York: Signet, 1989), 835.

5. American Psychiatric Association, *Diagnostic and Statistical Manual of Mental Disorders, 5th ed., DSM-5* (Washington, DC: American Psychiatric Publishing, 2013).

6. Simpson, 279.

7. Maria Konnikova, "Why We Need Answers," *New Yorker*, April 30, 2013, http://www.newyorker.com/tech/elements/why-we-need -answers.

BIBLIOGRAPHY

Adams, Ramon F. *Six-Guns and Saddle Leather: A Bibliography of Books and Pamphlets on Western Outlaws and Gunmen*. Mineola, NY: Dover Publications, 1954.

Alfred G. Packer Victims Exhumation Project: Lake City, Colorado, July 17, 1989. Washington, DC: Scientific Sleuthing Inc., 1989.

American Psychiatric Association. *Diagnostic and Statistical Manual of Mental Disorders, 5th ed., DSM-5*. Washington, DC: American Psychiatric Publishing, 2013.

Arens, W. *The Man-Eating Myth: Anthropology & Anthropophagy*. New York: Oxford University Press, 1979.

Armstrong, Betsy R. *Century of Struggle against Snow: A History of Avalanche Hazard in San Juan County, Colorado*. Boulder: University of Colorado Institute of Arctic and Alpine Research, 1976.

Askenasy, Hans. *Cannibalism: From Sacrifice to Survival*. Amherst, NY: Prometheus Books, 1994.

Bailyn, Bernard. *The Barbarous Years: The Peopling of British North America; The Conflict of Civilizations, 1600–1675*. New York: Alfred A. Knopf, 2012.

Banks, James E. *Alferd Packer's Wilderness Cookbook*. Palmer Lake, CO: Filter Press, 1969.

Bass, William, and Walter H. Birkby. "Exhumation: The Method Could Make All the Difference." *FBI Law Enforcement Bulletin* 47, no. 7 (July 1978): 6–11.

Bass, William, and Jon Jefferson. *Death's Acre: Inside the Legendary Forensic Lab the Body Farm Where the Dead Do Tell Tales*. New York: G. P. Putnam's Sons, 2003.

Bates, Charles Austin. *American Journalism from the Practical Side: What Leading Newspaper Publishers Say Concerning the Relations of Advertisers and Publishers and about the Way a Great Paper Should Be Made.* New York: Holmes, 1897.

Bates, Margaret. *A Quick History of Lake City, Colorado.* Colorado Springs, CO: Little London Press, 1973.

Becker, Cynthia S., and P. David Smith. *Chipeta: Queen of the Utes.* Lake City, CO: Western Reflections, 2006.

Bell, John C. *The Pilgrim and the Pioneer.* Lincoln, NE: International Printing Association, 1906.

Bender, Nathan E. "The Abandoned Scout's Revenge: Origins of the Crow Killer." *Annals of Wyoming: The Wyoming History Journal* 78, no. 4 (Autumn 2006): 2–17.

Benedict, Jeff. *No Bone Unturned: The Adventures of a Top Smithsonian Forensic Scientist and the Legal Battle for America's Oldest Skeletons.* New York: Harper, 2003.

Billington, R. A. *The American Frontiersman: An Inaugural Address Delivered Before the University of Oxford on 2 February 1954.* London: Oxford University Press, 1954.

Blue, Daniel. *Thrilling Narrative of the Adventures, Sufferings and Starvation of Pike's Peak Gold Seekers on the Plains of the West in the Winter and Spring of 1859.* Fairfield, WA: Ye Galleon Press, 1968.

Boggs, Johnny D. *Great Murder Trials of the Old West.* Plano, TX: Republic of Texas Press, 2003.

Bradford, William. *Of Plymouth Plantation.* New York: The Modern Library, 1981.

Breidinger, William J. *Shadows of the San Juans.* Bloomington, IN: iUniverse, 2009.

Brown, Daniel James. *The Indifferent Stars Above: The Harrowing Saga of a Donner Party Bride.* New York: Harper Perennial, 2010.

Brown, Robert L. *An Empire of Silver: A History of the San Juan Silver Rush.* Caldwell, ID: Caxton Printers, 1968.

———. *The Great Pikes Peak Gold Rush.* Caldwell, ID: Caxton Printers, 1985.

Bryson, Charles Lee. "'Packer the Cannibal' Case Nearly Fatal to Publishers." *Frontier Times* 9, no. 10 (July 1932): 441–42.

Buel, J. W. *The Border Bandits: An Authentic and Thrilling History of the Noted Outlaws, Jesse and Frank James, and Their Bands of Highwaymen. Compiled from Reliable Sources Only and Containing the Latest Facts in Regard to These Freebooters.* Saint Louis: Historical Publishing Company, 1881.

Burt, Olive Woolley. *American Murder Ballads and Their Stories.* New York: Oxford University Press, 1958.

———. *Ouray the Arrow.* New York: Julian Messner, 1953.

Collins, Gail. *Scorpion Tongues: Gossip, Celebrity, and American Politics.* New York: HarperCollins, 2007.

Constantine, Nathan. *A History of Cannibalism: From Ancient Cultures to Survival Stories and Modern Psychopaths.* Edison, NJ: Chartwell Books, 2006.

Crumpacker, Bunny. *The Sex Life of Food: When Body and Soul Meet to Eat.* New York: Thomas Dunne Books, 2006.

Cummins, Joseph, ed. *Cannibals: Shocking True Tales of the Last Taboo on Land and at Sea.* Guilford, CT: Lyons Press, 2001.

Darley, George M. *Pioneering in the San Juan.* Grand Rapids, MI: Fleming H. Revell, 1899.

David, Robert B. *Malcolm Campbell, Sheriff: The Reminiscences of the Greatest Frontier Sheriff in the History of the Platte Valley, and of the Famous Johnson County Invasion of 1892.* Casper, WY: Wyomingana, 1932.

Davis, Richard. *A Man to Cross Rivers With.* Ouray, CO: Western Reflections, 1999.

Decker, Peter R. *"The Utes Must Go!": American Expansion and the Removal of a People.* Golden, CO: Fulcrum, 2004.

Di Stefano, Diana. "Alfred Packer's World: Risk, Responsibility, and the Place of Experience in Mountain Culture, 1873–1907." *Journal of Social History* 40, no. 1 (Fall 2006): 181–204.

Donnelly, Mark P., and Daniel Diehl. *Eat Thy Neighbor: A History of Cannibalism.* Phoenix Mill, UK: Sutton, 2006.

Dorset, Phyllis Flanders. *The New Eldorado: The Story of Colorado's Gold and Silver Rushes.* New York: Macmillan, 1970.

Dow, James R., Roger L. Welsch, and Susan D. Dow, eds. *Wyoming Folklore: Reminiscences, Folktales, Beliefs, Customs, and Folk Speech*. Lincoln: University of Nebraska Press, 2010.

Dugan, Mark. *Bandit Years: A Gathering of Wolves*. Santa Fe, NM: Sunstone Press, 2007.

Duke, Thomas S. *Celebrated Criminal Cases of America*. San Francisco: James H. Barry, 1910.

Dunlay, Tom. *Kit Carson and the Indians*. Lincoln: University of Nebraska Press, 2000.

Evans, Colin. *A Question of Evidence: The Casebook of Great Forensic Controversies from Napoleon to O.J.* Hoboken, NJ: John Wiley & Sons, 2003.

Federal Writers' Project. *Colorado: A Guide to the Highest State*. New York: Hastings House, 1941.

Fenwick, Robert W. *Alfred Packer: The True Story of Colorado's Man-Eater*. Denver: *Empire Magazine* of the *Denver Post*, 1963.

Field, Kenneth S. *History of the American Academy of Forensic Sciences: 1948–1998*. West Conshohocken, PA: ASTM International, 1998.

Fisher, Vardis. *The Mothers*. Chicago: Sage Books, 1971.

Fisher, Vardis, and Opal Laurel Holmes. *Gold Rushes and Mining Camps of the Early American West*. Caldwell, ID: Caxton Printers, 1968.

Flanagan, Mike. *Out West*. New York: Harry N. Abrams, 1987.

Fowler, Gene. *Timber Line: A Story of Bonfils and Tammen*. Garden City, NY: Garden City, 1933.

France, L. B. *Reports of Cases Determined in the Supreme Court of the State of Colorado, Containing All Cases Decided at the December Term, 1883, the April Term, 1884, and the Special October Term, 1884*. Vol. 7. Chicago: Callaghan & Company, 1884.

Franzen, Jonathan. *How to Be Alone: Essays*. New York: Farrar, Straus and Giroux, 2003.

Frémont, John C. *Narrative of the Exploring Expedition to the Rocky Mountains in the Year 1842, and to Oregon and North Carolina in the Years 1843–'44*. Washington, DC: Henry Polkinhorn, 1845.

Fritz, Percy Stanley. *Colorado: The Centennial State*. New York: Prentice-Hall, 1941.

Gantt, Paul H. *The Case of Alfred Packer the Man-Eater.* Denver: University of Denver Press, 1952.

Garraty, John A., and Mark C. Carnes, eds. *American National Biography.* Vol. 3. New York: Oxford University Press, 1999.

Gay, Theressa. *James W. Marshall, the Discoverer of California Gold: A Biography.* Georgetown, CA: Talisman Press, 1967.

Gibbon, J. J. *In the San Juan: Sketches.* Lake City, CO: Western Reflections, 2008.

Gilliland, Mary Ellen. *Summit: A Gold Rush History of Summit County, Colorado.* Silverthorne, CO: Alpenrose Press, 1980.

Gorn, Elliott J. *Mother Jones: The Most Dangerous Woman in America.* New York: Hill and Wang, 2001.

Gorzalka, Ann. *Wyoming's Territorial Sheriffs.* Glendo, WY: High Plains Press, 1998.

Guetzkow, Harold Steere, and Paul Hoover Bowman. *Men and Hunger: A Psychological Manual for Relief Workers.* Elgin, IL: Brethren Publishing House, 1946.

Guttridge, Leonard F. *Ghosts of Cape Sabine: The Harrowing True Story of the Greely Expedition.* New York: G. P. Putnam's Sons, 2000.

Hafen, LeRoy. "Mountain Men—'Big Phil, the Cannibal.'" *Colorado Magazine* 8, no. 2 (March 1936): 53–58.

Hall, Frank. *History of the State of Colorado: Embracing Accounts of the Pre-Historic Races and Their Remains; the Earliest Spanish, French and American Explorations; the Lives of the Primitive Hunters, Trappers and Traders; the Commerce of the Prairies; the First American Settlements Founded; the Original Discoveries of Gold in the Rocky Mountains; the Development of Cities and Towns, with the Various Phases of the Industrial and Political Transition from 1858 to 1890.* In Four Volumes. Chicago: The Blakely Printing Company, 1891.

Hammett, Dashiell. *The Thin Man.* New York: Alfred A. Knopf, 1933.

Hanson, Neil. *The Custom of the Sea.* New York: John Wiley & Sons, 1999.

Hardcastle, Nate, ed. *Survive: Stories of Castaways and Cannibals.* New York: Thunder Mouth Press, 2001.

Harden, Mike. *Among Friends: The Best of Mike Harden*. N.p.: Wing and Prayer Publications, 1993.

Harris, Marvin. *Cannibals and Kings: The Origins of Culture*. New York: Vintage Books, 1991.

Harrison, Fred. *Hell Holes and Hangings*. Clarendon, TX: Clarendon Press, 1968.

Hayden, Peter V. "The Incredible Polly Pry." *Frontier Times* 51, no. 1 (December–January 1977): 16–19, 59.

Herron, Don. *The Dashiell Hammett Tour*. San Francisco: City Lights Books, 1991.

Hill, Alice Polk. *Tales of the Colorado Pioneers*. Denver: Pierson & Gardner, 1884.

Hill, William E. *The Mormon Trail: Yesterday and Today*. Logan: Utah State University Press, 1996.

Hodges, Joseph G. "The Legal Experiences of Mr. Alfred Packer." *Dicta* 19 (June 1942): 149–52.

Hodgson, Ken. *Lone Survivor*. New York: Pinnacle Books, 2001.

Hosokawa, Bill. *Thunder in the Rockies: The Incredible "Denver Post."* New York: William Morrow, 1976.

Hough, E. "Portraits of Three Westerners." *Field and Stream*, no. 9 (January 1904): 854.

Houston, Grant. *Lake City Reflections*. Gunnison, CO: B & B Printers, 1976.

Houston, Robert B., Jr. *Two Colorado Odysseys: Chief Ouray and Porter Nelson*. Lincoln, NE: printed by author, 2005.

Hubbell, Sue. "Polly Pry Did Not Just Report the News; She Made It." *Smithsonian Magazine* 21, no. 10 (January 1991): 48–56.

Hunt, Inez, and Wanetta W. Draper. *Horsefeathers and Applesauce: The Story of Frank Hamilton Rice*. Denver: Sage Publications, 1959.

Iverson, Kristen. *Molly Brown: Unraveling the Myth*. Boulder, CO: Johnson Books, 1999.

Jacobs, Pat. *Mountain Madman or Mountain Madness? Alfred Packer, Colorado Cannibal*. Lake City, CO: printed by author, 1965.

James, Stuart H., and Jon J. Nordby, eds. *Forensic Science: An Introduction to Scientific and Investigative Techniques*. 2nd ed. Boca Raton, FL: Taylor & Francis, 2005.

Jenkins, Philip. *Laying Down the Sword: Why We Can't Ignore the Bible's Violent Verses*. New York: HarperCollins, 2011.

Jocknick, Sidney. *Early Days on the Western Slope of Colorado, and Campfire Chats with Otto Mears, the Pathfinder*. Glorietta, NM: Rio Grande Press, 1968.

Kaplan, Michael. *Otto Mears: Paradoxical Pathfinder*. Silverton, CO: San Juan Book Company, 1982.

Kaplan, Michael David. *David Frakes Day: Civil War Hero and Notorious Frontier Newspaperman*. Jefferson, NC: McFarland, 2011.

Kreck, Dick. *Denver in Flames: Forging a New Mile High City*. Golden, CO: Fulcrum, 2000.

Kushner, Ervan F. *Alferd Packer: Cannibal! Victim?* Frederick, CO: Platte 'N Press, 1980.

———. *Otto Mears: His Life & Times, with Notes on the Alferd Packer Case*. Frederick, CO: Platte 'N Press, 1979.

Lavender, David. *The Big Divide: The Lively Story of the People of the Southern Rocky Mountains from Yellowstone to Santa Fe*. Edison, NJ: Castle Books, 2001.

Lee, Katie. *Ten Thousand Goddam Cattle: A History of the American Cowboy in Song, Story and Verse*. Albuquerque: University of New Mexico Press, 1976.

Leonard, Stephen J. *Lynching in Colorado, 1859–1919*. Boulder: University Press of Colorado, 2002.

Lindmier, Tom. *Drybone: A History of Fort Fetterman, Wyoming*. Glendo, WY: High Plains Press, 2002.

Look, Al. *Unforgettable Characters of Western Colorado*. Boulder, CO: Pruett Press, 1966.

Loerzel, Robert. *Alchemy of Bones: Chicago's Luetgert Murder Case of 1897*. Urbana: University of Illinois Press, 2003.

Maples, William R., and Michael Browning. *Dead Men Do Tell Tales: The Strange and Fascinating Cases of a Forensic Anthropologist*. New York: Doubleday, 1994.

Martin, Bernice, ed. *Frontier Eyewitness: Diary of John Lawrence, 1867–1908*. Saguache, CO: The Saguache County Museum, n.d.

Martin, Russell, and Lydia Nibley. *The Mysteries of Beethoven's Hair*. Watertown, MA: Charlesbridge, 2009.

Mazzulla, Fred, and Jo Mazzulla. *Al Packer: A Colorado Cannibal.* Denver: printed by authors, 1968.

McCaig, Donald. "The Bozeman Trail." *Smithsonian* 31, no. 7 (October 2000): 88.

McDevitt, Tom. *The Cannibal Boone Helm: Idaho–Utah 1858–1860.* Pocatello, ID: printed by author, 2008.

McGinniss, Joe. *Fatal Vision.* New York: Signet, 1989.

Monroe, Arthur W. *San Juan Silver: Historical Tales of the Silvery San Juan and Western Colorado.* Lake City, CO: Western Reflections, 2009.

Moore, Arthur K. *The Frontier Mind: A Cultural Analysis of the Kentucky Frontiersman.* Lexington: University Press of Kentucky, 1957.

Moore, Richard B. "Carib 'Cannibalism': A Study in Anthropological Stereotyping." *Caribbean Studies* 13, no. 3 (October 1973): 117–35.

Morgan, R. Kent. *Guide to the Indian War Battlefields in Eastern Wyoming, Nebraska and South Dakota.* Bloomington, IN: printed by author, 2006.

Moses, Albert L. "Judge Gerry's Sentence of Alfred Packer." *Dicta* 19 (July 1942): 169–71.

Nash, Jay Robert. *The Great Pictorial History of World Crime.* Vol. 1. Blue Ridge Summit, PA: Scarecrow Press, 2004.

Newman, Victoria R., and the Museum of Colorado Prisons. *Images of America: Prisons of Cañon City.* Charleston, SC: Arcadia, 2008.

Oldham, Ann. *Alfred G. Packer: Soldier, Prospector, Cannibal.* Davenport, IA: printed by author, 2005.

Pavich, Stella M. *Packer the Cannibal and Other Story Poems.* New York: Comet Press Books, 1961.

Petrinovich, Lewis. *The Cannibal Within.* New York: Aldine de Gruyter, 2000.

Pettit, Jan. *Utes: The Mountain People.* Boulder, CO: Johnson Books, 1990.

Philbrick, Nathaniel. *In the Heart of the Sea: The Tragedy of the Whaleship Essex.* New York: Penguin Books, 2000.

———. *Mayflower: A Story of Courage, Community, and War.* New York: Viking, 2006.

Porter, Olive Nagel. *A Remembrance of Alfred Packer*. N.p.: printed by author, 1965.

Portis, Charles. *True Grit*. New York: Simon & Schuster, 1968.

Price, Virginia, and John T. Darby. "Preston Nutter: Utah Cattleman, 1886–1936." *Utah Historical Quarterly* 32, no. 3 (Summer 1946): 232–51.

Rarick, Ethan. *Desperate Passage: The Donner Party's Perilous Journey West*. New York: Oxford University Press, 2008.

Rautman, Alison E., and Todd W. Fenton. "A Case of Historic Cannibalism in the American West: Implications for Southwestern Archaeology." *American Antiquity* 70, no. 2 (April 2005): 321–41.

Read, Piers Paul. *Alive: The Story of the Andes Survivors*. New York: Avon Books, 1975.

Rhine, Stanley. *Bone Voyage: A Journey in Forensic Anthropology*. Albuquerque: University of New Mexico Press, 1998.

Rhodes, Richard. *The Ungodly: A Novel of the Donner Party*. New York: Charterhouse, 1973.

Riffenburgh, Beau. *Pinkerton's Great Detective: The Amazing Life and Times of James McParland*. New York: Viking, 2013.

Riley, Marilyn Griggs. *High Altitude Attitudes: Six Savvy Colorado Women*. Boulder, CO: Johnson Books, 2006.

Ritter, Charles. "The Early History of Fort Fetterman." *Annals of Wyoming* 32, no. 2 (October 1960): 220–24.

Roberts, David. *A Newer World: Kit Carson, John C. Frémont, and the Claiming of the American West*. New York: Simon & Schuster, 2000.

Robinson, Michael F. *The Coldest Crucible: Arctic Exploration and American Culture*. Chicago: University of Chicago Press, 2006.

Rockwell, Wilson. *Sunset Slope*. Ouray, CO: Western Reflections, 1999.

———. *Uncompahgre Country*. Ouray, CO: Western Reflections, 1956.

———. *The Utes: A Forgotten People*. Ouray, CO: Western Reflections, 1956.

Root, George A. "Gunnison in the Early Eighties." *Colorado Magazine* 9, no. 6 (November 1932): 201–13.

Ross, Ishbel. *Ladies of the Press: The Story of Women in Journalism by an Insider*. New York: Harper & Brothers, 1936.

Russell, Sharman Apt. *Hunger: An Unnatural History*. New York: Basic Books, 2005.

Ruxton, George Frederick. *Life in the Far West*. Norman: University of Oklahoma Press, 1951.

Sachs, Jessica Snyder. *Corpse: Nature, Forensics, and the Struggle to Pinpoint Time of Death*. New York: Basic Books, 2001.

Sarah Platt Decker Chapter, DAR. *Pioneers of the San Juan Country*. Vol. 1. Colorado Springs, CO: The Out West Printing and Stationery Company, 1942.

Schama, Simon. *Dead Certainties: Unwarranted Speculations*. New York: Vintage Books, 1992.

Schoenberger, Dale T. *The Gunfighters*. Caldwell, ID: Caxton Printers, 1976.

Segrave, Kelly. *Lynchings of Women in the United States: The Recorded Cases, 1851–1946*. Jefferson, NC: McFarland, 2010.

Shirley, Gayle C. *More Than Petticoats: Remarkable Colorado Women*. Guilford, CT: Twodot Books, 2002.

Shores, Doc. *Memoirs of a Lawman*. Denver: Sage Books, 1962.

Silkenat, David. *Moments of Despair: Suicide, Divorce, and Debt in Civil War Era North Carolina*. Chapel Hill: University of North Carolina Press, 2011.

Simmons, Virginia McConnell. *The Ute Indians of Utah, Colorado and New Mexico*. Boulder: University Press of Colorado, 2000.

Simpson, A. W. Brian. *Cannibalism and the Common Law: A Victorian Yachting Tragedy*. London: Hambledon Press, 1994.

Siringo, Charles A. *Riata and Spurs: The Story of a Lifetime Spent in the Saddle as Cowboy and Ranger*. Boston: Houghton Mifflin, 1931.

Slatta, Richard W. *The Mythical West: An Encyclopedia of Legend, Lore, and Popular Culture*. Santa Barbara, CA: ABC-CLIO, 2001.

Smith, Gene, and Jayne Barry Smith, eds. *The Police Gazette*. New York: Simon & Schuster, 1972.

Smith, P. David. *Ouray: Chief of the Utes*. Ridgway, CO: Wayfinder Press, 1990.

Snow, Clyde Collins. "Forensic Anthropology." *Annual Review of Anthropology* 11 (1982): 97–131.

Speedlove, Earl. "Cannibals Leave Only Bones." *Real West* 7, no. 37 (September 1964): 24–26, 44–45.

Sprague, Marshall. *Colorado: A History.* New York: Norton, 1984.

——. *Massacre: The Tragedy at White River.* Lincoln: University of Nebraska Press, 1957.

Starrs, James E., and Katherine Ramsland. *A Voice for the Dead: A Forensic Investigator's Pursuit of the Truth in the Grave.* New York: G. P. Putnam's Sons, 2005.

Stewart, George R. *Ordeal by Hunger: The Story of the Donner Party.* Boston: Houghton Mifflin, 1988.

Stewart, T. D. *Essentials of Forensic Anthropology: Especially as Developed in the United States.* Springfield, IL: Charles C. Thomas, 1979.

——. "George A. Dorsey's Role in the Luetgert Case: A Significant Episode in the History of Forensic Anthropology." *Journal of Forensic Science* 23, no. 4 (October 1978): 786–91.

Stone, James W. *Report of the Trial of Prof. John W. Webster, Indicted for the Murder of Dr. George Parkman, before the Supreme Judicial Court of Massachusetts, Holden at Boston, on Tuesday, March 19, 1850.* Boston: Phillips, Sampson and Company, 1850.

Stover, Dawn. "Was It Murder?" *Popular Science* 254, no. 4 (April 1999): 78–81.

Sugg, Richard. *Mummies, Cannibals, and Vampires: The History of Corpse Medicine from the Renaissance to the Victorians.* London: Routledge, 2011.

Tannahill, Reay. *Flesh and Blood: A History of the Cannibal Complex.* New York: Stein and Day, 1975.

Temkin, Owsei. *The Falling Sickness: A History of Epilepsy from the Greeks to the Beginnings of Modern Neurology.* Baltimore: Johns Hopkins University Press, 1971.

Thompson, Thomas Gray. "Early Development of Lake City." *Colorado Magazine* 40, no. 2 (April 1963): 93–105.

Thompson, Virgil V. *1946 Brand Book: Twelve Original Papers Pertaining to the History of the West.* Denver: Westerners, 1947.

Tucker, E. F. *Otto Mears and the San Juans.* Montrose, CO: Western Reflections, 2003.

Turner, Christy G., II, and Jacqueline A. Turner. *Man Corn: Cannibalism and Violence in the Prehistoric American Southwest*. Salt Lake City: University of Utah Press, 1999.

Turner, Ralph F. "American Academy of Forensic Sciences Is Now Firmly Established." *Journal of Criminal Law and Criminology (1931–1951)* 41, no. 4 (November–December 1950): 477–78.

Twain, Mark. "Cannibalism in the Cars." In *The Complete Short Stories of Mark Twain*. New York: Bantam Books, 1957.

Ubelaker, Douglas, and Henry Scammell. *Bones: A Forensic Detective's Casebook*. Lanham, MD: M. Evans, 2006.

Unruh, John David. *The Plains Across: The Overland Emigrants and the Trans-Mississippi West, 1840–60*. Urbana: University of Illinois Press, 1982.

Wallace, Betty. *Gunnison: A Short, Illustrated History*. Denver: Sage Books, 1964.

———. *Gunnison Country*. Denver: Sage Books, 1960.

White, James Terry, ed. *The National Cyclopaedia of American Biography: Being the History of the United States as Illustrated in the Lives of the Founders, Builders, and Defenders of the Republic, and the Men and Women Who Are Doing the Work and Moulding the Thought of the Present Era*. Vol. 8. New York: James T. White, 1906.

Wigmore, John H. "The Luetgert Case." *American Law Review* 32 (March–April 1898): 187–207.

Willison, George. *Here They Dug the Gold*. New York: Reynal & Hitchcock, 1946.

Wise, Joe. *Cannibal Plateau*. Santa Fe, NM: Sunstone Press, 2002.

———. *A Sense of Place: A Conversation with Perk Vickers*. Lake City, CO: Western Reflections, 2007.

Wright, Carolyn, and Clarence Wright. *Tiny Hinsdale of the Silvery San Juan*. Denver: Big Mountain Press, 1964.

Younger, Cole. *The Story of Cole Younger, by Himself: Being an Autobiography of the Missouri Guerilla Captain and Outlaw, His Capture and Prison Life, and the Only Authentic Account of the Northfield Raid Ever Published*. Chicago: Henneberry, 1903.

INDEX